Learn Chinese through Songs and Rhymes

To my parents -

My Father,
whose spirit cheered me on throughout
the writing of this book,

and

My Mother,
who made me write pages and pages of
Chinese characters in my childhood

Lydia Lin

Cover design and all artwork are by the Author.
Except where noted, the Chinese translation of all original English lyrics
and the English translation of all original Chinese lyrics are by the Author.

The following songs and rhymes are original compositions by the Author:
"Happy Friends", "Half a Bucket of Rain", "Purple Spiders".

Many thanks to the members of my family for supplying some of the voices
in the audio files for this book. I am grateful for the availability of the many
time-honored songs in the public domain. As a reader, you may copy the
songs and rhymes in this book for your personal, non-commercial use.
Please give due credit to the composers. The supplemental audio files
for this book are stored on the Internet. You may download and save
the audio files to your hard drive, or burn them onto a CD for your
personal, non-commercial use only.

About the Author

Because of her father's occupation, Lydia Lin has lived in a few
different countries during her childhood and youth. Whenever her
family moved from one place to another, she and her siblings had
to deal with the issue of learning the language used at the new
school and, at the same time, maintaining a working knowledge
of their native tongue, Mandarin Chinese. Therefore, Lydia has
rich first-hand experiences to draw on for compiling this Chinese
language instruction book, even though her studies and job
functions have been in the fields of science and technology.

TABLE OF CONTENTS

The supplemental audio files for this book are stored in the
Microsoft® Windows Live™ SkyDrive.
You may download these files from the
URL listed on page 376 of this book.

1. Introduction

We know that repeated practicing plays an important role in learning any foreign language. However, it bores us to say something or recite a speech more than once. On the other hand, we usually don't mind listening to or singing a song over and over again. And once we've learned a song, we don't forget it. This is why I have translated quite a few traditional songs into Chinese and included them in this Chinese instruction book. The idea is to get you to repeat many of the Chinese phrases and sentences in an enjoyable and seemingly effortless way.

Each and every Chinese word in this book is accompanied by its English translation as well as phonetic marks that will help you sound it out correctly. In addition, you can listen to the supplemental audio files for this book, and check on your own Chinese pronunciation. In time, you will pick up enough words and expressions to be able to engage in a simple conversation.

Frankly, Chinese is a difficult language to master. Learning to speak Chinese is just part of the challenge. A much greater effort is called for to acquire the ability to read and write Chinese. Unlike the English words, which are made up of letters from the Roman alphabet, the Chinese words are not based on an alphabet. The Chinese characters are totally different from the written English, Spanish, German or French, and will look quite strange to you. Therefore, I don't expect you to be able to read a Chinese newspaper or to write a letter in Chinese any time soon. Nevertheless, the Chinese characters are provided for every lesson in this book. They are there if you choose to learn them. While listening to the audio files for this book and reading or singing along, if you also pay attention to the Chinese characters on the page, some of those Chinese characters will gradually become familiar and meaningful.

When learning your mother tongue, you find out what works and what doesn't from your daily interactions with other people who speak the language. You automatically apply the language rules that you have unknowingly acquired. Such a process takes time. Most people learning a second language do not have the luxury of spending a few years in the foreign country, or otherwise immersing in the language environment. Therefore, I have spelled out the grammar for you so you will be aware of the rules used in the sample sentences and dialogs in this book. Fortunately, you will see that the logic used in the Chinese language to get ideas across clearly is quite similar to that used in the English language.

Pronunciation

Although the Chinese characters can be classified into groups that can be distinguished by a number of basic building blocks, each Chinese character is a unique word, distinct from all the other characters. In fact, the Chinese people used to have to learn the pronunciation, or 发音 (fāyīn), for each and every character while they were developing the ability to read Chinese texts. This is an arduous process as there is little correlation between the Chinese characters and how they are pronounced. Fortunately, in modern times, phonetic systems have been devised that help the students to sound out and learn the Chinese characters. One such system is the standard pinyin, which is a Romanization system much like the English spelling. For example, 拼音 is the Chinese word for pinyin. It consists of two characters. 拼 means "put together". It is pronounced as "peen". 音 means "sounds". It is pronounced as "een". The pinyin notation for 拼音 is "pin1yin1" or "pīnyīn". If you are wondering about the significance of the special symbols or numerals in the pinyin notation, this subject will be addressed in the section below that is titled "The Five Tones".

Pinyin is a very useful tool for learning Chinese. It is especially intuitive to English-speaking learners. If you choose to just learn to speak Chinese, you need only pay attention to the pinyin notations in this book. If you are taking on the challenge to learn to read and write in Chinese, then the pinyin notations will help you pronounce the Chinese characters and associate the text with the sound.

Basically, each Chinese character is sounded out as one syllable. Each syllable may consist of a sole vowel sound, or it may contain one vowel sound flanked on one or both sides by a consonant sound. You can find the English equivalent for most of the sounds, although some others can only be roughly approximated. Please see the Romanization charts on the following pages to get an idea of the different sounds that you will be encountering. Actually, many of the pinyin notations are quite intuitive. You can refer back to these charts whenever you are not sure how to pronounce a pinyin. For the lessons contained in this book, you can learn the proper pronunciation of the Chinese words, phrases and sentences by listening to the associated media files.

Romanization of the Vowel Sounds using Standard Pinyin

See	Say	Example		
		Chinese Character	**Pinyin**	**Meaning**
a	**ah**	他	tā	he
ai	**I**	爱	ài	love
an	**Ann**ette	安	ān	safe, calm
ang	y**oung**	羊	yáng	goat, sheep
ao	**ou**ch	跑	pǎo	run, ran
e	lak**e**	客	kè	guest
ei	**ei**ght	黑	hēi	black
en	soft**en**	很	hěn	very
eng	str**ung**	等	děng	wait
i	**ee**l	你	nǐ	you
ia	As**ia**	家	jiā	home
ian	Appalach**ian**	天	tiān	sky
ie	**ye**llow	也	yě	also
iu	y**eo**man	九	jiǔ	nine
o	**o**range	我	wǒ	I, me
ong	s**ong**	红	hóng	red
ou	**owe**	有	yǒu	have
u	bl**ue**	不	bù	no
ua	**wah**	花	huā	flower
uai	Ha**waii**	快	kuài	quickly
ui	**way**	对	duì	correct
uo	**wo**k	多	duō	many
ü/uu	**ü** (a German umlaut)	绿	lǜ	green

When there is no danger of confusion, use a single "u" in place of "ü", such as in yú (鱼 fish) and qù (去 go). In general, read the "u" after j, q, x or y as "ü".

Romanization of the Consonant Sounds using Standard Pinyin

See	Say	Chinese Character	Pinyin	Meaning
		Example		
b	**b**ook	爸	bà	dad
c	i**ts**	草	cǎo	grass
ch	**ch**art	唱	chàng	sing
d	**d**ot	大	dà	big
f	**f**un	饭	fàn	rice (cooked)
g	**g**o	狗	gǒu	dog
h	**h**ow	好	hǎo	good
j	**j**eep	鸡	jī	chicken
k	**k**ing	看	kàn	see, watch
l	**l**and	来	lái	come
m	**m**om	妈	mā	mother
n	**n**o	拿	ná	take
p	**p**op	怕	pà	afraid
q	i**tch**	球	qiǔ	ball
r	**r**ent	人	rén	person
s	**s**un	三	sān	three (3)
sh	hu**sh**	山	shān	mountain
t	**t**ea	土	tǔ	soil, mud
v	(not used)			
w	**w**oo	五	wǔ	five
x	**sh**e	西	xī	west
y	**y**eah	牙	yá	tooth, teeth
z	**z**oom (more piercing)	坐	zuò	sit
zh	nu**dge**	站	zhàn	stand up

To pronounce the above "z" sound correctly, try making the "ts" sound with clenched front teeth.

The Five Tones

There are only five tones in Standard Mandarin Chinese, which is the official spoken Chinese. This is the result of an effort in the mid-20th century to standardize the language for all the people in the numerous provinces and districts of China. Although the Chinese people share a common written language, every province has its own local flavor of one of a number of distinct dialects, which, to a person from another region, can sound like a foreign language. Mandarin Chinese is based on the dialects spoken by the people in Northern China and Southwestern China. Because it has been standardized to use only five distinct tones and is stripped of most of the final stop consonants, standard Mandarin may sound mechanical to people who are used to hearing a more melodic tongue like French. On the other hand, having just five tones to deal with should be good news to a newcomer like you.

The five tones consist of four distinct main tones, plus one "silent" tone. The "silent" tone is not really silent. It is so called because it sounds soft and brief. Most printed textbooks indicate the four main tones by using diacritical marks above the syllable nucleus. Alternatively, you may indicate the four tones by placing the corresponding numerals at the end of the syllables. The tone mark is usually left out for the silent tone. With the tone number system, you may use "0" or "5", or the absence of a tone number, to represent the silent tone.

See		Say	Example
1	1st Tone	the "hee" in "hee-haw"	shan1 / shān mountain
2	2nd Tone	Yes?	yang2 / yáng goat, sheep
3	3rd Tone	the "per" in "perform"	pao3 / pǎo run, ran
4	4th Tone	Done!	diao4 / diào away
	Silent Tone	the "d" in "end"	le / le a word particle

Please familiarize yourself with the five tones by memorizing the following sentence:

山 羊 跑 掉 了. The mountain goat has run away.
Shān yáng pǎo diào le.

In the above sentence, 山羊 (shān yáng) is a goat. 跑掉 (pǎo diào) means to run away. 了 (le) is a particle that indicates the completion of an action.

The following English sentence is a close approximation of the five tones:

He will repent.
(1) (2) (3) (4) (0)

The importance of using the correct tones when speaking Chinese cannot be overemphasized. The same syllable sounded out in different tones can have totally different meanings. Just look at the following example, and you will see.

我 想 问 你. I would like to ask you.
Wǒ xiǎng wèn nǐ.

If you pronounce this sentence correctly, people will hear you say, "I would like to ask you." However, if you mispronounce the "wèn" and said "wěn" instead, people will hear this:

我 想 吻 你. I would like to kiss you.
Wǒ xiǎng wěn nǐ.

I do want to point out that when a Chinese hears a foreigner speak Chinese, he or she will usually make some allowance for the foreign accent and be able to make out the intended meaning. Therefore, please don't let the above example scare you from trying out your Chinese at every possible opportunity.

Exceptions in Intonation:

Certain Chinese word combinations are awkward to pronounce if you simply sound them out according to the tones normally assigned to them. The following rules of thumb take care of such special cases.

1. Whenever two 3rd tones come together, the first one is enunciated in the 2nd tone.

小鸟 Dickeybird 手表 Watch 老虎 Tiger

See:	xiǎo niǎo	shǒu biǎo	lǎo hǔ
Say:	**xiáo niǎo**	**shóu biǎo**	**láo hǔ**

See how much easier it is to say "xiáo niǎo" than "xiǎo niǎo"?

What if you encounter three 3rd tones in a sequence? Say the first one normally then apply the above rule to the remaining two characters, as in:

他想洗手   He wants to wash his hands.

See: tā xiǎng xǐ shǒu
Say: tā xiǎng xí shǒu

And what if you encounter four 3rd tones in a row? Simply, apply the above rule to each pair of third tones, as in:

我想洗手   I would like to wash my hands.

See: wǒ xiǎng xǐ shǒu
Say: wó xiǎng xí shǒu

2. Normally, 不 (bù), meaning "no" or "not", is pronounced in the 4th tone. For example:

不好   Not good; no.

bù hǎo

不行
bù xíng

Won't do; no way.

不想
bù xiǎng

Not feel like doing

When followed by a 4th-tone word, 不 is pronounced in 2nd tone.

不是	不要	不用	不会
bú shì	**bú yào**	**bú yòng**	**bú huì**
(be) not	don't want	not necessary	not able; won't happen

3. The silent tone is applied to the ending character of many expressions to make them sound more natural. Typically, when you see two identical characters in a row, the second one is made a silent tone, as in:

爸爸
bà ba

Dad

妈妈
mā ma

Mom

It is also customary to soften a character at the end of a familiar expression. For example, you would say, "yǐan jing" for 眼睛 (yǐan jīng eyes), and you would say, "ěr duo" for 耳朵 (ěr duō ears).

The word, 兒 (ér), means a son, a child, a youngster, or a small thing. It is pronounced in the second tone. The word, 子 (zǐ), which is pronounced in the third tone, also means a son, a child, an offspring, a seed, pr a small thing. In ancient times, it was used as a title of a respected person. For example:

女兒	nǚ ér	daughter (female child)
孔子	Kǒng zǐ	Confucius

兒 (ér) and 子 (zǐ) are often appended to another word to indicate smallness or cuteness. In this case, the suffix assumes a silent tone. Some common examples are:

花兒	huā er	small flower
羊兒	yáng er	lamb
兒子	ér zi	son
鼻子	bí zi	nose

Concatenation:

Up to this point, I have marked each individual Chinese character with its corresponding pinyin. Many Chinese "words" consist of two or more characters, similar to the polysyllable words in English. Therefore, the convention is to join together the pinyin notations for all the characters within a whole word, and follow certain orthographic rules, more or less, with respect to word formation and capitalization. One interesting rule is to change the suffix "er" to "r". Therefore, the pinyin for 花兒 (small flower) is "huār", and the pinyin for 羊兒 (small lamb) is "yángr". Notice how this smoothes out the enunciation of these words.

When there is ambiguity as to how to divide up a polysyllable word, an apostrophe is often inserted for clarity. So, in the rare case where you see an apostrophe in the pinyin notation, remember that it serves as the divider.

Now, with the help of the Romanization charts and knowledge about the five tones, you should be able to sound out any pinyin with ease. Why not give the following words a try?

一只 yī zhī	one (animal)	两只 liǎng zhī	two (animals)
老 lǎo	old	老虎 lǎohǔ	tiger
跑 paǔ ǎo	run	快 kuài	fast
跑得快 paǔ de kuài	run fast	没有 méiyǒu	have not, be without
耳朵 ěrduo	ear, ears	尾巴 wěiba	tail
眼睛 yǎnjing	eye, eyes	嘴吧 zuǐba	mouth
鼻子 bízi	nose	牙齿 yáchǐ	tooth, teeth
奇怪 qíguài	strange	真奇怪 zhēn qíguài	really strange

Please pay special attention to the difference between the harsher sound of 只 (zhī) and the softer sound of 子 (zi). When saying 眼睛 (yǎnjing), make sure that the "ing" sound rings in your mouth and does not sound like a plain "in". When saying 牙齿 (yáchǐ), make sure that the "chǐ" sound is thick and throaty and will not be confused with the "cǐ" sound. In fact, some Chinese people do not conform strictly to the standard Mandarin pronunciation rules. They pronounce "zhī" as "zī", "chī" as "cī", and "shī" as "sī". After you have become more familiar with Chinese, you will be able to make allowance for that.

And why stop here? Go ahead and read the lyrics to the following song aloud. Then sing it to the tune of "Brother John", which was originally a French nursery tune titled "Frère Jacques". The author of this popular Chinese version is unknown. I have added the word "odd" in the English lyrics to better fit the verses to the music.

Please note that 老虎 (lǎohǔ) does not necessarily mean an old tiger. Rather, 老虎 (lǎohǔ) is just a general term for tigers.

Two Tigers

tune: Frère Jacques

两只老虎

Liǎng Zhī Lǎohǔ

两只老虎, 两只老虎,

Liǎng zhī lǎohǔ, liǎng zhī lǎohǔ,

Two odd tigers, two odd tigers,

跑得快, 跑得快.

Pǎu de kuài, pǎu de kuài.

Running fast, running fast.

一只没有耳朵,

Yī zhī méiyǒu ěrduo,

One is missing the ears,

一只没有尾巴.

Yī zhī méiyǒu wěiba.

One is missing the tail.

真奇怪, 真奇怪.

Zhēn qíguài, zhēn qíguài.

Quite bizarre, quite bizarre.

OR *Very strange, very strange*

两只老虎, 两只老虎,
Liǎng zhī lǎohǔ, liǎng zhī lǎohǔ,

Two odd tigers, two odd tigers,

跑得快, 跑得快.
Pǎu de kuài, pǎu de kuài.

Running fast, running fast.

一只没有眼睛,
Yī zhī méiyǒu yǎnjing,

One is missing the eyes,

一只没有嘴巴.
Yī zhī méiyǒu zuǐba.

One is missing the mouth.

真奇怪, 真奇怪.
Zhēn qíguài, zhēn qíguài.

Quite bizarre, quite bizarre.

两只老虎, 两只老虎,
Liǎng zhī lǎohǔ, liǎng zhī lǎohǔ,

Two odd tigers, two odd tigers,

跑得快, 跑得快.
Pǎu de kuài, pǎu de kuài.

Running fast, running fast.

一只没有鼻子,
Yī zhī méiyǒu bízi,

One is missing the nose,

一只没有牙齿.
Yī zhī méiyǒu yáchǐ.

One is missing the teeth.

真奇怪, 真奇怪.
Zhēn qíguài, zhēn qíguài.

Quite bizarre, quite bizarre.

Chinese Characters

Understandably, the biggest hurdle in learning Chinese is the complexity of the Chinese characters, or 汉字 (hànzì). It will take great efforts and quite some time to master a basic set of commonly used Chinese words and characters. To be able to read newspapers requires the knowledge of 2000 to 3000 characters. This is but a small fraction of the 40,000 plus characters typically found in a large Chinese dictionary. While the people in Taiwan still use the traditional Chinese characters, those in China have switched over to the simplified version. I opted to use the simplified Chinese characters for this book, for the obvious reason that they generally contain fewer strokes, and are therefore easier for you to learn.

I have marked all the Chinese characters in this book with pinyin so that you will be able to learn to speak Chinese even if you choose not to learn the Chinese characters. In fact, it is possible to communicate in writing using only pinyin. However, ambiguities are apt to arise as the majority of Chinese characters have two or more homophones (words that sound exactly the same). If you are interested in learning how to write in Chinese, then it will be helpful to get a vocabulary book that shows the order in which the strokes in each character are executed. A useful reference book is "Reading & Writing Chinese" by William McNaughton and Li Ying (Simplified Character Edition, Tuttle® Publishing). You will also need to devote a great deal of time to "drawing" the commonly used Chinese characters repeatedly and learning them by heart. The secret to success? Practice, practice and practice.

In this book, the English translations provided for the Chinese text are those that go along with the context of the lessons. For the formal definition of each individual Chinese character, please refer to your Chinese dictionary.

Traditionally, Chinese documents were written in classical (or formal) Chinese, which is very terse and quite different from the spoken language. The modern written Chinese parallels the spoken Chinese. In general, what you write is what you would say, unless you are writing an official document, composing a classical poem, or you intend to flaunt your knowledge of classical Chinese. However, the modern Chinese language still employs quite a few of the classical Chinese words and expressions. Therefore, you will inevitably come across a few formal Chinese words in this book. You will also have an opportunity to learn to make use of some Chinese idioms to get your ideas across faster and more effectively.

Here are some examples of Chinese characters that originated from pictographs. If you would like to practice writing Chinese, you could start with these simple characters. The order of executing the strokes is generally from the top down and from left to right. With the "cross" shape, the horizontal stroke comes before the vertical stroke.

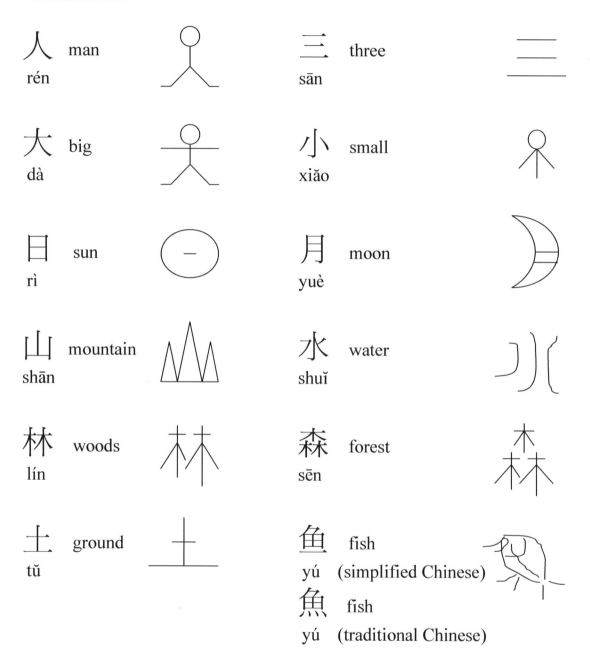

人　man
rén

三　three
sān

大　big
dà

小　small
xiǎo

日　sun
rì

月　moon
yuè

山　mountain
shān

水　water
shuǐ

林　woods
lín

森　forest
sēn

土　ground
tǔ

鱼　fish
yú　(simplified Chinese)

魚　fish
yú　(traditional Chinese)

Many Chinese characters are formed by combining two or more other characters. Following are a few interesting examples that appeal to common sense and are easy to understand:

小 + 大 = 尖   small on top of big = pointed, sharp
xiǎo   dà   jiān

羊 + 大 = 美   sheep + big = beautiful
yáng   dà   měi

女 + 子 = 好   female + person = good, nice
nǚ   zǐ   hǎo

不 + 正 = 歪   not + straight = slanted, crooked
bú zhèng wāi

木 + 子 = 李   wood/tree + seed = plums
mù   zǐ   lǐ   (a common Chinese last name)

人 + 言 = 信   man + word = trust, credibility,
rén   yán   xìn   word of honor, a letter

八 + 刀 = 分   eight cuts = divide, separate
bā   dāo   fēn

人 + 一 + 口 = 合   man + one + bite = combine, join,
rén   yī   kǒu   hé   together

合 + 手 = 拿   together + hands = hold, take
hé   shǒu   ná

Most Chinese dictionaries group the characters by radicals, which are the shared building blocks. Following are a few easily recognizable Chinese radicals:

口 mouth, opening, hole, entrance
kǒu

叫 call, shout   哈 ha *(a sound)*   唱 sing   哭 weep, cry
jiào   hā   chàng   kū

人 human being, person, people
rén

仁 kindness   你 you   信 trust, letter   仙 fairy
rén   nǐ   xìn   xiān

木 wood, wooden, tree, timber
mù

林 woods   森 forest   李 plum   桃 peach
lín   sén   lǐ   táo

足 foot, leg, sufficient
zú

跑 run   跳 jump   跌 fall   趴 lie prone
pǎo   tiào   dié   pā

Through the ages, many different styles have been adopted for writing and printing the Chinese characters. The ancient pictographs are, of course, obsolete. The Seal Script that was used in ancient dynasties are still found nowadays on personal and official seals. It will require some effort for most Chinese people to decipher the characters on these seals. The Clerical Script and the Weibei (found mostly on monuments and tomb stones) look similar to the traditional Regular Script. The difference among those can be compared to that between the Times New Roman font and the Courier New font. And similar to the sans serif fonts, there is also a Chinese sans serif font, the Black font, which can be compared to the Arial Black font. The Black font is used mostly for headlines, or on signs and placards.

Although people sometimes use their calligraphy brushes to write very neatly in Regular Script, most of the time they use the pen or pencil to write in Semi-cursive Script. If you copy a few characters from this book by hand, you would be writing in Semi-cursive Script. Some calligraphers and artists go a step further and turn the Chinese characters into an art form, which, with due respect, I liken to shorthand English. My own father left behind a few pieces of beautiful Chinese calligraphy work that he had created - some in Weibei style, others in Cursive Script. When I admire the scolls with the Cursive Script, I can almost feel the 气 (qì), or vital engergy, springing out at me but I honestly can't tell for sure what those animated scribbles stand for. It's like viewing a piece of abstract art.

So, what you see in this book is the simplified Regular Script. Still, there are various fonts used for printing the modern Chinese characters. Therefore, you will see slight variations among the different font types. For example, the Chinese word for "this" is 这 (zhè). It contains on its left side the radical that was derived from the character, 走 (zǒu), which means "to walk". Similarly, the word for "far" is 远 (yuǎn), which features the same radical on its left side. The diffence you are seeing is that between the typefaces used. Therefor, you may choose to always write this radical the way it looks in 远 (yuǎn).

The first three chapters of this book contain many Chinese characters in large font to give you an easy start. A smaller font size is used for the remaining chapters. Please keep in mind that the smaller Chinese characters in this book are still much enlarged compared to what you will find in a typical Chinese book.

Chinese Calligraphy

Before the modern pens, pencils and printing presses were invented, most Chinese documents were prepared using ink and paintbrushes. Chinese calligraphy, or 书法 (shūfǎ) is an enjoyable form of art in itself. You can try your hand at writing the Chinese characters by using a rounded paintbrush and bottled black ink. Plain typing paper is easier to work with. If you try your calligraphy on rice paper, you will need to use thick black ink, work fairly quickly, and pay close attention to the moisture control so the strokes do not bleed too much on the rice paper. As the Chinese brushes are made from the hair of animals, they are called 毛笔 (máobǐ), or "brushes made from hair", and doing Chinese calligraphy is also referred to as 写毛笔字 (xiě máobǐ zì), or brush writing.

The character 永 (yǒng) means "always", "forever" or "perpetually". It contains all of the eight different types of strokes that you will encounter in any Chinese character. You start with the *dot* at the top, make a *horizontal* stroke, turn a *corner* then make a *vertical* stroke, ending in a *hook*. The next stroke slants slightly *upward to the right;* then there is the *down-left* stroke. Now, a shorter *down-left* stroke, followed by the final *down-right* stroke. Hold the stem of the brush vertically, and keep the brush at the same level to maintain the even width of a long stroke. Notice how some of the strokes end in a fine point. Lift your brush gradually near the end of the stroke to achieve the point. See how gracefully the character is balanced on the paper. It takes years of practice to excel in Chinese calligraphy.

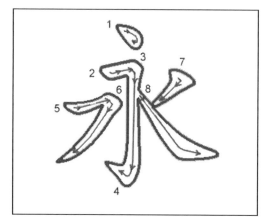

2. Me or I?

In English, you would say "I" when you are the doer of an action, and you would say "me" when you are the receiver of an action. In Chinese, it does not matter. "Me" and "I" are represented by the same Chinese character. Similarly, as you can see from the following list of personal pronouns, no distinction is made between "he" and "him", "she" and "her", or "they" and "them". On the other hand, there are a few variations for the second and third persons, but you can get by with using only the general term and ignoring the gender, the difference between humans and animals or inanimate objects, and the difference between mundanity and divinity.

我
wǒ
    I, me

你
nǐ
    You (singular, **general term**)
    (The radical on the left side denotes a man or a person.)

您
nín
    You (polite form)

妳
nǐ
    You (singular, female)
    (The radical on the left side denotes a female person.)

他
tā
    He, him (**general term**)
    (The radical on the left side denotes a man or a person.)

她
tā
    She, her (singular, female)

它
tā
    It (a thing)
    (The radical on top denotes a roof.)

牠
tā
    It (an animal)
    (The radical on the left side denotes an ox.)

祂
tā
    He/She (divinity)

我们　　　　　We, us
wǒmen

你们　　　　　You (plural, **general term**)
nǐmen

妳们　　　　　You (plural, female)
nǐmen

他们　　　　　They, them (plural, **general term**)
tāmen

她们　　　　　They, them (female)
tāmen

谁?　　　　　Who?
Shéi?

The song that you have learned in the "Introduction" contains a line that says:

一只没有尾巴.　　　　　One does not have a tail.
Yī zhī méiyǒu wěiba.

You could insert the word "tiger" after the "one", and say:

一只老虎没有尾巴.　　One tiger does not have a tail.
Yī zhī lǎohǔ méiyǒu wěiba.

You could also say:

牠没有尾巴.　　　　　It does not have a tail.
Tā méiyǒu wěiba.

没 (méi) means "not". If the tiger does have a tail then we should drop this character and say:

牠有尾巴.　　　　　It has a tail.
Tā yǒu wěiba.

24　　　　　　　　　　　2. Me or I?

Let's say the following out loud:

我有耳朵.   I have ears.
  Wǒ yǒu ěrduo.

我有眼睛.   I have eyes.
  Wǒ yǒu yǎnjing.

我有嘴巴.   I have a mouth.
  Wǒ yǒu zuǐba.

我有鼻子.   I have a nose.
  Wǒ yǒu bízi.

我有牙齿.   I have teeth.
  Wǒ yǒu yáchǐ.

As an exercise, substitute the "I" in the above sentences with each of the other pronouns that you have learned. When you use 谁 (Shéi? Who?), the sentence becomes a question, such as, "Who has ears?"

有 (yǒu) means "have", and 没有 (méiyǒu) means "not have" or "have not". 有没有 (yǒu méiyǒu) means "Have or have not?". For example:

牠有没有尾巴?   Does it have a tail or not?
  Tā yǒu méiyǒu wěiba?

When the parents say the following to a child, they are not really asking if their child has ears. Rather, they are chiding, "Why did you not heed my words?"

你有没有耳朵?   Do you have ears or not?
  Nǐ yǒu méiyǒu ěrduo?   (Why did you not listen to me?)

Up to this point, you have learned a few nouns (such as tiger, tail), pronouns (such as I, you) and verbs (run, have). You have also learned one adjective (two) and one adverb (fast). These are all essential components that make up a sentence. The main goal of this book is to enable you to speak Chinese in complete sentences. Obviously, the more words you know, the more sentences you will be able to make. Therefore, besides learning the sentence structures used in the Chinese language, you will also want to stock up on the words with which you can construct the sentences.

You may wish to start a vocabulary notebook of your own, and make an entry each time you have learned a new word either from this book or from somewhere else. A loose-leaf binder will work well because it lets you easily insert new pages and reorganize the existing pages in a way that will allow you to easily find what you need. Write each new word on a fresh page, along with its pinyin and English translation. Also write down a simple sentence with that word in it to show its usage. Revisit the page from time to time, as your vocabulary increases, to add more sophisticated sentences using that word.

I suggest that you organize this notebook into a few sections and add dividers that are labeled: **Nouns and Pronouns** (people, places, things and thoughts), **Adjectives** (words that describe the nouns), **Verbs** (actions), **Adverbs** (words that qualify the actions), **Conjunctives** (words that help connect clauses), and **Others** (particles, interjections, etc.). If you have a software program that lets you enter Chinese text into a computer file, then you could compile an electronic version of this vocabulary book. It is true that you will find many useful word lists in the book you are reading now, but you will definitely get a much greater sense of ownership with the words that you have collected yourself. For your reference, the abbreviations for some of the common parts of speech are listed below:

Part of Speech	Abbreviation	Examples
Noun	n.	house, mouse, tree
Adjective	adj.	beautiful, good, slow
Verb	v.	come, sit
Adverb	adv.	fast, slowly, quietly
Preposition	prep.	of, for, in
Conjunction	conj.	and, or, if, when
Interjection	interj.	Oh! Ah!

The Possessive Case of Pronouns

You form the possessive case of a personal pronoun by simply adding the particle 的 (de) to it, as shown below.

我的
wǒ de

My, of mine

你的
nǐ de

Your, of yours (singular)

他的
tā de

His, of his

她的
tā de

Her, of hers

它的, 牠的
tā de　,　tā de

Its (of a thing), its (of an animal)

祂的
tā de

His/Her, of his/of hers (divinity)

我们的
wǒmen de

Our, of ours

你们的
nǐmen de

Your, of yours (plural)

他们的
tāmen de

Their, of theirs

她们的
tāmen de

Their, of theirs (female)

谁的?
Shéi de?

Whose?

Let's say the following out loud. Please also try these sentences using some of the other personal pronouns:

我们的耳朵　　　　　　　　Our ears
wǒmen de ěrduo

我们的眼睛　　　　　　　　Our eyes
wǒmen de yǎnjīng

我们的嘴巴　　　　　　　　Our mouths
wǒmen de zuǐba

我们的鼻子　　　　　　　　Our noses
wǒmen de bízi

我们的牙齿　　　　　　　　Our teeth
wǒmen de yáchǐ

Often, the particle 的 (de) is omitted, as shown in the examples below:

我爸爸　　　　　　　　　　My dad
wǒ bàba

你妈妈　　　　　　　　　　Your mom
nǐ māma

他牙齿　　　　　　　　　　His teeth
tā yáchǐ

Have you noticed that we did not have to do anything special to form the plural of a noun? The same word 老虎 (lǎohǔ) is used whether there is one tiger or there are two tigers. Similarly, the same word 牙齿 (yáchǐ) is used to indicate one tooth or a mouthful of teeth. This is one of the nice things about Chinese grammar.

Linking Verbs

A linking verb associates a noun or pronoun with a complement. Following are the most commonly used linking verbs:

是 **(shì to be)** can be used to associate a noun or pronoun with another noun or pronoun. For example:

他是我的朋友.　　　　　He is my friend.
Tā shì wǒ de péngyǒu.

是 (shì to be) can also link a noun or pronoun with an adjective (description). In this case, however, 是 (shì to be) is usually omitted from the sentence. For example, for "I am tired", you would normally say:

我累了　　instead of:　　我是累了.
Wǒ lèi le.　　　　　　　Wǒ shì lèi le.

好像 **(hǎoxiàng seem, to appear to be)**, 感到 **(gǎndào feel)** , 感觉 **(gǎnjué feel)** or 觉得 **(juéde feel)** joins a noun or pronoun to an adjective only.

她好像累了.　　　　　She seems tired.
Tā hǎoxiàng lèi le.

我感到高兴.　　　　　I feel happy.
Wǒ gǎndào gāoxìng.

在 **(zài)** means "to be at some place" when it is used as a linking verb.

我们在家里.　　　　　We are at home.
Wǒmen zài jiālǐ.

Practice forming simple sentences by pairing up any term listed below on the left side with any term listed on the right side. You may wish to add the new words to the "Nouns" section of your vocabulary book.

我是 Wǒ shì	老师 lǎoshī	teacher(s)
你是 Nǐ shì	学生 xuéshēng	student(s)
我们是 Wǒmen shì	工程师 gōngchéngshī	engineer(s)
你们是 Nǐmen shì	工人 gōngrén	laborer(s)
他们是 Tāmen shì	护士 (看护) hùshì (kānhù)	nurse(s)
我不是 Wǒ bú shì	医生 (医师) yīshēng (yīshī)	doctor(s)
你不是 Nǐ bú shì	好人 hǎorén	good person (good people)
他也是 Tā yě shì	音乐家 yīnyuèjiā	musician(s)

不 (bú) means "not". 我不是医生 (wǒ bú shì yīshēng) means: "I am not a doctor". 也 (yě) means "also". 他也是音乐家 (Tā yě shì yīnyuèjiā) means: "He is also a musician."

问候 Greetings
Wènhòu

A: 你好吗? How are you?
Nǐ hǎo ma?

B: 我很好. 谢谢. I'm very fine. Thanks.
Wǒ hěn hǎo. Xièxiè.

你呢? 你好不好呢? And you? How about you?
Nǐ ne? Nǐ hǎo bùhǎo ne?

A: 我也很好. 谢谢. I'm fine also. Thanks.
Wǒ yě hěn hǎo. Xièxiè.

你哥哥呢? How about your brother?
Nǐ gēge ne?

他好不好呢? How is he doing?
Tā hǎo bù hǎo ne?

Note that 是 (shì) is implied in the above sentences that contain the "be" verb. For example, in "你好吗? (Nǐ hǎo ma?) " , the adjective connects directly to the pronoun without the intermediary "be" verb. To show courtesy to strangers or older people, replace "你 (nǐ)" with "您 (nín)". This will reflect on you as a refined and civilized person.

吗 (ma) and 呢 (ne or ní) are particles used to denote a question. 吗 (ma) is used only in a direct question, such as: "你好吗? (Nǐ hǎo ma?)" 呢 (ne or ní) is usually used after "whether or not", as in: "是不是呢? (Shì búshì ne? Is it or not?)"

Below, try pairing up any term on the left side with any term on the right side.

我在 Wǒ zài	家 jiā	home
你在 Nǐ zài	学校 xuéxiào	school
他在 Tā zài	公园里 gōngyuán lǐ	in the (public) park
我们在 Wǒmen zài	公车上 gōngchē shàng	on a public car (bus)
我们在 Wǒmen zài	巴士上 bāshì shàng	on the bus
你们在 Nǐmen zài	火车上 huǒchē shàng	on the train
他们在 Tāmen zài	街上 jiē shàng	on the street
我不在 Wǒ bú zài	草地上 cǎodì shàng	on the lawn
你不在 Nǐ bú zài	医院 yīyuàn yī yuàn	hospital
他也在 Tā yě zài	电影院 diànyǐngyuàn	movie hall
他不在 Tā bú zài	戏院 xìyuàn	theater

2. Me or I?

The following popular song originated from a German children's song, titled "Ach, Du Lieber Augustin". The composer of this song is unknown. The Chinese translation is very popular in Taiwan but the name of its author is unknown.

The More We Get Together
当我们同在一起
Dāng Wǒmen Tóng Zài Yīqǐ

当我们同在一起,
Dāng wǒmen tóng zài yīqǐ,

The more we get together,
Whenever we're together,

在一起, 在一起;
Zài yīqǐ, zài yīqǐ;

Together, together;
Together, together;

当我们同在一起,
Dāng wǒmen tóng zài yīqǐ,

The more we get together,
Whenever we're together,

其快乐无比.
Qí kuàilè wúbǐ.

The happier we'll be.
The joy is supreme.

你对著我笑嘻嘻.
Nǐ duì zhe wǒ xiàoxīxī.

For your friend is my friend,
You're smiling at me, "Hee, hee!"

我对著你笑哈哈.
Wǒ duì zhe nǐ xiàohāhā.

And my friend is your friend.
I'm smiling at you, "Ha, ha!"

当我们同在一起,
Dāng wǒmen tóng zài yīqǐ,

The more we get together,
Whenever we're together,

其快乐无比.
Qí kuàilè wúbǐ.

The happier we'll be.
The joy is supreme.

Let's look at some of the new words in this song.

当 (dāng) is the conjunctive "when".

同 (tóng) means "same" or "to have in common".

在一起 (zài yīqǐ) means "to be together", or "to be in the company of".

同在一起 (tóng zài yīqǐ) means "to be in the company of each other".

快乐 (kuàilè) is "happy (adj.)" or "happiness (n.)".

其 (chí) is a classical term that means "its", "his", "her", or "their". In this song, it refers to the state of being in each other's company.

无 (wú without) is the formal word for 没有 (méiyǒu have not, without). 比 (bǐ) is to compare. (See how the left side of the character kind of matches the right side.) 无比 (wúbǐ) literally translates to "no comparison". It means "beyond comparison".

对著 (duì zhe) means "directed at", as in:

他对著我笑.   He smiles at me.
Tā duì zhe wǒ xiào.

笑嘻嘻 (xiàoxīxī) and 笑哈哈 (xiàohāhā) are expressions that incorporate the sounds made when one laughs out loud.

As with the "Two Odd Tigers" song, I suggest that you first read the verses out loud a few times then sing the song. Sing the song a few times with the lyrics and pinyin in front of you. Then sing it without looking at the page, perhaps with an occasional peek or two. Sing it while taking a shower. Sing it while taking a walk. Sing it while making dinner. And pretty soon you will have all of these new words and expressions down pat. I hope someday you will get a chance to surprise a Chinese friend by singing a song in Chinese.

3. Family Members

The word 家 (jiā) means "family", "home" or "household". 家人 (jiārén) usually refers to the members of the immediate family, whereas 家族 (jiāzú) includes all kinfolk.

The Chinese make a clear distinction between the paternal and maternal relatives. The maternal relatives are considered "external relatives". For example, your father's father is your grandfather (祖父 zǔfù), while your mother's father is your "external grandfather" (外祖父 wàizǔfù). Unfortunately, this simple rule does not apply to the other relatives. As you will see in the following lists, your father's brother and your mother's brother have entirely different titles. Moreover, how you address your uncle or aunt would depend on whether he or she is older or younger than your father. Similarly, the word for "older sister" is different from the word for "younger sister"; and the word for "older brother" is different from the word for "younger brother".

Even a Chinese may sometimes pause a little before correctly referring to a distant relative. So, don't sweat over all the different family member names. Just learn a few essential ones then refer back to the lists on this and the following pages as necessary.

直系亲属 zhícì qīnshǔ Linear Relatives and Immediate Family

曾祖父	zēngzǔfù	Great-grandfather
曾祖母	zēngzǔmǔ	Great-grandmother
祖父	zǔfù	Grandfather
爷爷	yéye	Grandpa

祖母	zǔmǔ	Grandmother
奶奶	nǎinai	Grandma
父亲	fùqin	Father
爸爸	bàba	Dad
爹	diē	(same as above)
母亲	mǔqin	Mother
妈妈	māma	Mom
娘	niáng	(same as above)
丈夫	zhàngfū	Husband
先生	xiānsheng	(same as above; also means Mr.)
妻子	qīzi	Wife
太太	tàitai	(same as above; also means Mrs.)
哥哥	gēge	Elder Brother
姊姊	jiějie	Elder Sister
弟弟	dìdi	Younger Brother
妹妹	mèimei	Younger Sister
儿, 儿子	ér, érzi	Son
女儿	nǚér	Daughter
孙, 孙子	sūn, sūnzi	Grandson
孙女	sūnnǚ	Granddaughter

3. Family Members

曾孙	zēngsūn	Great-grandson
曾孙女	zēngsūnnǚ	Great-granddaughter
继父	jìfù	Stepfather
继母	jìmǔ	Stepmother
养父	yǎngfù	Adoptive Father, Foster Father
养母	yǎngmǔ	Adoptive Mother, Foster Mother
养子	yǎngzǐ	Adopted/Foster Son
养女	yǎngnǚ	Adopted/Foster Daughter

近亲 jìnqīn **Near Relatives**

伯父	bófù	Uncle (father's elder brother)
伯伯	bóbo	(same as above)
叔父	shúfù	Uncle (father's younger brother)
叔叔	shúshu	(same as above)
姑母	gūmǔ	Aunt (father's sister)
姑姑	gūgu	(same as above)
堂哥	tánggē	Elder Cousin (male)
堂姊	tángjiě	Elder Cousin (female)
堂弟	tángdì	Younger Cousin (male)
堂妹	tángmèi	Younger Cousin (female)

侄, 侄子	zhí, zhízi	Nephew (brother's son)
侄女	zhínǚ	Niece (brother's daughter)
甥, 甥子	shēng, shēngzi	Nephew (sister's son)
甥女	shēngnǚ	Niece (sister's daughter)

姻亲 yīnqīn **In-laws**

公公	gōnggong	Father-in-law (husband's father)
婆婆	pópo	Mother-in-law (husband's mother)
岳父	yuèfù	Father-in-law (wife's father)
丈人	zhàngrén	(same as above)
岳母	yuèmǔ	Mother-in-law (wife's mother)
丈母娘	zhàngmǔniáng	(same as above)
媳妇	xífù	Daughter-in-law
女婿	nǔxù	Son-in-law
伯母	bómǔ	Aunt (wife of father's elder brother)
叔母	shúmǔ	Aunt (wife of father's younger brother)
婶婶	shěnshen	Aunt (wife of father's younger brother)
姑丈	gūzhàng	Uncle (husband of father's sister)
嫂嫂	sǎosao	Sister-in-law (elder brother's wife)

姊夫	jiěfu	Brother-in-law (elder sister's husband)
弟媳	dìxí	Sister-in-law (younger brother's wife)
弟妹	dìmèi	(same as above)
妹婿	mèixù	Brother-in-law (younger sister's husband)

Some people say "弟妹 (dìmèi)" instead of "弟媳 (dìxí)" when referring to the younger brother's wife. This should not be confused with 弟妹们 (dì mèi mén), or 弟弟妹妹们 (dìdi mèimei mén), which refers to one's younger brothers and younger sisters.

密友 mìyǒu **Close Friends**

干爸爸	gānbàba	"Dry" Father (similar to a god-father)
干妈妈	gānmāma	"Dry" Mother (similar to a godmother)
干儿子	gānérzi	"Dry" Son (similar to a godson)
干女儿	gānnǚér	"Dry" Daughter(similar to a goddaughter)

外亲 wàiqīn **Maternal Relatives**

外 (wài) means "external" or "outside". Traditionally, the Chinese have adopted a male-centered mentality. As the male offspring normally carries the family name, he is much favored over a female offspring. In the province where I came from, if your newborn baby is a son, people will say jubilantly, "Congratulations!" If it's a girl, they will try to console you, "It's okay, too."

外曾祖父	wàizēngzǔfù	Great-grandfather
外曾祖母	wàizēngzǔmǔ	Great-gandmother
外祖父	wàizǔfù	Grandfather (mother's father)
外公	wàigōng	Grandpa
外祖母	wàizǔmǔ	Grandmother (mother's mother)
外婆	wàipó	Grandma
舅父	jiùfù	Uncle (mother's brother)
舅舅	jiùjiù	(same as above)
舅妈	jiùmā	Aunt (wife of mother's brother)
姨妈	yímā	Aunt (mother's sister)
阿姨	āyí	(same as above)
姨丈	yízhàng	Uncle (aunt's husband)
表哥	biǎogē	Elder Cousin (male)
表嫂	biǎosǎo	Elder Cousin's Wife
表姊	biǎojiě	Elder Cousin (female)
表姊夫	biǎojiěfū	Elder Cousin's Husband
表弟	biǎodì	Younger Cousin (male)
表弟媳	biǎodìxí	Younger Cousin's Wife
表妹	biǎomèi	Younger Cousin (female)
表妹婿	biǎomèixù	Younger Cousin's husband

3. Family Members

外孙	wàisūn		Grandson (daughter's son)	
外孙女	wàisūnnǚ		Granddaughter (daugheter's daughter)	
外曾孙	wàizēngsūn		Great-grandson	
外曾孙女	wàizēngsūnnǚ		Great-granddaughter	

As an exercise, use a pencil to join a pronoun on the left side to one of the nouns listed on the right side on the following page. Then write the English translation of the resulting term in the corresponding blank.

我的	wǒ de	祖父	zǔfù	_____
你的	nǐ de	外祖母	wàizǔmǔ	_____
他的	tā de	父亲	fùqīn	_____
我的	wǒ de	母亲	mǔqīn	_____
你们的	nǐmen de	姊姊	jiějie	_____
他们的	tāmen de	哥哥	gēge	_____

Following is a quotation of a simple rhyme written by 周伯阳 (Zhōu Bóyáng 1917-1984). It was set to music by his close friend, 苏春涛 (Sū Chuntáo 1918-2008), and became a popular Chinese children's song in Taiwan. Both gentlemen served as elementary school principals in Hsin-Chu, Taiwan, and enjoyed composing music. At a time when almost all children's songs sung in Taiwan were Japanese children's songs or translations thereof, these two gentlemen realized the importance of writing Taiwan's own children's songs.

Little Sister Totes a Doll
妹妹背著洋娃娃
Mèimei Bēi Zhe Yángwāwa

妹妹背著洋娃娃.　　　　Little sister is toting a doll.
Mèimei bēi zhe yángwāwa.

走到花园来看花.　　　　To the flower garden she strolls.
Zǒudào huāyuán lái kàn huā.　(Goes to the garden see the flowers.)

娃娃哭了, 叫妈妈.　　　　Dolly cries, and calls, "Mama!"
Wāwa kū le, jiào māma.

树上小鸟笑哈哈.　　　　On the tree, birds laugh, "Ha-ha!"
Shù shàng xiǎoniǎo xiàohāhā.　(The birds on the trees are laughing.)

娃娃 (wāwa) is a doll or a baby, while 洋娃娃 (yángwāwa) is a "foreign doll", most likely with blond hair and blue eyes. As most commercially available dolls are "foreign dolls", 洋娃娃 (yángwāwa) is a term generally used to refer to a doll. The word 洋 (yáng) means ocean or sea. Traditionally, many things from across the ocean receive the prefix 洋 (yáng). For example, potato is called 洋芋 (yángyú), or "foreign taro".

The above song contains a number of new nouns (names) and verbs (action words) that you could enter into your vocabulary book.

背著	bēi zhe	carrying on the back (v., progressive)
洋娃娃	yángwāwa	doll, foreign doll (n.)
走	zǒu	go, walk, leave (v.)

走到	zǒudào	walk to, go to (v. + prep.)
花园	huāyuán	flower garden (n.)
来	lái	come (v.)
看	kàn	see, look (v.)
花	huā	flower, flowers (n.)
哭	kū	weep, cry (v.)
叫	jiào	call, shout, ask to do something (v.)
树	shù	tree, trees (n.)
树上	shù shàng	on the tree, on the trees (adverbial phrase)
鸟	niǎo	bird, birds (n.)
小鸟	xiǎoniǎo	dickeybird; literally, little bird (adj. + n.)
笑	xiào	laugh (v.)

Notice that there are two wailing mouths, 口 (kǒu), and a teardrop in the word 哭 (kū). On the other hand, it looks like there is a pair of smiling eyes in the word 笑 (xiào).

The nouns and the verbs form the backbone of a sentence. Study the following simple sentences then make a couple of your own sentences using the words you have learned so far. On the left side, write the sentence in Chinese characters and pinyin, or just in pinyin, as you please. On the right side, write down the English translation.

In some of the sample sentences, I have appended the word 了 (le) to the verbs. This is an auxiliary word that helps to indicate that an action has transpired.

她背著娃娃.
Tā bēi zhe wāwa.

She is carrying a baby on her back.

我走到花园.
Wǒ zhǒu dào huāyuán.

I walk to the flower garden.

他来了.
Tā lái le.

He has come. He has arrived.

你叫他.
Nǐ jiào tā.

Call out to him.

他叫我来.
Tā jiào wǒ lái.

He asks me to come.

你弟弟哭了.
Nǐ dìdi kū le.

Your little brother is crying.

他们的母亲笑了.
Tāmen de mǔqin xiào le.

Their mother smiled.

_____   _____
_____   _____

_____   _____
_____   _____

4. Names of People

Each Chinese name is made up of a surname (family name) and a given name. The surname is usaully the same for everyone in the family, but the given name can be a combination of any characters.

Surnames

There is one fundamental difference between the Chinese and the English naming conventions - the Chinese surname, or 姓氏 (xìngshì), comes before the given name, not after it. Most of the Chinese surnames consist of just one character. Here are a few common ones:

Chinese	**Pinyin**	**Meaning**	**English Representation**
王	Wáng	King	Wang
李	Lǐ	Plum, prune	Lee
黄	Huáng	Yellow	Huang
陈	Chén	Display, old	Chen
林	Lín	Woods, forest	Lin
张	Zhāng	Open, spread, sheet	Zhang (often shown as Chang)
叶	Yè	Leaf	Yeh
苏	Sū	Revive	Su
白	Bái	White, pure	Bai
马	Mǎ	Horse	Ma
刘	Liú	(no particular meaning)	Liu
廖	Liào	(no particular meaning)	Liao

Following is a partial list of additional Chinese family names.

于 Yú	文 Wén	牛 Niú	毛 Máo	甘 Gān
方 Fāng	石 Shí	古 Gǔ	司 Sī	皮 Pí
汪 Wāng	宋 Sòng	安 Ān	周 Zhōu	米 Mǐ
何 Hé	柯 Kē	花 Huā	倪 Ní	胡 Hú
唐 Táng	吴 Wú	金 Jīn	章 Zhāng	施 shī
高 Gāo	汤 Tāng	范 Fàn	徐 Xú	许 Xǔ
袁 Yuán	贝 Bèi	温 Wēn	邱 Qiū	辜 Gū
连 Lián	应 Yìng	蔡 Cài	彭 Péng	夏 Xià
杨 Yáng	候 Hóu	邓 Dèng	陶 Táo	简 Jiǎn
郑 Zhèng	陆 Lù	潘 Pān	秦 Qín	贺 Hè
董 Dǒng	童 Tóng	赖 Lài	钱 Qián	谢 Xiè
毕 Bì	罗 Luó	庐 Lú	庞 Páng	姚 Yáo
蒋 Jiǎng	魏 Wèi	严 Yán	萧 Xiāo	顾 Gù
傅 Fù	赵 Zhào	曾 Zēng	戴 Dài	席 Xí
鲁 Lǔ	司马 Sīmǎ	公孙 Gōngsūn		

王先生 (Wáng xiānsheng) means "Mr. Wang", and 王太太 (Wáng tàitai) means "Mrs. Wang". In China and Taiwan, it's customary to address or refer to a male friend by his last name, such as in 老王 (Lǎo Wáng "Wang") and 老张 (Lǎo Zhāng "Zhang"). Just as with the word 老虎 (lǎohǔ tiger), here 老 (lǎo) does not mean old. It simply connotes an old friend, or 老朋友 (lǎo péngyǒu).

Given Names

The Chinese given names, or 名字 (míngzi), also contain just one or two characters. Why do the Chinese have such short names? There is an entertaining story written by Arlene Morsel and illustrated by Blair Lent, titled "Tiki Tiki Tembo", which offers a cute fictional explanation. If you know a young child, this would be a delightful book to read to him or her.

The fact is that each Chinese character actually represents one complete word. So, if you translate it into English, the one-syllable Chinese character often turns into a polysyllable English word. For example, 黄天虎 (Huáng Tiānhǔ), a three-syllable name, might be translated into English as: "Yellow Tiger from the Sky". This is why a ten-page report that's written in English could likely shrink to five or fewer pages after it has been translated into Chinese.

Traditionally, the names of the male children in a family have one character in common. Often, in the same family, the girls' names may also share one common character. Nowadays, most people name their children with any one or two characters that have auspicious meanings and sound good together with their family name. Small wonder that such words as "pearl", "jade", "flower", "beauty" and "fragrance" are popular in a girl's name, and "treasure", "strength", "courage", "prosperity" and "loyalty", in a boy's name. Another favorite character is "gold", although in Chinese, the word "gold" refers to metals in general. The Chinese believe that a good life depends on a proper balance of the vital forces of yin and yang as well as the five elements: metals, wood, water, fire, and soil. Therefore, if the fortuneteller says that your child is deficient in "metals", then you would want to give your child a name that contains the word 金 (jīn gold, or metals). Actually, the five elements do not simply refer to the corresponding physical entities, but are symbols employed in Chinese metaphysics.

In general, the Chinese do not call their elder family members by name. Rather, they respectfully address them by their order in the family hierarchy. For example, they would say something like, "Second Oldest Sister, are you coming?" On the other hand, they are free to call their younger siblings by name.

After you have become familiar with a fair number of Chinese characters and words you could make up a nice Chinese alias for yourself. If you can't wait, you could easily find a list of Chinese equivalents of English names on the Internet and pick one that corresponds to your name. The Chinese names provided in such a list are combinations of characters that sound somewhat like your English name and that don't have negative meanings. Over the years, the Chinese transliteration of some of the common English names have been standardized, such as Mary 玛莉 (Mǎlì),

彼得 (Bǐdé), Paul 保罗 (Bǎoluó), Lincoln 林肯 (Línkěn), and Washington 华盛顿 (Huáshèngdùn). Unless your last name is Lee, Lynn or Young, which translate nicely to 李 (Lǐ), 林 (Lín), or 杨 (Yáng), respectively, its Chinese equivalent could be a mouthful. For example, "Hilton" is translated as 希尔顿 (Xīrdùn). The extra syllable "ěr" is necessitated by the fact that there is not any Chinese character that ends in "l". You may choose to use the full phonetic translation of your last name. Or, you could just use the initial character of the transliteration to make it sound more like a Chinese last name. For example, "Mary Seton" could be translated as 玛莉席顿 (Mǎlì Xídùn), its English equivalent.

Or, we could use 席玛莉 (Xí Mǎlì), or 苏玛莉 (Sū Mǎlì), which sounds much more like a typical Chinese name.

Following is a Scottish folk song about one of the four maids-in-waiting of Mary Guise, Queen Consort of James V. The "me" refers to Mary Hamilton, for whom there was no record in the Scottish history. There was, however, an incident in Russia involving a Mary Hamilton. No matter that the balladiers might have had their historical facts mixed up, this heart-breaking song aptly reflects the sorrow of a young lady who was about to be executed. The original lyrics are italicized.

The Four Marys
四位玛莉
Sì Wèi Mǎlì

昨夜有四位玛莉.
Zuóyè yǒu sì wèi Mǎlì.

Last night there were four Marys.

今夜将剩下三位.
Jīnyè jiàng shèngxià sān wèi.

Tonight there'll be but three.
Tonight there will remain three.

你看苏玛莉,
Nǐ kàn Sū Mǎlì,

There was Mary Seton,
Look at Mary S.,

白玛莉,
Bái Mǎlì,

Mary Beaton,
Mary B.,

柯玛莉.
Kē Mǎlì.

Mary Carmichael,
Mary C.,

他们都为我流泪.
Tāmen dōu wèi wǒ liú lèi.

And me.
They are all weeping for me.

Note that 昨夜 (zuóyè last night) and 今夜 (jīnyè tonight) share the character 夜 (yè), which means "night". 昨 (zuó) stands for "yester-", and 今 (jīn) indicates the present. By pairing each character listed below on the left side to each of the characters on the right side, you will obtain the words for today, this evening, tonight, tomorrow, tomorrow evening, tomorrow night, yesterday, last evening, and last night.

今	jīn	today, the present time (adv.)	天	tiān	day (n.)
明	míng	tomorrow, next (in time)	晚	wǎn	evening (n.)
昨	zuó	yesterday (adv.), yester-	夜	yè	night (n.)

When talking about years, 去 (qù) is used to indicate the past year.

今年	jīnnián	The current year
明年	míngnián	Next year
去年	qùnián	Last year

In the above, 去 (qù) is used as an adjective that means "past or gone". This word does double-duty as a verb that means "go away" or "remove". It is the opposite of 来 (lái come, or coming in the future).

When talking about months, you would just say "this month", "the previous month" and "the following month".

这個月 zhège yuè   this month

上個月 shàng ge yuè   the previous month

下個月 xià ge yuè   next month

See the difference between the words 上 (shàng above, previous) and 下 (xià below, following) ? These two should be easy to remember.

In the following sentence, 为我 (wèi wǒ) means "for me". It comes before the verb 流泪 (liú lèi weep, shed tears). This is one example where the word order is distinctly different in English and Chinese.

他们都为我流泪.   They are all weeping for me.
Tāmen dōu wèi wǒ liú lèi.

Practice this sentence pattern by using the nouns and pronouns that you have already learned. The word 都 (dōu all) is used here as an adverb to emphasize that the action or description pertains to two or more subjects. With the singular nouns and pronouns, you would omit the word 都 (dōu). For example:

妈妈为你流泪.   Mom weeps for you.
Māma wèi nǐ liú lèi.

她为你流泪.   She weeps for you.
Tā wèi nǐ liú lèi.

玛莉和我都为他流泪.   Mary and I both weep for him.
Mǎlì hé wǒ dōu wèi tā liú lèi.

和 (hé) means "and" or "along with". Many people in Taiwan pronounce it as "hàn".

5. Keeping Count

Arabic numerals are used extensively in China. If you were in China and didn't know how to say, for example, "three hundred and sixty-five", you could always manage by jotting down "365" on a piece of paper. Nevertheless, it will be helpful to know the Chinese numerals and be able to read, for instance, the price tags at a local store or the menu plastered on a wall at a small local eatery.

You already know the first four numerals in Chinese. Do you recognize them in the following sentences and expressions?

一只没有耳朵.
Yī zhī méiyǒu ěrduo.

One is missing the ears.

两只老虎
Liǎng zhī lǎohǔ

Two old tigers

剩下三位.
Shèng xià sān wèi.

There remain *three*.

四位玛莉
Sì wèi Mǎlì

Four Marys

Now, you should never say 两只人 (liǎng zhī rén), or 四只玛莉 (sì zhī Mǎlì). It would be disrespectful. 只 (zhī) is a unit for counting animals, eyes, ears, limbs, fingers, toes, and a few other things, but not people. 個 (gè) is a general unit that can be safely applied to discrete entities. It is okay to say 两個老虎 (liǎng gè lǎohǔ) or 四個玛莉 (sì gè Mǎlì). However, it is more polite to say 四位玛莉 (sì wèi Mǎlì). 位 (wèi) means "seat", "place", or "position". It is also used as a unit for counting people in a respectful way. In fact, the Chinese use specific units for counting different things. I will talk about this in the next chapter, and also show you how to say "a dozen eggs" and "a flock of sheep" in Chinese.

两 (liǎng) is the colloquial way of saying "two" in Chinese, as in:

两 只 老 虎   Two tigers
liǎng zhī lǎohǔ

两 只 眼 睛   Two eyes
liǎng zhī yǎnjing

两個人   Two persons
liǎng ge rén

二 (èr) is the formal word for "two". It is the one used in mathematical expressions. When counting to four in Chinese, you would say:

一, 二, 三, 四   1, 2, 3, 4
yī, èr, sān, sì

And, the Chinese expression for "one out of two (one half)" is:

二分之一
èr fēn zhī yī

You have seen the word 分 (fēn divide, a fraction of) in the chapter titled "Introduction", under "Chinese Characters". To express any fraction, just put the divisor in front of 分 (fēn) and put the numerator at the end. For example:

三分之二   two out of three parts (2/3)
sān fēn zhī èr

四分之一   one out of four, one-fourth, a quarter (1/4)
sì fēn zhī yī

By the way, in some Chinese dialects, 四 (sì four) is pronounced in the third tone and sounds exactly like 死 (sǐ dead). Therefore, the number 4 is considered inauspicious by the Chinese, like the number 13 in English.

An important fraction to know is 1/100: 百分之一 (bǎi fēn zhī yī), where 百 (bǎi) is "hundred". Hence, three percent (3%) is: 百分之三 (bǎi fēn zhī sān).

The Chinese word for "numbers", "numerals" or "figures" used in counting is: 数字 (shù zì). However, when referring to house numbers or phone numbers, you would use: 号码 (hàomǎ). For example, 电话号码 (diànhuà hàomǎ) is the telephone number, and 房间号码 (fángjiān hàomǎ) is the room number. Please make sure you stress the fourth tone in 号码 (hàomǎ number), so this word will not be misconstrued as: 好吗? (Hǎo ma? Is it okay?)

To form the ordinal numbers, simply add the word 第 (dì ranking) to each numeral. 第一 (dìyī) means the first, 第二 (dìèr) means the second, 第三 (dìsān) means the third, and so on.

第一名 (dìyī míng) means placing first, as in a competition.

第一步 (dìyī bù) means "Step #1", such as in a procedure.

第三楼 (dìsān lóu) means the third floor.

第一次 (dìyīcì) means the first time.

世界 (shìjiè) is the world. 大战 (dàzhàn) means big war. Therefore, WWII translates to: 第二次世界大战 (dìèr cì shìjièdàzhàn)

You will need the following words for doing arithmetic:

加	jiā	Add
减	jiǎn	Subtract (also means "to reduce")
乘	chéng	Multiply (also means "to ride on a vehicle")
除	chú	Divide (also means "to remove")

Days of the Week

With the exception of Sunday, each day of the week is named by its sequence number. Monday is "Weekday 1", Tuesday is "Weekday 2", and so on.

Both 周 (zhōu) and 星期 (zīngqī) mean "week". Therefore, there are two formal ways of saying each day of the week. 日 (rì sun) and 天 (tiān sky, heaven) both mean "day".

周一 zhōuyī	or	星期一 xīngqīyī		Monday
周二 zhōuèr	or	星期二 xīngqīèr		Tuesday
周三 zhōusān	or	星期三 xīngqīsān		Wednesday
周四 zhōusì	or	星期四 zīngqīsì		Thursday
周五 zhōuwǔ	or	星期五 xīngqīwǔ		Friday
周六 zhōuliù	or	星期六 xīngqīliù		Saturday
周日 zhōurì	or	星期日 xīngqīrì	or 星期天 xīngqītiān	Sunday
周末 zhōumò	or	星期末 xīngqīmò		Weekend

Practice saying the days of the week by using the following sentence pattern:

星期天见!
Xīngqītiān jiàn!   See you on Sunday!

There is also an informal way of saying each day of the week that is associated with religious worship.

礼拜 (lǐbài) means "worship". Monday would be the first day of worship, Tuesday, the second day of worship, and so on.

礼拜一   Monday
lǐbàiyī

礼拜二   Tuesday
lǐbàièr

礼拜三   Wednesday
lǐbàisān

礼拜四   Thursday
lǐbàisì

礼拜五   Friday
lǐbàiwǔ

礼拜六   Saturday
lǐbàiliù

礼拜日   or   礼拜天   Sunday
lǐbàirì   lǐbàitiān

Now you know how to count to six in Chinese, and you can probably write the first three numerals in Chinese with your eyes closed. Please fill in the blanks below. Do both the Chinese characters and the pinyin if you can.

_____, _____, _____, _____, _____, _____   1, 2, 3, 4, 5, 6
   yī   _____ _____ _____ _____ _____ (pinyin)

Months of the Year

The month is represented by the character for the moon, which is 月 (yuè moon).

The months of the year, 月份 (yuèfèn), are named by their sequence numbers. January is the first month, February is the second month, and so on.

一月 yīyuè	January	七月 qīyuè	July
二月 èryuè	February	八月 bāyuè	August
三月 sānyuè	March	九月 jiǔyuè	September
四月 sìyuè	April	十月 shíyuè	October
五月 wǔyuè	May	十一月 shíyīyuè	November
六月 liùyuè	June	十二月 shíèryuè	December

闰月 (rùnyuè) means "leap month", and 闰年 (rùnnián) means "leap year".

Dates

Although the word "day" can be represented by 天 (tiān sky, heaven) or 日 (rì sun), 日 (rì) is used when naming the days on the calendar, or 日期 (rìqī date).

一日 1st yī rì	九日 9th jiǔ rì	十七日 17th shíqī rì	二十五日 25th èrshíwǔ rì
二日 2nd èr rì	十日 10th shí rì	十八日 18th shíbā rì	二十六日 26th èrshíliù rì
三日 3rd sānrì	十一日 11th shíyī rì	十九日 19th shíjiǔ rì	二十七日 27th èrshíqī rì
四日 4th sì rì	十二日 12th shíèr rì	二十日 20th èrshí rì	二十八日 28th èrshíbā rì
五日 5th wǔ rì	十三日 13th shísān rì	二十一日 21st èrshíyī rì	二十九日 29th èrshíjiǔ rì
六日 6th liù rì	十四日 14th shísì rì	二十二日 22nd èrshíèr rì	三十日 30th sānshí rì
七日 7th qī rì	十五日 15th shíwǔ rì	二十三日 23rd èrshísān rì	三十一日 31st sānshíyī rì
八日 8th bā rì	十六日 16th shíliù rì	二十四日 24th èrshísì rì	

In a date, the month is named first, followed by the day of the month, as in:

三月十二日　　March 12th
sān yuè shíèr rì

六月六日　　June 6th
liù yuè liù rì

The word for "year" is 年 (nián). To say a given year in Chinese, simply translate each numeral. For example, the year 1986 translates to:

一九八六年
yī niǔ bā liù nián

The year 2009 translates to:

二〇〇九年
èr líng líng niǔ nián

Although the word for "zero" is 零 (líng), nowadays, instead of writing out this complex character, people simply use the round "〇" symbol to represent "zero".

Following are two dates complete with the year, month and day. Note that the year always comes first, then the month, then the day.

一九八六年三月十二日   March 12th, 1986
yī niǔ bā liù nián sānyuè shíér rì

二〇〇九年八月二十日   August 20th, 2009
èr líng líng jiǔ nián bāyuè èrshí rì

二〇〇九年 is customarily read as "两千零九年 (liǎng qiān líng jiǔ nián).
Later in this chapter, you will learn that 千 (qiān) means "a thousand".

The Chinese Zodiac

The Chinese have chosen twelve animals to symbolize the year in which a person is born. The cycle repeats itself indefinitely. The order is said to be based on the outcome of a race among all the animals. Originally, the ox thought it was the first to reach the finish line, but then the rat jumped off its back and finished first. Anyway, here are twelve animals you can enter into the "Nouns" section of your vocabulary binder. Keep in mind, though, that the dragon is not an extant animal, but a mythical being.

一九六○年 yī jiǔ liù líng nián	1960	鼠 shǔ	Rat	一九六七年 yī jiǔ liù qī nián	1967	羊 yáng	Ram
一九六一年 yī jiǔ liù yī nián	1961	牛 niú	Ox	一九六八年 yī jiǔ liù bā nián	1968	猴 hóu	Monkey
一九六二年 yī jiǔ liù èr nián	1962	虎 hǔ	Tiger	一九六九年 yī jiǔ liù jiǔ nián	1969	鸡 jī	Rooster
一九六三年 yī jiǔ liù sān nián	1963	兔 tù	Hare	一九七○年 yī jiǔ qī líng nián	1970	狗 gǒu	Dog
一九六四年 yī jiǔ liù sì nián	1964	龙 lóng	Dragon	一九七一年 yī jiǔ qī yī nián	1971	猪 zhū	Boar
一九六五年 yī jiǔ liù wǔ nián	1965	蛇 shé	Snake	一九七二年 yī jiǔ qī èr nián	1972	鼠 shǔ	Rat
一九六六年 yī jiǔ liù liù nián	1966	马 mǎ	Horse	and so on . . .			

The following nursery rhyme from the Sichuan Province in China will help you brush up on your math. Read it slowly at first then gradually increase the speed and see how fast you can say it without twisting your tongue.

Counting the Frogs
数青蛙
Shǔ Qīngwā

一只青蛙一张嘴，

Yī zhī qīngwā yī zhāng zuǐ,

One frog , one mouth,

两只眼睛四条腿.

Liǎng zhī yǎnjing sì tiáo tuǐ.

Two eyes and four legs.

扑通一声跳下水.

Pū tōng yī shēng tiàoxià shuǐ.

Making a splashing sound,
It jumps into the water.

两只青蛙两张嘴，

Liǎng zhī qīngwā liǎng zhāng zuǐ,

Two frogs, two mouths,

四只眼睛八条腿.

Sì zhī yǎnjing bā tiáo tuǐ.

Four eyes and eight legs.

扑通! 扑通! 跳下水.

Pū tōng! Pū tōng! Tiàoxià shuǐ.

Splash! Splash!
They jump into the water.

三只青蛙三张嘴，

Sān zhī qīngwā sān zhāng zuǐ,

Three frogs, three mouths,

六只眼睛十二条腿.

Liù zhī yǎnjing shíèr tiáo tuǐ.

Six eyes and twelve legs.

扑通! 扑通! 扑通! 跳下水.

Pū tōng! Pū tōng! Pū tōng! Tiàoxià shuǐ.

Splash! Splash! Splash!
They jump into the water.

青蛙 (qīngwā) is a frog.

扑通 (pū tōng)is just a combination of characters used to mimic the plopping sound.

一声 (yī shēng) means "a sound", or literally, "one sound". 扑通一声 (pū tōng yī shēng) is a common expression used to portray how something or somebody drops or jumps into water with a loud splash.

跳 (tiào) means "to jump". 下 (xià) means "down", "below" or "to descend". Obviously, 跳下 (tiàoxià) means "to jump down".

水 (shuǐ) is water. By the way, 跳水 (tiàoshuǐ) refers to the sport of diving.

You know that 张 (Zhāng) is a common Chinese surname. This word has a few different meanings - to open, to spread, to stretch, to display, or to exaggerate. It is also a unit of measure for a sheet of paper, a desk, a chair, a bed, as well as a face or a mouth. For example, 一张嘴 (yī zhāng zuǐ) is one mouth.

条 (tiáo) is a strip, a band, a slip of paper, or any long narrow piece that's usually not stiff. It is also used as a unit for a street, a rope, a ribbon, a wire, a tail, a whip, a ship, a song, a fish, a dog, or a leg. For example, 四条腿 (sì tiáo tuǐ) means four legs.

Time of Day

时间 (shíjiān) means "time" or "time period". The units of time are:

时 (shí time) or 点 (diǎn point)　　an hour

刻 (kè carved mark)　　　　　　　a quarter of an hour

分 (fēn division)　　　　　　　　　a minute

秒 (miǎo second)　　　　　　　　a second

When telling the time, you would say the hour first, followed by the number of quarters or minutes then by the number of seconds, as in the following examples:

十二点一刻 　*or*	12点15分	12:15:00
shíèr diǎn yī kè	shíèr diǎn shíwǔ fēn	(a quarter past 12)
三点二十分 　*or*	3点20分	3:20:00
sān diǎn èrshí fēn	sān diǎn èrshí fēn	
八点五分十秒 　*or*	8点5分10秒	8:05:10
bā diǎn wǔ fēn shí miǎo	bā diǎn wǔ fēn shí miǎo	

The word for "a half" is 半 (bàn), as in:

十二点半 　*or*	12点30分	12:30:00
shíèr diǎn bàn	shíèr diǎn sānshí fēn	

The word 分 (fēn) is often dropped if it is the last character and follows a two-digit number, as in 三点二十 (sān diǎn èrshí 3:20:00).

差 (chā) means "shy of". This is how you would say "ten minutes to eight":

八点差十分 　*or*	差十分八点	ten minutes short of eight
bā diǎn chā shí fēn	chā shí fēn bā diǎn	

The following terms indicate the time periods into which a day is customarily divided:

清早 qìngzǎo	early morning	早上 *or* 早晨 zǎoshàng zǎochén	morning
上午 shàngwǔ	before noon	中午 zhōngwǔ	noon, mid-day
下午 xiǎwǔ	afternoon	傍晚 bàngwǎn	towards evening
黃昏 huánghūn	dusk, twilight	晚上 wǎnshàng	evening
半夜 bànyè	midnight	深夜 shēnyè	late night (deep into the night)

You already know that 上 (shàng) means "above" or "before", and 下 (xià) means "below" or "following". The word for "middle" is 中 (zhōng), and it is used in 中午 (zhōngwǔ mid-day). However, for midnight, 半 (bàn, half) is used to indicate that it is half through the night.

When saying the time in Chinese, always place the time period before the time of the day, as in:

早上八点   eight in the morning (8:00 a.m.)
zǎoshàng bā diǎn

So, how would you say "ten past eight in the evening (8:10 p.m.)"?

_____ _____ _____ _____ _____

_____ _____ _____ _____ _____ _____ (pinyin)

Working with Larger Numbers

As you can see from the following list, the Chinese denominations do not correspond exactly to the English denominations. For example, "one million" in English is usually expressed as "one hundred ten thousands" in Chinese.

百	bǎi	hundred
千	qiān	thousand
万	wàn	ten thousand
十万	shí wàn	hundred thousand
百万	bǎiwàn	million
兆	zhào	million, mega-
千万	qiānwàn	ten million
万万	wànwàn	hundred million (colloquial)
亿	yì	hundred million (formal)
十亿	shí yì	billion

This is how you would say, "There are 365 days in a year."

一年有三百六十五天.

Yī nián yǒu sān bǎi liùshíwǔ tiān.

And, this is how you would say, "I'm a millionaire." (Don't we all wish? ☺)

我是百万富翁.

Wǒ shì bǎiwànfùwēng.

When one or more denominations are missing, you would fill in with a single "zero", which is the word 零 (líng). For example:

一千零一夜   One Thousand and One Nights (*Arabian Nights*)

Yī quiān líng yī yè

Money

Money is called 钱 (qián) or 金钱 (jīnqián). 紙币 (zhǐbì) is paper currency, while 钱币 (qiánbì) and 硬币 (yìngbì) refer to coins. The US dollar is called 美金 (měijīn). Credit cards are called 信用卡 (xìnyòngkǎ).

Listed below are the units of Chinese currency along with a few examples. Note that there is not an equivalent for the nickel, the quarter, or the half-dollar.

元 (yuán)	dollar	十元	shí yuán	ten dollars
角 (jiǎo)	dime	三角钱	sān jiǎo qián	three dimes
分 (fēn)	penny	一分钱	yī fēn qián	one penny

Colloquially, 毛 (máo hair, fur) is often used instead of 角 (jiǎo horn); and 块 (kuài piece) is used instead of 元 (yuán). For example:

五块三毛钱   or   五块三   five dollars and three dimes
wǔ kuài sān máo qián   wǔ kuài sān

角 (jiǎo), 分 (fēn) and 毛 (máo) are often dropped when doing so does not lead to ambiguity.

台币 (táibì), New Taiwan Dollar, or NT$, is used in Taiwan. For example, the following expressions all refer to NT$20.

二十元   or   二十圆   or   二十块台币
èrshí yuán   èrshí yuán   èrshí kuài táibì

人民币 (rénmínbì People's Money), the renminbi, or RMB, is used in China. For example:

一百元   or   一百人民币   100 Chinese dollars or 100 RMB
yī bǎi yuán   yī bǎi rénmínbì

Exercise:

Please read the following Chinese characters or pinyin aloud then draw a line to join each expression with the correct English translation on the right-hand side. When in doubt, please review the lessons that have been covered so far instead of going directly to the answer sheet on the next page.

你好吗?
Nǐ hǎo ma?

Are you coming on Wednesday?

我哥哥是有钱人.
Wǒ gēge shì yǒuqiánrén.

My brother is a rich man.

他是百万富翁.
Tā shì bǎiwànfùwēng.

Do you have 50 U. S. dollars?

你们礼拜三來吗?
Nǐmen lǐbàisān lái ma?

How are you?

我们十二点半到.
Wǒmen shíèr diǎn bàn dào.

We will each get one half.

我有二十块钱.
Wǒ yǒu èrshí kuài qián.

We will arrive at 12:30.

他有两百人民币.
Tā yǒu liǎng bǎi rénmínbì.

He is a millionaire.

下星期天见.
Xià xíngqītiān jiàn.

See you next Sunday.

我们一人一半.
Wǒmen yī rén yī bàn.

I have twenty dollars.

你有五十块美金吗?
Nǐ yǒu wǔshí kuài měijīn ma?

He has 200 RMB.

Answer:

你好吗?
Nǐ hǎo ma?

How are you?

我哥哥是有钱人.
Wǒ gēge shì yǒuqiánrén.

My brother is a rich man.

他是百万富翁.
Tā shì bǎiwànfùwēng.

He is a millionaire.

你们礼拜三來吗?
Nǐmen lǐbàisān lái ma?

Are you coming on Wednesday?

我们十二点半到.
Wǒmen shíèr diǎn bàn dào.

We will arrive at 12:30.

我有二十块钱.
Wǒ yǒu èr shí kuài qián.

I have twenty dollars.

他有两百人民币.
Tā yǒu liǎng bǎi rénmínbì.

He has 200 RMB.

下星期天见.
Xià xíngqītiān jiàn.

See you next Sunday.

我们一人一半.
Wǒmen yī rén yī bàn.

We will each get one half.
(We will share this half-and half.)

你有五十块美金吗?
Nǐ yǒu wǔshí kuài měijīn ma?

Do you have 50 U. S. dollars?

5. Keeping Count

6. Units for Counting

One way to find out about the quantity of something is to ask, "How many?" or "How much?" For example:

有多少老虎?   How many tigers are there?
Yǒu duōshǎo lǎo hǔ?

有多少人?   How many people are there?
Yǒu duōshǎo rén?

有多少水?   How much water is there?
Yǒu duōshǎo shuǐ?

To answer such a question with a definite quantity, you would need to supply a unit associated with that quantity. When talking about the quantity of fluids or masses of material, we usually count the containers of such items. For example, we don't say "one water", but "one cup of water, and we don't say "a rice", but "a bowl of rice". The Chinese do the same, but they go one step further. They even assign different units to countable discrete entities like people and tigers. It can be challenging to learn and remember all the commonly used units and measures. However, as I have mentioned before, **for discrete items, it is generally safe to use** 个 **(gè) as the counting unit**. So, either of the following will work:

有两只老虎 .   There are two tigers.
Yǒu liǎng zhī lǎohǔ.

有两个老虎.   There are two tigers.
Yǒu liǎng gè lǎohǔ.

The Chinese word for "unit" is 单位 (dānwèi). Many commonly used units are listed below, and a number of examples are provided with the name of each unit. As you will see, you can refer to some things by more than one unit. From now on, whenever you look at or touch an item, ask yourself, "What is this called in Chinese?" Also find out what would be the appropriate unit to use with that item.

If you do not wish to concern yourself with the proper use of the various units at this time then just skim through this chapter, pick out the nouns that might interest you and add them to your vocabulary book.

Discrete Items

Here is a sample of commonly used units for counting discrete items. If you like, you may substitute the count of "one" with a different number, such as "three". The noun remains absolutely the same no matter the count.

个 (gè) an individual person or item

This is the most commonly used unit for counting individual things. You may pass the other units on a first reading of this book, but please be sure to learn this one.

Please note that when used as a unit of counting, 个 (gè) takes on the silent tone. Therefore, I will switch the pinyin notation to "ge" for this unit of counting.

一个
yī ge

男人 man
nánrén

女人 woman
nǔrén

小孩
xiǎohái

鼻子 nose
bízi

眼睛 eye
yǎnjing

东西 thing, creature
dōngxi

盘子 plate, dish
pánzi

杯子 cup
bēizi

瓶子 bottle, jar
píngzi

国家 country
guójiā

苹果 apple
píngguǒ

故事 story
gùshì

位 (wèi)   position, placement

This is a more respectful way of referring to individuals.

一位
yī wèi

老师 teacher
lǎoshī

同学 classmate
tóngxué

先生 gentleman
xiānsheng

只 (zhī) single one

This unit applies to most animals and bugs. Interestingly, they are also used for counting your eyes, ears and limbs.

一只	手 hand	脚 leg	狗 dog
yī zhī	shǒu	jiǎo	gǒu
	猫 cat	鸡 chicken	老鼠 mouse
	māo	jī	lǎoshǔ

头 (tóu) head

This unit mostly applies to the larger animals that are raised on a farm or ranch. A farmer or rancher would often boast of the number of heads of animals that he has.

一头	母牛 cow	猪 hog, pig	公羊 ram (male goat)
yī tóu	mǔniú (female)	zhū	gōngyáng

种 (zhǒng) variety, type, kind

一种	花 flower	苹果 apple	问题 problem
yī zhǒng	huā	píngguǒ	wèntí

块 (kuài) piece, a square of

一块	布 cloth	石头 rock	牛排 steak
yī kuài	bù	shítóu	niúpái
	毛巾 towel	土地 land	肥皂 bar soap
	máojīn	tǔdì	féizào

本 (běn) book

一本	书 book	字典 dictionary	电话簿 phone book
yī běn	shū	zìdiǎn	diànhuàbù

页 (yè) page

| 一页
yī yè | 书 book
shū | 报告 report
bàogào | 广告 advertisement
guǎnggào |

张 (zhang) opening, sheet, spread

| 一张
yī zhāng | 支票 cheque
zhīpiào | 纸 paper
zhǐ | 纸巾 paper napkin
zhǐjīn |
| | 名片 calling card
míngpiàn | 床 bed
chuáng | 信用卡 credit card
xìnyòngkǎ |

封 (fēng) envelope

| 一封
yī fēng | 信 letter
xìn | 请帖 invitation
qǐngtiě (qǐngtiē) | 情书 love letter
qínshū |

支 (zhī) branch, twig, stick

This unit is used for stick-like things as well as songs.

| 一支
yī zhī | 笔 pen
bǐ | 扫把 broom
sàobǎ | 枪 gun
qiāng |
| | 笛子 flute
dízi | 歌 song
gē | 曲子 tune, melody
qǔzi |

件 (jiàn) item

This unit is used for garments, documents and events.

| 一件
yī jiàn | 衣服 garment
yīfu | 大衣 overcoat
dàyī | 公文 official document
gōngwén |

长裤 trousers   消息 news   事 matter, event
chángkù   xiāoxí   shì

套 (tào) case, set, suit

一套   工具 tools   洋装 dress   西装 suit
yī tào   gōngjù   yángzhuāng   xīzhuāng

朵 (duǒ) floweret

一朵   云 cloud   枚瑰花 rose   梅花 plum blossom
yī duǒ   yún   méigui huā   méihuā

株 (zhu) stem or stalk of a standing plant

一株   树 Tree   枚瑰 rose   青菜 vegetable
yī zhū   shù   méigui   qīngcài
                   (In Taiwan, say méigùi.)

棵 (kē)   count of a plant

一棵   树 Tree   枚瑰 rosebush   青菜 vegetable
yī kē   shù   méigui   qīngcài

条 (tiáo) twig, strip, long narrow piece

一条   船 boat, ship   路 road   皮带 leather belt
yī tiáo   chuán   lù   pídài

                绳子 rope   香肠 sausage   面包 loaf of bread
                shéngzi   xiāncháng   miànbāo

根 (gēn) root, long piece

一根　　　棍子 stick　　　香蕉 banana　　　木材 logs, lumber
yī gēn　　gùnzi　　　　xiāngjiāo　　　mùcái

粒 (lì) grain, granule

一粒　　　米 rice　　　糖果 candy　　　沙 sand
yī lì　　　mǐ　　　　tángguǒ　　　shā

颗 (kē) rounded piece

一颗　　　蛋 egg　　　糖果 candy　　　牙 tooth
yī kē　　　dàn　　　　tángguǒ　　　yá
　　　　　石头 rock　　　星 star　　　　高丽菜 cabbage
　　　　　shítou　　　xīng　　　　gāolìcài

枚 (méi) a unit for small things

一枚　　　蛋 egg　　　子弹 bullet　　　邮票 stamp
yī méi　　dàn　　　　zǐdàn　　　　yóupiào

片 (piàn) flat thin piece, flake, slice

一片　　　云 cloud　　　树叶 leaf　　　西瓜 watermelon
yī piàn　　yún　　　　shùyè　　　　xīguā

把 (bǎ) grip, handle

一把　　　刀 knife　　　剪刀 scissors　　　锯子 saw
yī bǎ　　　dāo　　　　jiǎndāo　　　jùzi

段 (duàn) section

一段
yī duàn

故事 story
gùshì

历史 history
lìshǐ

影片 movie
yǐngpiàn

场 (yī chǎng) scene, location

一场
yī chǎng

虚惊 false alarm
xūjīng

电影 movie
diànyǐng

表演 performance
biǎoyǎn

份 (yī fèn) portion, share

一份
yī fèn

报纸 newspaper
bàozhǐ

点心 snacks
diǎnxīn

炒饭 fried rice
chǎofàn

遗产 inheritance
yíchǎn

工作 job
gōngzuò

公文 official paper
gōngwén

台 (tái) stand, platform

一台
yī tái

电脑 computer
diànnǎo

机器 machine
jīqì

电风扇 electric fan
diànfēngshàn

The terms used for many electrical appliances start with the word 电 (diàn electricity). Some other examples are: 电话 (diànhuà telephone), 电视 (diànshì television), 电灯 (diàndēng lighting fixture) and 电梯 (diàntī elevator, or "electric ladder").

辆 (liàng) unit for vehicles

一辆
yī liàng

跑车 racecar
pǎochē

单车 bicycle
dānchē

汽车 automobile
qìchē

The word 部 (bù) is also used as a measure for cars and machines. For example: 一部计程车 (yī bù jìchéngchē a taxi cab).

架 (jià) frame

一架
yī jià

喷射机 jet plane
pēnshèjī

飞机 airplane
fēijī

直升机 helicopter
zhíshēngjī

栋 (jià) ridgepole, unit for buildings

一栋
yī dòng

办公室 office
bàngōngshì

房子 house
fángzi

大厦 large building
dàshà

座 (zuò) seat, pedestal

一座
yī zuò

山 mountain
shān

桥 bridge
qiáo

大楼 tall building
dàlóu

花园 garden
huāyuán

庙 temple
miào

佛像 statue of
fóxiàng Buddha

It's customary to pronounce "一 (yī)" in the second tone when it is followed by a character with the fourth tone. For example, when you see 一位 (yī wèi), say "yí wèi". 一个 (yī gè) is usually pronounced as "yí ge". **Also, it's customary to pronounce "一 (yī)" in the fourth tone when it is followed by a character with the first, second or third tone.** For example, 一只 (yī zhī) is pronounced as "yì zhī", 一条 (yī tiáo) is pronounced as "yì tiáo", and 一本 (yī běn) is pronounced as "yì běn".

Nevertheless, it is okay if you always pronounce 一 (yī) in the first tone.

Finger-guessing Game
猜拳
Cāiquán

There is a hand-gesture game that is very popular among the Chinese children. The two competing parties chant: "剪刀, 石头, 布! (Jiǎndāo, shítou, bù!)" On the last syllable, they simultaneously thrust out a finger gesture representing one of the following:

剪刀 scissors   石头 rock   布 fabric
jiǎndāo   shítou   bù

The gestures are compared to determine the winner. The scissors cut the fabric, the fabric wraps the rock, and the rock blunts the scissors. In itself, this game is fun to play and a great exercise for the mind. It also often used to decide who gets to start a game, win a prize or have the other party do his or her bidding.

猜 (cāi) means to guess. 拳 (quán) is a fist.

As an exercise, please search the list of units in the previous pages and find the proper units for 剪刀 (jiǎndāo scissors), 石头 (shítou rocks) and 布 (bù).

Multiple Discrete Items

Yes, there are Chinese words that correspond to such English words as: "a pair of", "a couple of", and "a dozen".

一双 a pair of   手 hands   脚 feet   腿 legs
yī shuāng   shǒu   jiǎo   tuǐ

眼睛 eyes   手套 gloves   筷子 chopsticks
yǎnjing   shǒutào   kuàizi

鞋 shoes   皮靴 boots
xié   píxuē

一对 a pair of   耳环 earrings   情人 lovers   鸭 ducks
yī duì   ěrhuán   qíngrén   yā

一双 (yī shuāng) and 一对 (yī duì) have the same meaning. However, some words are customarily used with one term rather than the other. Also, these terms are only used with things that are usually paired, like eyes, shoes or a pair of male and female ducks. To talk about "a couple of" anything else, you would simply say, "two of", like 两只 (liǎng zhī), 两个 (liǎng ge), 两片 (liǎng piàn), and so on.

一打 a dozen   鸡蛋 eggs   饼干 cookies   枚瑰花 roses
yī dǎ   jīdàn   bǐnggān   méigui huā

半打 a half dozen   鸡蛋 eggs   饼干 cookies   汽水 soda pops
bàn dǎ   jīdàn   bǐnggān   qìshuǐ

半 (bàn) means a half. Please note that 一打 (yī dǎ) and 半打 (bàn dǎ) only apply to objects that are customarily sold by the dozen, such as eggs, cookies and soda pops. You would never use these terms on people. The correct way to say "a dozen or so people" is 十几个人 (shí jǐ ge rén), which means "ten plus a few people". The correct way to say "a dozen or so books" is 十几本书 (shí jǐ běn shū), or 十来本书 (shí lái běn shū), which means "ten plus a few books".

When things are bunched together, they are referred to by different group measures, depending on what they are and how they are gathered together. Following are a few examples:

一包 a bag/package of yī bāo	食品 food shípǐn	饼干 cookies bǐnggān	铅笔 pencils qiānbǐ
一盒 a box of yī hé	糖果 candies tángguǒ	雪茄 cigar xuějiā	珠宝 jewelry zhūbǎo
一串 a string/cluster of yī chuàn	项链 necklace xiàngliàn	葡萄 grapes pútáo	事件 events shìjiàn
一堆 a heap of yī duī	杂志 magazines zázhì	衣服 clothing yīfu	东西 things dōngxi
一叠 a stack of yī dié	文件 documents wénjiàn	盘子 plates pánzi	光碟 CDs guāngdié
一把 a bunch of yī bǎ	青菜 vegetables qīngcài	香蕉 bananas xiāngjiāo	米 rice mǐ
一挂 a bunch of yī guà (hung items)	香蕉 bananas xiāngjiāo	项链 necklace xiàngliàn	葡萄 grapes pútáo
一束 a small bundle of yī shù	葱 green onions cōng	枚瑰花 roses méigui huā	花 flowers huā
一扎 a small bundle of yī zhá	钞票 paper bills chāopiào	文件 document wénjiàn	信件 mail xìnjiàn

一捆 a bundle of
yī kǔn

稻草 hay
dàocǎo

电线 cables
diànxiàng

毛巾 towels
máojīn

一卷 a roll of
yī juǎn

纸巾 paper towels
zhǐjīn

布 fabric
bù

寿司 sushi
shòusī

Luckily, a group of people or animals is always referred to as 一群 (yī qún):

一群人 a group of people
yī qún rén

一群鸟 a flock of birds
yī qún niǎo

一群羊 a herd of sheep
yī qún yáng

一群鱼 a school of fish
yī qún yú

一群狼 a pack of wolves
yī qún láng

一群鹿 a drove of deer
yī qún lù

Again, it's customary to pronounce "一 (yī)" in the second tone when it is followed by a character with the fourth tone, as with 一串 (yī chuàn), 一挂 (yī guà), and 一束 (yī shù). And, it's customary to pronounce "一 (yī)" in the fourth tone when it is followed by a character with the first, second or third tone, as with 一包 (yī bāo), 一群 (yī qún), and 一卷 (yī juǎn).

Therefore, when you see 一堆 (yī duī a pile of), you would say "yì duī". But when you see 一大堆 (yī dà duī a large pile of), you would say "yí dà duī".

At the break of dawn, the night-shift banana harvesters are loading the goods onto the boats; they are ready to go home. Why not sing the following Jamaican folk song along with them?

Banana Boat Song

香蕉船歌

Xiāngjiāo Chuán Gē

嘿唷, 天亮罗!
Hēi yō, tiān liàng luó!

Day, oh! Day oh!
(Hey, oh! The day is dawning.)

天亮了, 我就要回家去.
Tiān liàng le, wǒ jiùyào huíjiā qù.

Daylight come an' I wanna go home.
(When the day breaks, I'll go home.)

嘿唷, 天亮罗!
Hēi yō, tiān liàng luó!

Day, oh! Day oh!

天亮了, 我就要回家去.
Tiān liàng le, wǒ jiùyào huíjiā qù.

Daylight come an' I wanna go home.

六挂, 七挂,
Liù guà, qī guà,

Six-hand, seven-hand,

八挂串.
Bā guà chuàn.

Eight-hand bunch.

天亮了, 我就要回家去.
Tiān liàng le, wǒ jiùyào huíjiā qù.

Daylight come an' I wanna go home.

六挂, 七挂,
Liù guà, qī guà,

Six-hand, seven-hand,

八挂串.
Bā guà chuàn.

Eight-hand bunch.

天亮了, 我就要回家去.
Tiān liàng le, wǒ jiùyào huíjiā qù.

Daylight come an' I wanna go home.

来吧! 稽查先生.
Lái ba! Jīchá xiānsheng.

Come, Mr. Tally Man,
(Come, Mr. Inspector,)

来算我的香蕉.
Lái suàn wǒ de xiāngjiāo

Tally me banana.
(Come and count my banana.)

天亮了, 我就要回家去.
Tiān liàng le, wǒ jiùyào huíjiā qù.

Daylight come an' I wanna go home.

来吧! 稽查先生.
Lái ba! Jīchá xiānsheng.

Come, Mr. Tally Man,
(Come, Mr. Inspector,)

来算我的香蕉.
Lái suàn wǒ de xiāngjiāo.

Tally me banana.
(Come and count my banana.)

天亮了, 我就要回家去.
Tiān liàng le, wǒ jiùyào huíjiā qù.

Daylight come an' I wanna go home.

嘿! 我说天, 我说天,
Hēi! Wǒ shuō tiān, wǒ shuō tiān,

Day! Me say day, me say day,
(Hey! I say day, I say day, I say day,)

我说天, 我说天,
Wǒ shuō tiān, wǒ shuō tiān,

Me say day, me say day,

我说天, 我说天唷!
Wǒ shuō tiān, wǒ shuō tiān yō!

Me say day, me say day, oh!

天亮了, 我就要回家去.
Tiān liàng le, wǒ jiùyào huíjiā qù.

Daylight come an' I wanna go home.

天亮了, 我就要回家去.
Tiān liàng le, wǒ jiùyào huíjiā qù.

Daylight come an' I wanna go home.

You may say 一挂香蕉 (yī guà xiāngjiāo) or 一把香蕉 (yī bǎ xiāngjiāo) for one hand of bananas, each single banana being like a finger on a hand. 一串香蕉 (yī chuàn xiāngjiāo) is a bunch or stem made up of several hands or tiers of bananas.

Exercise:

1. Fill in the proper measure for the following items:

两___狗 2 dogs   三___书 3 books   一___衣服 1 garment

liǎng___ gǒu   sān ___ shū   yī ____ yīfu

一___信 a letter   一___人 a person   五___香蕉 5 bananas

yī ____ xìn   yī _____ rén   wǔ ____xiāngjiāo

2. Please translate the following sentences into English.

你是一个好人.

Nǐ shì yī ge hǎorén.

_____

她是一位老师.

Tā shì yī wèi lǎoshī.

_____

妹妹看到两朵枚瑰花.

Mèimei kàndào liǎng duǒ méigui huā.

_____

我吃了一颗蛋和四片面包.

Wǒ chī le yī kē dàn hé sì piàn miànbāo.

_____

三只青蛙有三张嘴和十二条腿.

Sān zhī qīngwā yǒu sān zhāng zuǐ hé shíèr tiáo tuǐ.

_____

Answer:

1. Fill in the proper measure for the following items:

两只狗 2 dogs   三本书 3 books   一件衣服 1 garment
liǎng zhī gǒu   sān běn shū   yī jiàn yīfu

一封信 a letter   一个人 a person   五根香蕉 5 bananas
yī fēng xìn   yī ge rén   wǔ gēn xiāngjiāo

2. Please translate the following sentences into English.

你是一个好人.
Nǐ shì yī ge hǎorén.
You are a good person.

她是一位老师.
Tā shì yī wèi lǎoshī.
She is a teacher.

妹妹看到两朵枚瑰花.
Mèimei kàndào liǎng duǒ méigui huā.
Little sister saw two roses.

我吃了一颗蛋和四片面包.
Wǒ chī le yī kē dàn hé sì piàn miànbāo.
I ate one egg and four slices of bread.

三只青蛙有三张嘴和十二条腿.
Sān zhī qīngwā yǒu sán zhāng zuǐ hé shíèr tiáo tuǐ.
Three frogs have three mouths and twelve legs.

7. *Half a Bucket of Rain*

We all know that there are different ways to look at things. A pessimist tends to dwell on what has been lost, where as an optimist delights in what remains in hand. I made the following rhyme to illustrate this point.

Half a Bucket of Rain
半桶雨
Bàn Tǒng Yǔ

呼呼冬风，
Hūhū dōngfēng,

雨下半桶．
Yǔ xià bàn tǒng.

它是半满，
Tā shì bàn mǎn,

还是半空？
Háishì bàn kōng?

Winter wind is blasting;

There's half a bucket of rain.

Is it half full,

Or really half drained?

呼呼 (hū hū) mimics the sound of blowing winds. 呼 (hū) means to exhale or to call. 吸 (xī) means to inhale, suck in, absorb or attract. 呼吸 (hūxī) means to breathe. 呼喊 (hūhǎn) means to call out or shout.

冬 (dōng) is winter and 风 (fēng) means wind. 雨 (yǔ) is rain. 下 (xià) means to descend or fall.

You know that 半 (bàn) means a half. Therefore, 半桶 (bàn tǒng) is half a bucket, 半满 (bàn mǎn) is half full, and 半空 (bàn kōng) is half empty.

是 (shì) and 还是 (háishì) is a pair of words that you could use to pose a question with two alternatives.

Mass Quantities

Things that you cannot count individually are referred to by volume, by weight, by their shapes, or by the containers used to hold them. For example:

一点 yī diǎn	a drop/bit of	水 water shuǐ	盐 salt yán	消息 news xiāoxí
一滴 yī dī	a drop of	水 water shuǐ	眼泪 tears yǎnlèi	血 blood xuě
一匙 yī chí	a spoonful of	糖 sugar táng	盐 salt yán	酱油 soy sauce jiàngyóu
一盘 yī pán	a dish of	菜 food cài	牛肉 beef niúròu	面 noodles miàn
一碗 yī wǎn	a bowl of	饭 rice fàn	汤 soup tāng	豆浆 soymilk dòujiāng
一杯 yī bēi	a cup of	水 water shuǐ	牛奶 milk niúnǎi	茶 tea chá
一瓶 yī píng	a bottle of	水 water shuǐ	油 oil yóu	酒 wine jiǔ
一罐 yī guàn	a can of	汽水 soda qìshuǐ	果汁 fruit juice guǒzhī	沙丁鱼 sardines shādīngyú
一袋 yī dài	a sack of	米 rice mǐ	面粉 flour miànfěn	沙 sand shā
一桶 yī tǒng	a bucket of	水 water shuǐ	汽油 gasoline qìyóu	啤酒 beer píjiǔ
一股 yī gǔ	a gust/whiff of	臭味 stench chòuwèi	傲气 arrogance àoqì	冷风 cold wind lěngfēng
一团 yī tuán	a glob of	饭 rice fàn	棉花 cotton miánhuā	糟 mess zāo
一片 yī piàn	an expanse of	雾 fog wù	草地 lawn cǎodì	人海 huge crowd rénhǎi

7. Half a Bucket of Rain

Table of Conversions

The metric system of measurement units is used in most Asian countries. In the following conversion chart, 等于 (děngyú) means " is equal to". 大约 (dàyuē) and 差不多 (chàbuduō) both mean "roughly" or "approximately".

一大匙等于三小匙.
Yī dà chǐ děngyú sān xiǎo chǐ.

1 tablespoonful = 3 teaspoonfuls

一公斤大约等于二点二磅.
Yī gōngjīn dàyuē děngyú èr diǎn èr bàng.

1 kg is approximately 2.2 lbs.

一磅等于十六盎士.
Yī bàng děngyú shíliù àngshì.

1 pound = 16 ounces

一公升差不多是一夸脱.
Yī gòngshēng chàbuduō shì yī kuātuō.

1 liter is approximately 1 quart.

一加仑等于四夸脱.
Yī jiālún děngyú sì kuātuō.

1 gallon = 4 quarts

一夸脱等于四杯.
Yī kuātuō děngyú sì bēi.

1 quart = 4 cups

四分之一杯等于四大匙.
Sì fēn zhī yī bēi děngyú sì dà chǐ.

1/4 cup = 4 tablespoonfuls

一尺等于十二寸.
Yī chǐ děngyú shíèr cùn

1 foot = 12 inches

一寸等于二点五四厘米.
Yī cùn děngyú èr diǎn wǔ sì límǐ.

1 inch = 2.54 centimeter

一公尺大约是三点三尺.
Yī gōngchǐ dàyuē shì sān diǎn sān chǐ.

1 meter is approximately 3.3 feet.

一公里大约等于零点六二哩.
Yī gōnglǐ dàyuē děngyú líng diǎn liù èr lǐ.

1 km is approximately 0.62 mile.

尺 is the short form of 英尺 (yīngchǐ), where 英 (yīng) stands for "British".
寸 is the short form of 英寸 (yīngcùn). Meter is 米 (mǐ) or 公尺(gōngchǐ).

How Many Again?

When asking about the quantity of something, you may use 多少 (duōshǎo how many, how much) in combination with the unit for the item of interest, as in:

有多少只老虎? How many tigers are there?
Yǒu duōshǎo zhī lǎohǔ?

有多少个人? How many people are there?
Yǒu duōshǎo ge rén?

有多少杯水? How many cups of water are there?
Yǒu duōshǎo bēi shuǐ?

Such questions are easy to answer, because all you have to do is to supply the quantity in the same unit.

有两只老虎. There are two tigers.
Yǒu liǎng zhī lǎohǔ.

有五十个人. There are fifty persons.
Yǒu wǔshí ge rén.

有六杯水. There are six cups of water.
Yǒu liù bēi shuǐ.

The word 几 (jǐ how many) can also be used to inquire about the quantity. It is always followed by the unit used for the item of interest. For example:

有几只老虎？　　　　　　　How many tigers are there?
Yǒu jǐ zhī lǎohǔ?

有几个人？　　　　　　　　How many persons are there?
Yǒu jǐ ge rén?

有几杯水？　　　　　　　　How many cups of water are there?
Yǒu jǐ bēi shuǐ?

As days, weeks, hours, minutes and seconds are themselves units of time, you may omit the word 个 (ge) after 几 (jǐ) when asking about the duration of time in these units. In fact, as shown below, the unit 个 (ge) is usually not used with 天 (tiān days), 分 (fēn minutes), and 秒 (miǎo seconds). Some examples follow.

几天？　　　　　　　　　　How many days?
Jǐ tiān?

几个星期？　or 几星期？　　How many weeks?
Jǐ ge xīngqī?　　　Jǐ xīngqī?

几个小时？　or 几小时？　　How many hours?
Jǐ ge xiǎoshí?　　　Jǐ xiǎoshí?

几分钟？　　　　　　　　　How many minutes?
Jǐ fēnzhōng?

几秒钟？　　　　　　　　　How many seconds?
Jǐ miǎozhōng?

You know that 月 (yuè month) is also a unit of time. However, you must say "几个月？(Jǐ ge yuè?)" when you are asking, "How many months?" because "几月？" (Jǐ yuè?) will be taken to mean, "Which month?" Such ambiguity does not exist with the other units of time.

7. Half a Bucket of Rain

It is interesting that the word 几 (jǐ) means "how many" as well as "several" or "a few". Therefore, if you remove the question marks from the previous set of questions, you will get the following statements:

有几只老虎.   There are several tigers.
Yǒu jǐ zhī lǎohǔ.

有几个人.   There are several people.
Yǒu jǐge rén.

有几杯水.   There are several cups of water.
Yǒu jǐ bēi shuǐ.

几天.   A few days.
Jǐ tiān.

几个星期.   Several weeks.
Jǐge xīngqī.

几个月.   Several months.
Jǐge yuè.

几个小时.   A few hours.
Jǐge xiǎoshí.

几分钟.   A few minutes.
Jǐ fēnzhong.

几秒钟.   A few seconds.
Jǐ miǎozhong.

Here, 几个 (jǐge) is interpreted as the word "several", hence the concatenated pinyin.

Rough Estimates

When you don't need to quantify something in terms of units, you could use such words as "a few", "many", "a little", or "much" to describe it. The Chinese don't fuss about differentiating between "many" and "much", or "a few" and "a little". You know that 多少 (duōshǎo) means both "how many" and "how much". Similarly, when there is plenty of something, whether it is water or trees, you can use 许多 (xǔduō lots of) as an approximation. For example:

许多水   a lot of water   许多树   many trees
xǔduō shuǐ   xǔduō shù

许多知识   much knowledge   许多人   many people
xǔduō zhīshì   xǔduō rén

And, when there is little of something, you can use 很少 (hěn shǎo scanty) to describe it. For example:

很少水   little water   很少树   very few trees
hěn shǎo shuǐ   hěn shǎo shù

很少知识   scanty knowledge   很少人   very few people
hěn shǎo zhīshì   hěn shǎo rén

Now, when the quantity falls somewhere in between, 一些 (yīxiē) would be the word to use. For example:

一些水   a little water   一些树   a few trees
yīxiē shuǐ   yīxiē shù

一些知识   some knowledge   一些人   a few people
yīxiē zhīshì   yīxiē rén

This and That

The Chinese word for "this" is 这 (zhè). The word for "that" is 那 (nà). When you talk about this thing or that thing, you will also need to use the proper unit for the thing. Following are some examples.

这个人 this person
zhège rén

那个人 that person
nàge rén

这封信 this letter
zhè fēng xìn

那封信 that letter
nà fēng xìn

这杯牛奶 this cup of milk
zhè bēi niúnǎi

那杯牛奶 that cup of milk
nà bēi niúnǎi

这盘菜 this dish of food
zhè pán cài

那盘菜 that dish of food
nà pán cài

Remember that the singular and plural forms of the nouns in Chinese are the same. So how can you tell if someone is talking about one single unit or multiple units of that item? Obviously, if a group measure such as 群 (qún) is used, plurality is indicated, such as in 这群人 (zhè qún rén this group of people) and 那群人 (nà qún rén that group of people). Generally, though, when one talks about multiple items, one would use 这些 (zhèxiē these) or 那些 (nàxiē those), as in the following examples.

这些人   these people
zhèxiē rén

那些人   those people
nàxiē rén

这些树   these trees
zhèxiē shù

那些树   those trees
nàxiē shù

这些文件   these documents
zhèxiē wénjiàn

那些文件   those documents
nàxiē wénjiàn

Which and What?

The word 哪 (nǎ) is formed by adding the radical 口 (kǒu mouth) to the character 那 (nà that, or that which). It is used in posing the question, "Which?"

哪一天?   Which day?
Nǎ yītiān?

哪一位先生?   Which gentleman?
Nǎ yī wèi xiānsheng?

哪些人?   Which people?
Nǎxiē rén?

You may also pose the question by using 什么 (shénme), which is the Chinese word for "what". For example:

你看到什么人?   What person (whom) did you see?
Nǐ kàndào shénme rén?

Suppose you want to answer that you saw everybody. You would say,

我看到每个人.   I saw every person.
Wǒ kàndào měi ge rén.

每 (měi) means "every" or "each". You would follow it with the proper unit for the thing you are talking about. Here is another example:

每一盘菜都好吃.   Every single dish was delicious.
Měi yī pán cài dōu hǎochī.

The word "一" (yī one) is often dropped after 每 (měi), except when it is needed for emphasis, as in "every single".

The word 各 (gè) sounds like 个 (gè), but it is not a unit of measure. Like the word, 每 (měi), it means "each" or "every". However, there is a fine distinction between 各 (gè) and 每 (měi).

每 (měi) is used for indicating every one of all the items in a group of items, such as in:

每个人   every person
měi ge rén

每盘菜   every dish of food
měi pán cài

On the other hand, 各 (gè) refers to the distinct individuals or kinds of items in a group, as shown in the following examples.

各个人   each individual person
gè ge rén

各种花   each of all kinds of flowers
gè zhǒng huā   (various kinds of flowers)

各位先生, 各位女士.   Gentlemen and Ladies!
Gè wèi xiānsheng, gè wèi nǚshì.

Sorry, ladies, in the Chinese culture, the gentlemen come first.

8. Feelings and Personalities

Undeniably, each one of us is a bundle of feelings, 感觉 (gǎnjué), and emotions, 情感 (qínggǎn). We may be able to tell how some people feel by observing their facial expression or body language, but we can usually understand them better if they articulate their feelings through spoken or written language. Through the ages, many gifted people have been able to express their feelings and emotions through songs and poems. When we sing or read those songs and poems, we can often relive the sentiments of their composers.

Do you share the philosophy contained in the following song? The tune as well as the lyrics are credited to Eliphalit Oram Lyte in the publication "The Franklin Square Song Collection (1881, New York)".

Row, Row, Row Your Boat
摇, 摇, 摇小船
Yáo, Yáo, Yáo, Xiǎo Chuán

摇, 摇, 摇小船, Yáo, yáo, yáo xiǎo chuán,	*Row, row, row your boat,* Row, row, row the little boat,
漂流小河中. Piāoliú xiǎohé zhōng.	*Gently down the stream.* Drifting in the stream.
好快活! 好快活! Hǎo kuàihuó! Hǎo kuàihuó!	*Merrily, merrily,* How happy! How happy!
好快活! 好快活! Hǎo kuàihuó! Hǎo kuàihuó!	*Merrily, merrily,* How happy! How happy!
人生本如梦. Rénshēng běn rú mèng.	*Life is but a dream.* Life is just like a dream.

摇 (yáo) means "to shake", "to rock" or "to move back and forth". 摇船 (yáochuán) means to row a boat. 摇手 (yáoshǒu) is waving one's hand.

漂 (piāo) is to float and drift. 流 (liú) means "to flow", "to move from place to place", "a stream of water" or "a current". 流汗 (liúhàn) is to sweat, 流血 (liúxuě) is to bleed, and 流鼻水 (liúbíshuǐ) is to have a runny nose.

快 (kuài) means "fast", "quick", "sharp" or "happy". 活 (huó) means "life" or "to live". 快活 (kuàihuó) means "living happily", or simply, "happy". 好快活 (hǎo kuàihuó) means "quite happy", "so happy" or "very happy".

小 (xiǎo) is "small". 河 (hé) is river. Put these two words together, and you will get 小河 (xiǎohé), which is "a small river", or "a stream".

As you know, 人 (rén) refers to "a person", "people" or "humans". 生 (shēng) has many different meanings, among which are: "life", "to live", "to generate", and "unripe". 人生 (rénshēng) means "life".

本 is the abbreviation of 本来 (běnlái), which means "originally", "after all", "it goes without saying", or "of course".

如 (rú) is the formal word for "seeming like" or "being like". In everyday speech, you would say 像 (xiàng, seems like), 好像 (hǎoxiàng seems much like), or 就像 (jiùxiàng is just like).

梦 (mèng) means "dreams". The common units used for dreams are 一个 (yī ge one) or 一場 (yī chǎng a location, a scene of).

Putting it all together, the verse "人生本如梦. (Rénshēng běn rú mèng.)" translates to: "After all, life is like a dream." In every day speech, you would say:

人生本来就像一場梦.

Rénshēng běnlái jiù xiàng yī chǎng mèng.

After all, life is just like a dream.

In the above song, "好快活! (Hǎo kuài huó! So happy!)" stands alone as an exclamation. You may use many other adjectives in the same way. For example:

好饱!	Hǎo bǎo!	(I'm) quite full!
好饿!	Hǎo è!	(I'm) quite hungry!
好累!	Hǎo lèi!	So tired!

To form a complete sentence, simply add a noun or a pronoun, as in:

我好累!	Wǒ hǎo lèi!	I'm so tired!

很 (hěn) means "very". For example:

他很饿了.	Tā hěn è le.	He is (already) very hungry.
我们很累.	Wǒmen hěn lèi.	We're very tired.

If you are not full, not hungry, or not tired, then add the word 不 (bù not) before the adjective to get the opposite meaning. For example:

我不饿.	Wǒ bú è.	I'm not hungry.
我们不累.	Wǒmen bú lèi.	We're not tired.

Note that in these sentences, the linking verb, 是 (shì to be), is only implied. Please remember this general rule: **Omit 是 (shì to be) when it links the subject to an adjective or a descriptive phrase expressing a feeling or an emotion.**

However, do not omit 是 (shì) when it links the subject to a noun complement. For example, do not omit 是 (shì) from the following sentences:

8. Feelings and Personalities   97

他是个音乐家.
Tā shì ge yīnyuèjiā.

He is a musician.

他是我的先生.
Tā shì wǒ de xiānsheng.

He is my husband.

她是我的太太.
Tā shì wǒ de tàitai.

She is my wife.

那是我的小孩.
Nà shì wǒ de xiǎohái.

That's my kid (child).

Also, do not omit the word, 是 (shì) when it serves as the abbreviation for 真是 (zhēn shì), and is used to convey the meaning of "truly so" or "actually so". When reading the following sentences, please put the emphasis on the word, 是 (shì).

是呀! 她是很得意.
Shì yā! Tā shì hěn déyì.

Yes, she is (actually) elated
(cocky with her success).

是啊! 看来他是生病了.
Shì ā! Kànlái tā shì shēngbìng le.

Yes, it does look like he is ill.

对呀! 他是爱打网球.
Duì yā! Tā shì ài dǎ wǎngqiú.

That's right, he does love
to play tennis.

As mentioned previously in Chapter 2, you could use the linking verb, "feel", to join an adjective to the noun it describes. In Chinese, there are several words that correspond to the linking verb, "feel": 感觉 (gǎnjué), 感到 (gǎndào) and 觉得 (juéde). All of these words have the same meaning and can be used interchangeably in a sentence.

The following examples feature a few more common feelings and emotions. Please pay attention to how these adjectives are used in the sentences.

他很<u>兴奋</u>.
Tā hěn xīngfèn.

He is very excited.

山姆<u>高兴</u>.
Shānmǔ gāoxìng.

Sam is glad.

他们很<u>欢喜</u>.
Tāmen hěn huānxǐ.

They are very happy.

他很<u>满意</u>.
Tā hěn mǎnyì.

He is pleased (satisfied).

尼克好<u>生气</u>.
Níkè hǎo shēngqì.

Nick was so mad(angry).

莉莉很<u>失望</u>.
Lìlì hěn shīwàng.

Lily is very disappointed.

她很<u>害羞</u>.
Tā hěn hàixiū.

She is very shy.

他们很<u>窘</u>.
Tāmen hěn jiǒng.

They were embarrassed.

我很<u>烦恼</u>.
Wǒ hěn fánnǎo.

I'm vexed (or worried).

我很<u>后悔</u>.
Wǒ hěn hòuhuǐ.

I feel regretful.

汉斯今天很<u>伤心</u>.
Hànsī jīntiān hěn shāngxīn.

Hans feels very sad today.

小妹妹很<u>开心</u>.
Xiǎo mèimèi hěn kāixīn.

Little sister is happy.

他嫉妒你.　　　　　　　　He is envious of you.
Tā jìdù nǐ.

艾伦说: "我害怕."　　　　Ellen said, "I'm scared."
Āilún shuō: "Wǒ hàipà."

祝愉快.　　　　　　　　　Hope you'll have fun.
Zhù yúkuài.

祝你生日快乐.　　　　　　We wish you a Happy Birthday.
Zhù nǐ shēngrì kuàilè.

海伦感到不耐烦.　　　　　Helen got impatient
Hǎilún gǎndào bú nàifán.　 (Helen felt impatient.)

马特感到惊讶.　　　　　　Matt was surprised.
Mǎtè gǎndào jīngyà.　　　 (Matt felt surprised.)

我们都为他感到悲哀.　　　We all felt sad for him.
Wǒmen dōu wèi tā gǎndào bēiāi.

我觉得不舒服.　　　　　　I feel sick. (I don't feel well.)
Wǒ juéde bù shūfu.　　　　I con't feel comfortable.

安迪觉得无聊.　　　　　　Andy feels bored.
Āndí juéde wúliáo.

轻松一点.　　　　　　　　Be relaxed a little. (Relax.)
Qīngsōng yīdiǎn.

镇静一点.　　　　　　　　Calm down.
Zhènjìng yīdiǎn.

不要紧张.　　　　　　　　Don't be nervous.
Búyào jǐnzhāng.　　　　　 (Take it easy.)

不要慌张.　　　　　　　　Don't be flustered.
Búyào huāngzhāng.

路易说: "我无所谓."
Lùyì shuō: "Wǒ wúsuǒwèi."

Louis said, "I'm indifferent."
(Either way is fine with me.)

不在乎 (bú zàihu) and 不介意 (bú jièyì) also mean being indifferent.

Personal Characteristics

As you have seen, one way to use an adjective is to place it after the linking verb, 是 (shì), which is usually omitted. For example:

他很聪明.
Tā hěn cōngmíng.

He is very intelligent.
(Here, the linking verb is omitted.)

The other way is to place it before the noun it describes, as in:

他是个聪明的人.
Tā shì ge cōngmíng de rén.

He is an intelligent person.
(He is a smart person.)

他是个高大的人.
Tā shì ge gāodà de rén.

He is a tall and big person.
(He is a stout person.)

凯瑟是个快乐的孩子.
Kǎisè shì ge kuàilè de háizi.

Cathy is a happy child.

Here, the particle 的 (de) is a word-ending for adjectives, much like the "ive" in "supportive", the "y" in "spongy", or the "ing" in "aging population". This particle is usually dropped when the adjective is placed after the linking verb, as in our first example:

他很聪明.
Tā hěn cōngmíng.

He is very intelligent.

In such a sentence, both 是 (shì) and 的 (de) are omitted.

The easy way to form the antonym (opposite word) of an adjective is to add the word 不 (bù not) before it. For example, 不聪明 (bù cōngmíng) means "not smart", and 不胖 (bú pàng) means "not fat". Of course, you could also use the Chinese equivalent of "stupid" and "slender", respectively, as shown below:

愚笨	yúbèn	stupid, foolish
瘦	shòu	slender, skinny

Following are additional words that you might use to describe yourself and other people. The personal characteristics listed in the two columns are the opposites of each other. As they say in China, "yin" and "yang" must be balanced in the world. You are not expected to learn all these adjectives by heart at this time. The next time you need a word to characterize someone, you know where to find it.

好 hǎo	good	坏 huài	bad
高 gāo	tall	矮 ǎi	short
胖 pàng	plump, fat	瘦 shòu	slender, skinny
年老 niánlǎo	old	年轻 niánqīng	young
美丽 měilì	beautiful	丑陋 chǒulòu	ugly
聪明 cōngmíng	clever	愚笨 yúbèn	foolish
乐观 lèguān	optimistic	悲观 bēiguān	pessimistic

健康 jiànkāng	healthy	虚弱 xūruò	feeble, in poor health
强壮 qiángzhuàng	strong, stout	衰弱 shuāiruò	weak, feeble, frail
坚强 jiānqiáng	firm, strong-willed	软弱 ruǎnruò	feeble, ineffectual
勇敢 yǒnggǎn	brave, courageous	胆小 dǎnxiǎo	cowardly, gutless
认真 rènzhēn	earnest	随便 suíbiàn	casual
细心 xìxīn	careful, attentive	粗心 cūxīn	careless, thoughtless
能干 nénggàn	competent, capable	无能 wúnéng	incompetent
精明 jīngmíng	shrewd, sharp, astute	糊涂 hútu	muddle-headed
勤劳 qínláo	diligent	懒惰 lǎnduò	lazy
正直 zhèngzhí	decent, righteous	邪恶 xiéè	wicked
诚实 chéngshí	honest	狡猾 jiǎohuá	sly, canny
真诚 zhēnchéng	sincere, truthful	虚伪 xūwěi	hypocritical

富有 fùyǒu	rich	贫穷 pínqióng	poor
节俭 jiéjiǎn	frugal	浪费 làngfèi	extravagant
慷慨 kāngkǎi	generous	小气 xiǎoqì	stingy, petty
大方 dàfāng	generous, gracious	拘谨 jūjǐn	reserved, standoffish
沉默 chénmò	reticent	多嘴 duōzuǐ	talkative, garrulous
活泼 huópō	vivacious, lively	沉闷 chénmèn	dull
热情 rèqíng	affectionate, enthusiastic	冷漠 lěngmò	cold and detached
有趣 yǒuqù	interesting	讨厌 tǎoyàn	disagreeable
滑稽 huájī	funny	呆板 dāibǎn	rigid
幽默 yōumò	humorous	严肃 yánsù	serious, solemn
客气 kèqì	courteous, polite	无礼 wúlǐ	rude, impolite
和气 héqì	amiable, agreeable	暴躁 bàozào	irascible

8. Feelings and Personalities

温和 wēnhé	gentle	凶猛 xiōngméng	ferocious
温柔 wēnróu	warm and gentle	刚硬 gāngyìng	strong and firm
善良 shànliáng	kind-hearted	残忍 cánrěn	cruel
仁慈 réncí	kind, merciful	无情 wúqíng	merciless, heartless
忠实 zhōngshí	loyal, faithful	善变 shànbiàn	fickle, unpredictable
优雅 yōuyǎ	elegant, neat	粗鲁 cūlǔ	rough, rude, boorish
饱学 bǎoxué	learned, knowlegeable	无知 wúzhī	ignorant

Exercise:

1. Please search the list of adjectives in the previous pages for the appropriate word to fill into the blanks in the following sentences. Here again you can see that there are basically two ways to use an adjective in a sentence. One is to place it after the linking verb, such as the omitted 是 (shì to be), and the other is to place it before the noun it describes.

今天我很 _____ _____.　　　　　I'm very glad today.

Jīntiān wǒ hěn _____.

他_____ _____ 吗?　　　　　Is he pleased (satisfied)?

Tā _____ ma?

我好_____!　　　　　I'm so tired!

Wǒ hǎo _____!

杰克说我_____ _____.　　　　　Jack said that I am stingy.

Jiékè shuō wǒ _____.

不要_____ _____.　　　　　Don't be too courteous.

Búyào _____.　　　　　(Make yourself at home.)

他是个_____ _____的男人.　　He is a stout man.

Tā shì ge _____ de nárén.

马克是个_____ _____的人.　　Mark is a generous person.

Mǎkè shì ge _____ de rén.

2. Now, change the descriptive words in a couple of the English sentences then find the appropriate Chinese adjectives for them.

Answer:

1. Completing the given sentences:

今天我很高兴.
Jīn tiān wǒ hěn gāoxìng.

I'm very glad today.

他满意吗?
Tā mǎnyì ma?

Is he pleased (satisfied)?

我好累!
Wǒ hǎo lèi!

I'm so tired!

杰克说我小气.
Jiékè shuō wǒ xiǎoqì.

Jack said that I am stingy.

不要客气.
Búyào kèqì.

Don't be too courteous.
(Please make yourself at home.)

他是个强壮的男人.
Tā shì ge qiángzhuàng de nánrén.

He is a stout man.

马克是个慷慨的人.
Mǎkè shì ge kāngkǎi de rén.

Mark is a generous person.

2. Additional sentences:

他伤心吗?
Tā shāngxīn ma?

Does he feel sad?

马克是个热情的人.
Mǎkè shì ge rèqíng de rén.

Mark is an affectionate person.

8. Feelings and Personalities

9. Colors and Other Attributes

When you talk about things, besides stating the quantity, you may also wish to describe how they look and feel. In this chapter, you will learn various groups of descriptive words as well as how to form your own descriptive phrases to characterize people and things. At this time, don't worry about memorizing all the adjectives listed here. You can always come back to these word lists or check your dictionary when you need to look for a particular adjective. For now, choose a few that interest you. The more often you use these words, the sooner they will sink in.

Colors

The Chinese word for "color" is: 色彩 (sècǎi), 颜色 (yánsè), or simply, 色 (sè). 彩色的 (cǎisè de) means "in color" or "colorful", while 黑白的 (hēibái de) means "black & white". 黑白 (hēibái) also refers to "right and wrong".

Following are the names of a few common colors:

黑色 Black hēisè	褐色 Brown hésè	棕色 Brown zōngsè
红色 Red hóngsè	粉红色 Pink fěnhóngsè	橘黄色 Yellowish Orange júhuángsè
橙色 Orange chéngsè	橘色 Orange júsè	橘红色 Reddish Orange júhóngsè
黄色 Yellow huángsè	绿色 Green lǜsè	蓝色 Blue lánsè
靛色 Indigo Blue diànsè	紫色 Violet zǐsè or Purple	青色 Blue or Green qīngsè
天蓝色 Sky-blue tiānlánsè	白色 White báisè	雪白色 Snow-white xuěbáisè

金色 Gold   银色 Silver   灰色 Gray
jīnsè   yínsè   huīsè

So, to describe a red flower, you might say:

红色的花   hóngsè de huā   red-colored flower

Or simply:

红花   hóng huā   red flower

Similarly, "blue sky" would be:

蓝色的天   lánsè de tiān   *or*   蓝天   lán tiān

And "white clouds" would be:

白色的云   báisè de yún   *or*   白云   bái yún

Some colors are named after the objects usually associated with them.

天蓝	tiēnlán	sky-blue
雪白	xuěbái	snow-white
血红	xuěhóng	blood-red
碧绿	bìlǜ	jade-green, bluish green
铁青	tiěqīng	ashen, cobalt, ghastly (iron-blue)

Did you notice that 雪 (xuě snow) and 血 (xuě blood) sound exactly the same but have totally different meanings? The Chinese language is replete with such homophones. There will be no ambiguity in the written Chinese as the characters are different. With the spoken language, it is the context in which the words are found that allows people to interpret them correctly. This is one reason why the modern Chinese language liberally employs multi-character expressions to help reduce the confusion. For example, 亮 (liàng) means "bright". There are at least four other characters that have the same pronunciation: 量 (liàng quantity), 辆 (liàng a unit for vehicles), 谅 (liàng forgive), and 晾 (liàng to dry in air). Therefore, when they mean: "bright", people might say: 很亮 (hěn liàng very bright), 明亮 (míng liàng clear and bright), 光亮 (guāngliàng shiny as light), or 雪亮 (xuě liàng bright as snow).

Following are a few sample sentences that incorporate various colors.

我看到蓝色的天.
Wǒ kàndào lánsè de tiān.

I see the blue sky.

我看到白色的云.
Wǒ kàndào báisè de yún.

I see the white clouds.

我看到红色的太阳.
Wǒ kàndào hóngsè de tàiyáng.

I see the red sun.

我看到银色的月亮.
Wǒ kàndào yínsè de yuèliàng.

I see the silver moon.

我在绿色的草地上.
Wǒ zài lǜsè de cǎodì shàng.

I am on the green lawn.

我有只灰色的猫.
Wǒ yǒu zhī huīsè de māo.

I have a gray cat.

我有只灰猫.
Wǒ yǒu zhī huī māo.

I have a gray cat.

你的眼睛是褐色的.
Nǐ de yǎnjing shì hésè de.

Your eyes are brown.

她的眼睛不是褐色的.
Tā de yǎnjing búshì hésè de.

Her eyes are not brown.

9. Colors and Other Attributes   111

他有金色的头发.
Tā yǒu jīnsè de tóufǎ.

He has golden hair.

他有金发.
Tā yǒu jīn fǎ.

He has golden hair.

他的狗是咖啡色的.
Tā de gǒu shì kāfēisè de.

His dog is coffee-colored.

我要那块紫色的布.
Wǒ yào nà kuài zǐsè de bù.

I want that piece of purple fabric.

这张纸巾是粉红色的.
Zhè zhāng zhǐjīn shì fěnhóngsè de.

This sheet of napkin is pink.

天黑了.
Tiān hēi le.

It's getting dark.
(The sky is turning black.)

彩色相片好看.
Cǎisè xiàngpiàn hǎokàn.

Color photos look nice.

彩虹有七个颜色:
Cǎihóng yǒu qī ge yánsè:

The rainbow has seven colors:

红, 橙, 黄, 绿, 蓝, 靛, 紫
hóng, chéng, huáng, lǜ, lán, diàn, zǐ

red, orange, yellow, green, blue,
indigo, violet.

白雪公主
Bái Xuě Gōngzhǔ

"White Snow" Princess
(Snow White)

Exercise:

Please fill each blank below with the color of your choice.

我的眼睛是_____色的.
Wǒ de yǎnjing shì _____ sè de.

My eyes are _____.

我的汽车是_____色的.
Wǒ de qìchē shì _____ sè de.

My car is _____.

这朵_____枚瑰很好看.
Zhè duǒ _____ méigui hěn hǎokàn.

This _____ rose looks nice.

我有一件_____色的衣服.
Wǒ yǒu yī jiàn _____ sè de yīfu.

I have a _____ garment.

树上有只_____色的鸟.
Shù shàng yǒu zhī _____ sè de niǎo.

There's a ____ bird on the tree.

In this 19th Century nursery rhyme, 小 (xiǎo little) and 白 (bái white) are two separate adjectives that describe the lamb that went to school.

Mary Had A Little Lamb
玛莉有只小白羊
Mǎlì Yǒu Zhī Xiǎo Bái Yáng

玛莉有只小白羊,
Mǎlì yǒu zhī xiǎo bái yáng,

Mary had a little lamb,
(Mary had a little white lamb,)

小白羊, 小白羊.
Xiǎo bái yáng, xiǎo bái yáng,

Little lamb, little lamb.

玛莉有只小白羊,
Mǎ lì yǒu zhī xiǎo bái yáng,

Mary had a little lamb,

它雪白又光亮.
Tā xuěbái yòu guāngliàng.

Its fleece is white as snow.
(It's snowy white and shiny bright.)

小朋友都哈哈笑,
Xiǎopéngyǒu dōu hāhā xiào,

It made the children laugh and play,
(All the children are laughing,)

哈哈笑, 哈哈笑.
Hāhā xiào, hāhā xiào.

Laugh and play, laugh and play.
(Laughing, laughing.)

小朋友都哈哈笑,
Xiǎopéngyǒu dōu hāhā xiào,

It made the children laugh and play,
(All the children are laughing,)

看小羊在学校.
Kàn xiǎo yáng zài xuéxiào.

To see a lamb at school.

朋友 (péngyǒu) are friends. In Chinese, the term "little friends" refers to children. If you don't know the name of a child, you may address him or her as "little friend", or 小朋友 (xiǎopéngyǒu).

Appearance

Following are a number of other attributes that you can see with your eyes.

大 dà	big, great, important	小 xiǎo	small, insugnificant
多 duō	many, much	少 shǎo	few, little
长 cháng	long	短 duǎn	short
高 gāo	high, tall	低 dī	low
宽 kuān	wide	窄 zhǎi	narrow
方 fāng	square	圆 yuán	round
直 zhí	straight	弯 wān	bent, curved
粗 cū	wide, coarse	细 xì	slender, fine
厚 hòu	thick	薄 báo	thin, filmy
尖 jiān	pointed	扁 biǎn	flattened, squashed
凸 tū	protruding	凹 āo	recessed
深 shēn	deep	浅 qiǎn	shallow
轻 qīng	light	重 zhòng	heavy

上 shàng	at the top, above	下 xià	at the bottom, beneath
左 zuǒ	on the left side	右 yòu	on the right side
前 qián	at the front	后 hòu	at the back
里 lǐ	inside	外 wài	outside
横 héng	horizontal	竖 shù	vertical
直立 zhílì	upright, erect	歪斜 wāixié	slanted
满 mǎn	full	空 kōng	empty
正 zhèng	upright, set right	反 fǎn	upside down, reversed
新 xīn	new	旧 jiù	used, old
完整 wánzhěng	intact, complete	破 pò	broken
亮, 明亮 liàng, míngliàng	bright, shiny	暗, 黑暗 àn, hēiàn	dark, dim
整齐 zhěngqí	tidy	杂乱 záluàn	messy
干净 gānjìng	clean	脏, 肮脏 zāng, āngzāng	dirty
好看 hǎokàn	nice-looking, pretty	难看 nánkàn	bad-looking, ugly
美丽 měilì	beautiful	刺眼 cìyǎn	unsightly

9. Colors and Other Attributes

Texture and Feel

Certain properties of things can only be sensed by touching and feeling.

平滑 pínghuá	level and smooth	粗糙 cūcāo	rough, coarse
脆弱 cuìruò	fragile, weak	坚固 jiāngù	strong, sturdy
软，柔软 ruǎn, róu ruǎn	soft, pliable	硬 yìng	tough, hard
钝 dùn	blunt	利，锐利 lì ruìlì	razor-sharp
温暖 wēnnuǎn	warm, temperate	寒冷 hánlěng	cold
热 rè	hot, enthused	凉 liáng	cool
烫 tàng	scorching	冰冷 bīnglěng	ice-cold, freezing
干 gān	dry	湿 shī	wet
浓 nóng	thick, condensed	稀 xī	diluted
舒适 shūshì	comfortable	不舒适 bù shūshì	uncomfortable
安逸 ānyì	cozy, at ease	难受 nánshòu	unbearable
松 sōng	loose	紧 jǐn	tight

Now, you can see why the elastic band is called: 松紧带 (sōngjǐndài).

Here is a spiritual that helps you practice some of the adjectives that you have learned.

Rock-a My Soul
呵护我的心灵
Hēhù Wǒ de Xīnlíng

把我的心放在
Bǎ wǒ de xīn fàng zài

Rock-a my soul in the
Place my heart in the

天父的怀抱里.
Tiānfù de huàibào lǐ.

Bosom of Abraham.
Bosom of our Heavenly Father.

把我的心放在
Bǎ wǒ de xīn fàng zài

Rock-a my soul in the
Place my heart in the

天父的怀抱里.
Tiānfù de huàibào lǐ;

Bosom of Abraham.
Bosom of our Heavenly Father.

把我的心放在
Bǎ wǒ de xīn fàng zài

Rock-a my soul in the
Place my heart in the

天父的怀抱里.
Tiānfù de huàibào lǐ.

Bosom of Abraham.
Bosom of our Heavenly Father.

噢! 多么安逸!
Ō! Duōme ānyì!

Oh! Rock-a my soul.
Oh! How comfy it feels.

那么高,
Nàme gāo,

So high,

你没法儿越过去.
Nǐ méifǎr yuè guòqù.

You can't get over it.

那么低,　　　　　　　　　　*So low,*
Nàme dī,

你没法儿蹚过去.　　　　　　*You can't get under it.*
Nǐ méifǎr zuān guòqù.

那么宽,　　　　　　　　　　*So wide,*
Nàme kuān,

你没法儿绕过去.　　　　　　*You can't get 'round it.*
Nǐ méifǎr rào guòqù.

噢! 无忧无虑!　　　　　　　*Oh! Rock-a-my soul.*
Ō! Wúyōuwúlǜ!　　　　　　　Oh! No more worries.

把我的心放在　　　　　　　*Rock-a my soul in the*
Bǎ wǒ de xīn fàng zài　　　　Place my heart in the

天父的怀抱里.　　　　　　　*Bosom of Abraham.*
Tiānfù de huàibào lǐ.　　　　　Bosom of our Heavenly Father.

把我的心放在　　　　　　　*Rock-a my soul in the*
Bǎ wǒ de xīn fàng zài　　　　Place my heart in the

天父的怀抱里.　　　　　　　*Bosom of Abraham.*
Tiānfù de huàibào lǐ.　　　　　Bosom of our Heavenly Father.

把我的心放在　　　　　　　*Rock-a my soul in the*
bǎ wǒ de xīn fàng zài　　　　Place my heart in the

天父的怀抱里.　　　　　　　*Bosom of Abraham.*
Tiānfù de huàibào lǐ.　　　　　 Bosom of our Heavenly Father.

噢! 多么欢喜!　　　　　　　*Oh! Rock-a my soul.*
Ō! Duōme huānxǐ!　　　　　　Oh! How joyful it is.

呵护 (hēhù) means to protect and look after. 心灵 (xīnlíng) is the soul. 心 (xīn) is the heart.

You have probably guessed that 天父 (tiānfù) means "Heavenly Father". 天父的 (tiānfù de) means "Heavenly Father's".

怀抱 (huáibào) is the bosom. 里 (lǐ) means "in" or "inside".

The word 把 (bǎ) has multiple meanings. Here it serves to point out the target of the action 放 (fàng to put, to place). The first two lines of the lyrics could be translated as: "Take my heart and put it into the Heavenly Father's bosom."

As with 很 (hěn very), 那么 (nàme) is frequently used to modify an adjective. 那么高 (nàme gāo) translates to: "that high" or "so high". Correspondingly, 这么高 (zhème gāo) translates to: "this high" or "so high".

法 (fǎ) is a method or a rule. 没法儿 (méifǎer) means "no way to", or "cannot".

In the following phrases, 过去 (guòqù) means "passing by".

越过去 (yuè guòqù) is to get over something.

躜过去 (zuān guòqù) is to pass under something.

绕过去 (rào guòqù) is to go around something.

When used as a noun, 过去 (guòqù) means "the past".

无忧无虑 (wúyōuwúlǜ) is a phrase that means no worries and no concerns; in otherwords, carefree.

Tastes, Smells, and Sounds

Use the following words to describe what you have tasted, smelled or heard.

甜 tián	sweet	苦 kǔ	bitter
淡 dàn	mild, not salty	咸 xián	salty
酸 suān	sour	辣 là	spicy hot
涩 sè	astringent	腥 xīng	fishy, smelly
清淡 qīngdàn	light and subtle	油腻 yóunì	rich, heavy, greasy
好吃, 可口 hǎochī, kěkǒu	delicious, tasty	难吃 nánchī	unpalatable
香 xiāng	fragrant, appetizing	臭 chòu	stinking, smelly
芬芳 fēnfāng	sweet-scented	无味 wúwèi	bland, plain
悦耳 yuèěr	mellifluous	刺耳 cìěr	strident
好听 hǎotīng	pleasant to hear	难听 nántīng	unpleasant to hear
小声 xiǎoshēng	gentle/soft (sound)	大声 dàshēng	loud
安静 ānjìng	quiet	吵闹 chǎonào	noisy
宁静 níngjìng	serene, tranquil	热闹 rènào	bustling, busy

Exercise:

Please fill each blank below with the appropriate adjective.

我看到很_____人. I saw many people.
Wǒ kàndào hěn _____ ren.

我的汽车很_____. My car is big.
Wǒ de qìchē hěn _____.

啊! 这朵枚瑰很_____ _____. Ah! This rose looks beautiful.
Ā! Zhè duǒ méigui hěn _____.

一碗_____ _____汤. A bowl of sour-spicy soup.
Yī wǎn _____ _____ tāng. (Hot & Sour Soup)

桂花很_____. Sweet osmanthus flowers are fragrant.
Guìhuā hěn _____.

那一盘面 _____ _____. That dish of noodles is tasty.
Nà yī pán miàn _____.

这支歌_____ _____. This song sounds good.
Zhè zhī gē _____.

这座庙很_____ _____. This temple is quiet.
Zhè zuò miào hěn _____.

Answer:

Please fill each blank below with the appropriate adjective.

我看到很多人.
Wǒ kàndào hěn duō rén.

I saw many people.

我的汽车很大.
Wǒ de qìchē hěn dà.

My car is big.

啊! 这朵枚瑰很美丽.
Ā! Zhè duǒ méigui hěn měilì.

Ah! This rose looks beautiful.

一碗酸辣汤.
Yī wǎn suānlàtāng.

A bowl of sour-spicy soup
(Hot & Sour Soup)

桂花很香.
Guìhuā hěn xiāng.

Sweet osmanthus flowers are fragrant.

那一盘面好吃.
Nà yī pán miàn hǎochī.

That dish of noodles is tasty.

这支歌好听.
Zhè zhī gē hǎotīng.

This song sounds good.

这座庙很安静.
Zhè zuò miào hěn ānjìng.

This temple is quiet.

For your information, 桂花 (Guìhuā Sweet osmanthus) is also known as sweet olive. It is a shrub that produces an abundance of tiny fragrant pale yellow flowers, which are often used to flavor teas, plum juices, sweet cakes and dumplings.

Attributes of Intangibles

Here are some words for describing status, quality, value, events and such.

好 hǎo	good	坏 huài	bad
真 zhēn	true, real	假 jiǎ	false, fake
容易 róngyì	easy	困难 kùnnán	difficult
简单 jiǎndān	simple	复杂 fùzá	complicated
可笑 kěxiào	laughable	可悲 kěbēi	lamentable
有趣 yǒuqù	interesting	乏味 fáwèi	uninteresting
严重 yánzhòng	serious, grave	轻微 qīngwei	minor (In Taiwan, say qīngwéi.)
卫生 wèishēng	sanitary	不卫生 bú wèishēng	unsanitary
幸运 xìngyùn	lucky, fortunate	不幸 búxìng	unfortunate
成功 chénggōng	successful	失败 shībài	unsuccessful
平常 píngcháng	ordinary	特别 tèbié	special
昂贵, 贵 ángguì, guì	expensive	便宜 piányí	inexpensive
高级 gāojí	premium quality	低级 dījí	shoddy, sub-standard

高贵 gāoguì	noble, elite	低贱 dījiàn	lowly, humble
上流 shàngliú	high-class, refined	下流 xiàliú	low-class, lewd
合理 hélǐ	rational	无理 wúlǐ	irrational
公平 gōngpíng	equitable	不公平 bù gōngpíng	unfair
合法 héfǎ	legal	违法 wéifǎ	illegal
安全 ānquán	safe	危险 wēixiǎn	dangerous (In Taiwan, say wéixiǎn.)
晴朗 qíngláng	sunny (weather)	恶劣 èliè	bad, foul (weather)

Please note that many Chinese adjectives can also be used as nouns. For example, 卫生 (wèishēng), as an adjective, means "sanitary". As a noun, it means "sanitation". Similarly, 安全 (ānquán) could mean "safe" or "safety". The following sentences illustrate this point.

这家饭店不卫生.
Zhè jiā fàndiàn bú wèishēng.

This restaurant is not sanitary.

大家要注意卫生.
Dàjiā yào zhùyì wèishēng.

Everyone must pay attention to sanitation.

这房子很安全.
Zhè fángzi hěn ānquán.

This house is very safe.

请注意交通安全.
Qǐng zhùyì jiāotōng ānquán.

Please pay attention to traffic safety.

Exercise:

Can you successfully haggle for a computer that you want to buy by using some of the words that you have learned in the previous chapters? The clerk starts first.

这是一台 ___ ___ 的电脑.　　This is a premium-quality computer.
Zhè shì yī tái _____ de diànnǎo.

多少 ____?　　How much (money) is it?
Duōshǎo _____?

八千人民币.　　$8000 RMB.
Bā qiān rénmínbì.

太 ___ 了!　　Too expensive!
Tài _____ le!

价钱很 ___ ___呀!　　The price is quite reasonable!
Jiàqián hěn_____ yā!

___ ___ 一点, 好 ___?　　(Make it) A little cheaper, okay?
_____ yīdiǎn, hǎo _____?

___ ___ 元.　　$7000 Yuan (RMB).
___ ___ yuán.

好吧! ___ ___. 谢谢.　　All right. Thanks.
Hǎo ba! _____. Xièxiè.

可以用 ___ ___ ___ 吗?　　May I use credit card?
Kěyǐ yòng _____ma?

可以.　　That's fine.
Kěyǐ.

Answer:

这是一台高级的电脑.
Zhè shì yī tái gāojí de diànnǎo.

This is a premium-quality computer.

多少钱?
Duōshǎo qián?

How much (money) is it?

八千人民币.
Bā qiān rénmínbì.

$8000 RMB.

太贵了!
Tài guì le!

Too expensive!

价钱很合理呀!
Jiàqián hěn hélǐ yā!

The price is quite reasonable!

便宜一点好吗?
Piányí yīdiǎn hǎo ma?

(Make it) A little cheaper, okay?

七千元.
Qī qiān yuán.

$7000 Yuan (RMB).

好吧! 谢谢.
Hǎo ba! Xièxiè.

All right. Thanks.

可以用信用卡吗?
Kěyǐ yòng xìnyòngkǎ ma?

May I use credit card?

可以.
Kěyǐ.

That's fine.

9. Colors and Other Attributes

10. Your Eyes are Shiny as the Pearls

You are not limited to describing people and things using only the "canned" generic terms. In fact, you can form a descriptive phrase from any specifics about the person or thing you are describing as long as the resulting sentence makes sense. For example, you know that 树上 (shù shàng) means "on the tree". You can form an adjective phrase by adding the particle "的 (de)" to it, as shown below:

树上的小鸟   the dickeybird on the tree
shù shàng de xiǎoniǎo

Similarly, add the word-ending "的 (de)" to 五月 (wǔyuè May) and you would get the descriptive phrase "in May", as in:

五月的花好看.   Flowers in May are pretty.
Wǔyuè de huā hǎokàn.

Many common descriptive phrases contain the word 有 (yǒu to have, to own), followed by a noun, such as:

有钱的   rich (having money)
yǒuqián de
有礼貌的   polite (displaying politeness)
yǒu lǐmào de
有良心的   conscientious (having conscience)
yǒu liángxīn de

Naturally, there is a corresponding set of descriptive phrases that start with 没有 (méiyǒu have not, lacking), or 没 (méi have not, lacking), such as:

没有钱的   poor (without money)
méiyǒu qián de
没有礼貌的   impolite (lacking politeness)
méiyǒu lǐmào de

没良心的   unscrupulous (devoid of conscience)
méi liángxīn de

Let's try a sentence with a descriptive clause in it:

"The man who has a big house came to see me."

In Chinese, it goes like this:

那个有大房子的人來看我.
Nàge yǒu dà fángzi de rén lái kàn wǒ.

In this example, the main sentence is:

那个人來看我.   That man came to see me.
Nàge rén lái kàn wǒ.

And the descriptive phrase is used to tell us something about "that man":

有大房子的   with a big house (having a big house)
yǒu dà fángzi de

So, you see that by adding the magic word-ending "的 (de)", we could turn just about any phrase or clause into a descriptive phrase or clause. Note, however, that in Chinese, the descriptive phrase always comes before the noun it modifies, where as in English, the descriptive phrase or clause follows the noun that it modifies.

As another example, let's say, "Come and see that tiger!"

来看那只老虎!
Lái kàn nà zhī lǎohǔ!

If we wish to elaborate that that tiger runs fast, we could say, "Come and see that tiger that runs fast." And we would insert the phrase 跑得快的 (pǎo de kuài de that which runs fast) before the noun, tiger.

来看那只跑得快的老虎!
Lái kàn nà zhī pǎo de kuài de lǎohǔ!

You will be able to form many such descriptive phrases after you have learned more action words.

The following folk song from Xinjiang, China, will show you how to describe the facial features of a pretty young lady.

Lift Your Veil
掀起你的盖头来
Xiānqǐ Nǐ de Gàitóu Lái

掀起你的盖头来.
Xiānqǐ nǐ de gàitóu lái.

Lift the veil that covers your head.

让我看看你的眉.
Ràng wǒ kàn kàn nǐ de méi.

Let me look at your fine brows.

你的眉儿细又长啊!
Nǐ de méi er xì yòu cháng a!

Your eyebrows are long and slender,
(Your eyebrows are slender and long,)

好像那树上的弯月亮.
Hǎoxiàng nà shù shàng de wān yuèliàng.

Just like the curved moon on the tree.

我的眉儿细又长啊!
Wǒ de méi er xì yòu cháng a!

My eyebrows are long and slender,
(My eyebrows are slender and long,)

好像那树上的弯月亮.
Hǎoxiàng nà shù shàng de wān yuèliàng.

Just like the curved moon on the tree.

掀起你的盖头来.
Xiānqǐ nǐ de gàitóu lái.

Lift the veil that covers your head.

让我看看你的眼.
Ràng wǒ kàn kàn nǐ de yǎn.

Let me look at your fine eyes.

你的眼儿黑又亮啊!
Nǐ de yǎn er hēi yòu liàng a!

Your cute eyes are dark and shiny,

好像那珍珠一般样.
Hǎoxiàng nà zhēnzhū yībān yàng.

Just like the lovely precious pearls.

我的眼儿黑又亮啊!
Wǒ de yǎn er hēi yòu liàng a!

My cute eyes are dark and shiny,

好像那珍珠一般样.
Hǎoxiàng nà zhēnzhū yībān yàng.

Just like the lovely precious pearls.

掀起你的盖头来.
Xiānqǐ nǐ de gàitóu lái.

Lift the veil that covers your head.

让我看看你的嘴.
Ràng wǒ kàn kàn nǐ de zuǐ.

Let me look at your fine mouth.

你的嘴儿红又小啊!
Nǐ de zuǐ er hóng yòu xiǎo a!

Your mouth is ruby and so tiny,

好像那五月的鲜樱桃.
Hǎoxiàng nà wǔyuè de xiān yīngtáo.

Just like a cherry fresh in May.

我的嘴儿红又小啊!
Wǒ de zuǐ er hóng yòu xiǎo a!

My mouth is ruby and so tiny,

好像那五月的鲜樱桃.
Hǎoxiàng nà wǔyuè de xiān yīngtáo.

Just like a cherry fresh in May.

掀起你的盖头来.
Xiānqǐ nǐ de gàitóu lái.

Lift the veil that covers your head.

让我看看你的脸.
Ràng wǒ kàn kàn nǐ de liǎn.

Let me look at your fine face.

你的脸儿红又圆啊！
Nǐ de liǎn er hóng yòu yuán a!

好像那苹果到秋天.
Hǎoxiàng nà píngguǒ dào qiūtiān.

我的脸儿红又圆啊！
Wǒ de liǎn er hóng yòu yuán a!

好像那苹果到秋天.
Hǎoxiàng nà píngguǒ dào qiūtiān.

Your face is pretty, red and chubby,

Just like an apple in the fall.

My face is pretty, red and chubby,

Just like an apple in the fall.

In songs, 的 is often pronounced as "di" rather than "de", understandably because "duh" doesn't sound that great when accentuated in a song.

In the old Chinese tradition, marriages were mostly arranged, and the groom was not allowed to see the bride's face until after the wedding ceremony. The bride would wear a festive red costume and let someone escort her through the wedding ceremony, all the time with a large red veil draped over her headdress, concealing her face from everyone. It was only after all the guests had departed and the couple had retired to their own room that the groom would be permitted to see his bride for the first time. It appears that the groom in our song is quite pleased with what he sees, and the bride cheerfully echoes the praises lavished on her.

掀 (xiān) means "to lift", and 起 (qǐ) can be interpreted as "up". 掀起 (xiānqǐ) means "to lift up" or "to uncover". 盖头 (gàitóu) specifically refers to the veil that is part of the traditional bride's wedding costume.

让 (ràng) means "to let", "to allow" or "to yield to". "让我看看 (ràng wǒ kànkan)" is a commonly used expression that says, "Let me take a look."

眉 (méi) means "eyebrows". 眉儿 (méir) means "cute, little eyebrows". In this song, we do not join the pinyin for 儿 (er) to the preceding word because we need the extra syllable to match the music.

又 (yòu) means "again", or "both …. and ….". This word is commonly used to associate multiple adjectives with the same noun.

You already know that 好像 (hǎoxiàng) means "seems like". This word is often paired with 一样 (yīyàng same), or 一般 (yībān), with the object of likeness sandwiched in between. For example,

好像珍珠一般   just like the pearls.
hǎoxiàng zhēnzhū yībān

好像苹果一样   just like the apples
hǎoxiàng píngguǒ yīyàng

The song uses "一般样 (yībān yàng)" because it needs an extra character to go with the musical note.

秋天 (qiūtiān) is autumn, when the apples ripen and blush.

11. Let's Get Into Action

Knowing the names of a few things and an assortment of descriptions, you can now paint many still pictures with words. Yet, to animate the pictures, you will need the help of action words (verbs). Action is what makes the world go around, and the verb is the backbone of a sentence.

You have already come across a few verbs, such as 跑 (pǎo run), 跳 (tiào jump), 哭 (kū weep), and 叫 (jiào call, shout), as shown in the following sentences:

两只老虎跑得快.　　　　Two tigers run fast.
Liǎng zhī lǎohǔ pǎo de kuài.

一只青蛙跳下水.　　　　A frog jumped into water.
Yī zhī qīngwā tiào xià shuǐ.

娃娃哭了, 叫妈妈.　　　　The doll cries, and calls "mama".
Wāwa kū le, jiào māma.

These and a number of other common verbs will be covered in this and the next few chapters. Additional action words will pop up in subsequent chapters. Clearly, it is impossible to discuss all the Chinese characters and words in this one book. Also, each of the characters and words you learn here may occur in many other words and phrases that are not found in this book. Nevertheless, after you have mastered a basic set of commonly used characters and words, when you see them in a new expression, they may help you make out the meaning of the new expression.

In Chinese, there is no distinction between a plural noun and a singular noun. Similarly, the verb stays the same whether it is used with multiple subjects or a single subject. So, you would use the same word 跑 (pǎo run) whether you are talking about one tiger running, or one hundred tigers running.

In English, you may change a verb into a noun by appending the suffix "ing". For example, "sing" is a verb, and "singing" may be used as a noun. In Chinese, many action words double as nouns without requiring any effort on your part.

The following is arguably the most popular children's rhyme in Taiwan. Its author's name is unknown.

Pedicab
三轮车
Sānlúnchē

三轮车, 跑得快.   Pedicab, running fast.
Sānlúnchē, pǎo de kuài.

上面坐一位老太太.   On it sits an old lady.
Shàngmiàn zuò yī wèi lǎo tàitai.

要五毛, 给一块.   Asked for 5 dimes, she gives a buck.
Yào wǔ máo, gěi yī kuài.

你说奇怪不奇怪?   Tell me, isn't it crazy?
Nǐ shuō qíguài bù qíguài?   (Say, is it strange or not?)

轮 (lún) is a wheel, and 车 (chē) is a vehicle. 三轮车 (sānlúnchē) is a three-wheeled cart that is basically a large tricycle. The driver pedals in front, and one or two passengers sit in the back. When it rains, the driver puts on his raincoat and deploys the collapsible awning for the passengers. The pedicabs were a popular means of transportation in Asia in the last century. These man-powered vehicles have gradually been replaced by the modern taxicabs.

How many action words do you see in the Pedicab rhyme? They are described below.

跑   **pǎo**   **run, run away, run errands, a run (n.)**

她跑得快; 我追不上.   She runs fast; I can't catch up.
Tā pǎo de kuài; wǒ zhuī bú shàng.

小马跑到花园.   The colt ran to the flower garden.
Xiǎo mǎ pǎo dào huāyuán.

The word 跑 (pǎo) also functions as a noun, as in 长跑 (chángpǎo long-distance running) and 短跑 (duǎnpǎo dash, sprint). On the other hand, marathon is transliterated as 马拉松 (mǎlāsōng). 追 (zhuī) is to chase after or to pursue. 追女友 (zhuī nǚyǒu) means to court a girl friend.

坐	**zuò**	**sit, or travel by (vehicle)**

请坐.   Sit down, please.
Qǐng zuò.

你坐这儿.   You sit over here.
Nǐ zuò zhèr.

他坐在我的座位上.   He is sitting in my seat.
Tā zuò zài wǒ de zuòwèi shàng.

我坐火车去纽约.   I ride the train to New York.
Wǒ zuò huǒchē qù Niǔyuē.

Please note that, although 坐 (zuò sit) and 座 (zuò seat) sound the same, the verb 坐 (zuò sit), and the noun 座 (zuò seat) are two different words.

要	**yào**	**want, ask for, want to, should, important (adj.), essence (n.), important person or thing (n.)**

他要面子嘛!   Well, he is keen on face-saving.
Tā yào miànzi ma!

这件事很重要.   This matter is very important.
Zhè jiàn shì hěn zhòngyào.

他是主要的客人.   He is the main guest.
Tā shì zhǔyào de kèrén.

他是一位<u>要人</u>.　　　　　He is a VIP (Very Important Person).
Tā shì yī wèi yàorén.

那小孩<u>要求</u>五毛.　　　　That kid asks for 5 dimes.
Nà xiǎohái yāoqiú wǔ máo.

In 要求 (yāoqiú), the word 要 (yāo) is pronounced in the first tone.

As 要 (yào) also means to want to do something, it can be used in combination with any other action word. For example:

我要坐这儿.　　　　　I would like to sit here.
Wǒ yào zuò zhèr.

你<u>要不要</u>坐火车去?　　Would you like to go there by train?
Nǐ yào bú yào zuò huǒchē qù?

我<u>正要</u>打电话给你.　　I was just going to phone you.
Wǒ zhèng yào dǎdiànhuà gěi nǐ.

你要注意.　　　　　You must pay attention.
Nǐ yào zhùyì.　　　　　You must be careful about this.

To tell someone not to do something, you could say "不要 (búyào)" or "别 (bié)". Therefore, 不要跑 (búyào pǎo) and "别跑 (bié pǎo)" both mean "Don't run."

给　　　gěi　　　**give, provide, provision (n.), to, for, by (prep.)**

别给他!　　　　　Don't give (it) to him!
Bié gěi tā!

我给那小孩一本书.　　I gave that kid a book.
Wǒ gěi nà xiǎohái yī běn shū.

In the following example, 给 (gěi) functions as a preposition:

他借给我一本书.　　　　　He loaned a book to me.
Tā jiè gěi wǒ yī běn shū.

我忘了还书给他.　　　　　I forgot to return the book to him.
Wǒ wàng le huán shū gěi tā.

她给我写了一封信.　　　　She wrote a letter to me.
Tā gěi wǒ xiě le yī fēng xìn.

我送给他一个礼物.　　　　I gave to him a present.
Wǒ sòng gěi tā yī ge lǐwù.

As a verb, the word 得 (dé) means "to get", "to obtain", or "to gain". We could follow the above sentence with:

他<u>得到</u>一个礼物.　　　　He received a gift.
Tā dédào yī ge lǐwù.

说　　　　　**shuō**　　　　**say, speak, talk, explain, scold,**
　　　　　　　　　　　　　　speech (n.), exposition (n.), doctrine (n.)

她说她不来.　　　　　　　She said she would not come.
Tā shuō tā bù lái.

不要<u>说话</u>.　　　　　　　Don't talk. (Don't say a word.)
Búyào shuōhuà.

他在看<u>小说</u>.　　　　　　He is reading a novel (a "trivial book").
Tā zài kàn xiǎoshuō.

Suppose you want to say, "She said to me she would not come." You would need to know the Chinese word for the preposition, "to", or "with". In fact, there are several of them.

The following example uses the word: 对 (duì to, face to face, opposite, to reply, to be correct).

她对我说她不来.   She said to me she would not come.
Tā duì wǒ shuō tā bù lái.

The following sentences employ different prepositions to ask the same question.

你对他说什么?   What did you say to him?
Nǐ duì tā shuō shénme?

你向他说什么?   What did you say to him?
Nǐ xiàng tā shuō shénme?

你和他说什么?   What did you speak with him about?
Nǐ hé tā shuō shénme?

你同他说什么?   What did you speak with him about?
Nǐ tóng tā shuō shénme?

你跟他说什么?   What did you say to him?
Nǐ gēn tā shuō shénme?

你给他说什么?   What did you say to him?
Nǐ gěi tā shuō shénme?

Please fill the blanks in the following sentences with the appropriate words:

老太太_____我一块钱.   The old lady gave me one dollar.
Lǎo tàitai _____ wǒ yī kuài qián.

我不_____坐这儿.   I don't want to sit here.
Wǒ bú _____ zuò zhèr.

她_____我说她不来.   She told me she would not come.
Tā _____ wǒ shuō tā bù lái.

Following is a slapstick rhyme some Chinese children like to recite. Even young minds know there is some pleasure to be had in getting an edge over the others, if only in words.

How's That Again?

不要吵, 不要闹.　　　　　　　　Don't make a fuss,
Búyào shǎo, búyào nào.　　　　　 And don't complain.

听我老爷讲公道:　　　　　　　　What's fair and just?
Tīng wǒ lǎoyé jiǎng gōngdào.　　　 Hear me, the master, explain:

我坐椅子, 你坐地.　　　　　　　 I'll sit on the chair,
Wǒ zuò yǐzi, nǐ zuò dì.　　　　　　 And you on the floor.

我吃苹果, 你吃心.　　　　　　　 I'll eat the apple,
Wǒ chī píngguǒ, nǐ chī xīn.　　　　 And you can have the core.

You could try inserting some other nouns into this rhyme. For example:

我坐床上, 你坐地.　　　　　　　 I'll sit on the bed,
Wǒ zuò chuáng shàng, nǐ zuò dì.　　 And you on the ground.

我吃香蕉, 你吃皮.　　　　　　　 I'll eat the banana,
Wǒ chī xiāngjiāo, nǐ chī pí.　　　　 And you can have the peel.

老爷 (lǎoyé) is the master of the house, a bureaucrat, a lord or an older gentleman. On the other hand, the lady of the house is called: 太太 (tàitai). The sons and daughters of the master of the house would be addressed by the servants as: 少爷 (shàoyé young master) and 小姐 (xiǎojiě Miss), respectively. If you have watched Chinese movies or situation comedies, you would most likely have heard these terms before.

The five new action words in the above slapstick rhyme all involve the mouth and the ears.

吵　　　　　chǎo　　　　　**make a noise, argue, quarrel, a squabble (n.)**

不要吵.　　　　　　　　　Be quiet. Calm down.
Búyào chǎo.

她吵著要一个洋娃娃.　　She clamored for a doll.
Tā chǎo zhe yào yī ge yángwāwa.

闹　　　　　nào　　　　　**make a noise, stir up trouble, vent, suffer from, a loud noise (n.)**

他们大吵大闹.　　　　　They made much row.
Tāmen dàchǎodànào.

他们闹病.　　　　　　　They are ill.
Tāmen nàobìng.

听　　　　　tīng　　　　　**hear, listen to, obey**

我听到电话响了.　　　　I heard the phone ring.
Wǒ tīngdào diànhuà xiǎng le.

我的狗很听话.　　　　　My dog is obedient.
Wǒ de gǒu hěn tīnghuà.

听说 (tīngshuō) literally translates to "hear say". It is always used as a verb, and means: "I heard some people say".

听说他周六不来.　　　　I heard that he is not coming on Saturday.
Tīngshuō tā zhōuliù bù lái.

没听说过.
Méi tīngshuō guò.

Never heard of that before.

| 讲 | **jiǎng** | **speak, talk, explain, scold, speech (n.)** |

你讲什么?
Nǐ jiǎng shénme?

What are you saying?

我要同他讲和.
Wǒ yào tóng tā jiǎnghé.

I want to make peace with him.

他不讲道理.
Tā bù jiǎng dàolǐ.

He cannot be reasoned with.
(He is unreasonable.)

我们要听他的演讲.
Wǒmen yào tīng tā de yǎnjiǎng.

We want to listen to his speech.

| 吃 | **chī** | **eat, have a meal, soak up, incur, a snack (n.)** |

他要吃早点.
Tā yào chī zǎodiǎn.

He wants to eat breakfast.

我吃了两碗面.
Wǒ chī le liǎng wǎn miàn.

I ate two bowls of noodles.

The traditional Chinese character for noodles is 麵 (miàn), showing the radical 麥 (mài wheat), on the left side. The character 面 (miàn) means face, facet or surface. It has been adopted as the simplified Chinese character for noodles. This sort of ambiguity is one of the drawbacks of using the simplified Chinese characters.

Snacks are called 点心 (Diǎnxīn), 零吃 (língchī) or 零食 (língshī). Here, 零 (líng) means "odd" or "piecemeal". Many Chinese eateries serve the so-called "small meals", 小吃 (xiǎochī light meals), which can range from simple entrées to an assortment of dim-sums. Dim-sum is 点心 (Diǎnxīn) in Cantonese dialect.

Now, 吃 (chī) is "to eat" and 醋 (cù) is "vinegar", but 吃醋 (chīcù) means feeling sour, or resentful, because one is jealous of a rival in love. As an example:

她<u>吃醋</u>了.   She got jealous.
Tā chīcù le.

Verbal Activities

Besides 吃 (chī to eat), 喝 (hē to drink), and 说 (shuō to speak) there are quite a few other things you could do by using your mouth. Most of these action words contain the radical 口 (kǒu mouth).

请	**qǐng**	**"Please", ask for a favor, invite, a request (n.)**

请大家不要吵.   Everybody, please don't make so much noise.
Qǐng dàjiā búyào chǎo.

今天我<u>请客</u>.   The meal is on me today.
Jīntiān wǒ qǐngkè.   (I'm hosting the party.)

今天我请了三位客人.   I invited three guests today.
Jīntiān wǒ qǐng le sān wèi kèrén.

他不听我的<u>请求</u>.   He turns a deaf ear to my request.
Tā bù tīng wǒ de qǐngqiú.

The traditional Chinese character for 请 (qǐng) is 請 (qǐng). On the left side of the traditional Chinese character is the radical 言 (yán), which stands for speech, word or language. In the simplified character 请 (qǐng), you don't see 口 (kǒu mouth) anymore. This is another drawback of using simplified Chinese characters.

问   **wèn**   **ask a question, inquire about, ask about**

这问题, 你问他好了.   As for this question, go ask him.
Zhè wèntí, nǐ wèn tā hǎo le.

他问候你.   He gives his regards to you.
Tā wènhòu nǐ.   (He inquires after you.)

请问, 现在几点?   Please, what time is it?
Qǐngwèn, xiànzài jǐ diǎn?

请问, 这样好吗?   (May I ask:) Is it okay this way?
Qǐngwèn, zhèyàng hǎo ma?

答   **dá**   **reply, answer, a response (n.)**

好, 我答应帮忙你.   All right, I consent to help you.
Hǎo, wǒ dāyìng bāngmáng nǐ.

我答应你的要求.   I grant you your wish.
Wǒ dāyìng nǐ de yāoqiú.

请回答我.   Please answer me.
Qǐng huídá wǒ.

我听到他的回答.   I heard his reply.
Wǒ tīngdào tā de huídá.

答对了!   You got it! (You answered correctly.)
Dá duì le!

Here, 对 (duì) means "correct" or "correctly". Please also note that the first tone is used in 答应 (dāyìng to agree, to promise).

告诉　　**gàosù**　　　　**tell, let know**

<u>告诉</u>我, 他在哪儿?　　Tell me, where is he?
Gàosù wǒ, tā zài nǎr?

请你不要<u>告诉</u>他.　　Please don't tell him.
Qǐng nǐ búyào gàosù tā.

唱　　**chàng**　　　　**sing, or song (n.)**

我听到他<u>唱歌</u>.　　I heard him sing (a song).
Wǒ tīngdào tā chànggē.

他唱的歌很好听.　　The song he sings sounds very good.
Tā chàng de gē hěn hǎotīng.

他们的<u>合唱</u>很好听.　　Their chorus sounds great.
Tāmen de héchàng hěn hǎotīng.

叫　　**jiào**　　　　**shout, call, name, order, a scream (n.)**

他高声<u>尖叫</u>.　　He shrieked at the top of his lungs.
Tā gāoshēng jiānjiào.

这<u>叫</u>什么?　　What's this called (named)?
Zhè jiào shénme?

我<u>叫</u>他们不要吵.　　I told them to stop making
Wǒ jiào tāmen búyào chǎo.　　so much noise.

声 (shēng) is "voice" or "sound". 音 (yīn) is "sound". These characters are

typically used in combination with other characters. For example, 高声

(gāoshēng) means "loud", 音乐 (yīnyuè) is music, and 声音 (shēngyīn) simply means "voice" or "sound".

| 喊 | hǎn | **shout, call, yell, a scream (n.)** |

他们<u>大喊大叫</u>.
Tāmen dàhǎn dàjiào.

They shouted and yelled loudly.

他喊了三声.
Tā hǎn le sān shēng.

He called out three times.

我听到他们的<u>喊叫</u>.
Wǒ tīngdào tāmen de hǎnjiào.

I heard their screams.

| 哭 | kū | **cry, weep, crying (n.)** |

妹妹哭了.
Mèimei kū le.

Little sister is weeping.

我听到娃娃的<u>哭喊</u>.
Wǒ tīngdào wáwa de kūhǎn.

I heard the baby's crying.

痛 (tòng) means pain, sorrow or painful. 痛哭 (tòngkū) means to cry bitterly.

| 笑 | xiào | **laugh, smile, laugh at, ridicule, a laugh (n.), a smile (n.)** |

他<u>又哭又笑</u>.
Tā yòukūyòuxiào.

He cried and laughed at the same time.

不要笑不幸的人.
Búyào xiào búxìng de rén.

Do not make fun of the unfortunate.

她向我<u>微笑</u>.
Tā xiàng wǒ wēixiào.

She smiled at me. (In Taiwan, say "wéixiào" instead of "wēixiào".)

她的微笑很甜.
Tā de wēixiào hěn tián.

Her smiles are sweet.

谈　　　　tán　　　　**talk, chat, discuss, a discussion (n.)**

我要和他谈一件事.
Wǒ yào hé tā tán yī jiàn shì.

I'd like to discuss a matter with him.

我和他谈好了.
Wǒ hé tā tán hǎo le.

I've come to an agreement with him.

大家愉快地谈话.
Dàjiā yúkuài de tánhuà.

We chat together pleasantly.

大家愉快地谈天.
Dàjiā yúkuài de tántiān.

We chat together pleasantly.

讨　　　　tǎo　　　　**demand, beg for, incur, discuss**

那小孩在街頭讨饭.
Nà xiǎohái zài jiētóu tǎofàn.

That kid begs for food on the street.

我们大家一起讨论.
Wǒmen dàjiā yīqí tǎolùn.

We all discuss together.

他们在讨价.
Tāmen zài tǎojià.

They are bargaining.

吐　　　　tù　　　　**vomit, spit out**

那娃娃吐了.
Nà wāwa tù le.

That baby threw up.

尝 **cháng** **taste, try the flavor of**

尝尝这盘鸡.   Try (taste) this dish of chicken.
Cháng cháng zhè pán jī.

他想尝试新的经验.   He wants to try a new experience.
Tā xiǎng chángshì xīn de jīngyàn.

道歉 **dàoqiàn** **apologize, an apology (n.)**

我向你道歉, 好不好?   Let me apologize to you, all right?
Wǒ xiàng nǐ dàoqiàn, hǎo bùhǎo?

这是你的错;   This is your fault;
Zhè shì nǐ de cuò;

你应该道歉.   you should apologize.
Nǐ yīnggāi dàoqiàn.

对不起.   I'm sorry.
Duìbùqǐ.

The word 道 (dào) has a few different meanings: road, way, doctrine, principle, say, and talk. 歉 (qiàn) means apology. 道歉 (dàoqiàn) can be used as a verb (to make any apology) or as a noun (an apology).

错 (cuò wrong, a mistake) is the opposite of 对 (duì correct, right). "你错了. (Nǐ cuò le.)" means: "You are wrong." "我错了. (Wǒ cuò le.)" means: "I'm mistaken." When you have done something wrong, you could also admit it by saying, "我错了. (Wǒ cuò le.)"

The next three lessons will cover additional groups of action words. On a first reading of this book, you may skim over these verbs and learn just a few that interest you the most. Come back later to study the remaining ones.

Exercise:

Fill in the blanks with the appropriate words to complete a simple rhyme fashioned after the "Pedicab" rhyme. Put the Chinese characters on the first row, and the pinyin on the second row of each verse. You may use the index at the end of this book to help locate the words you need.

_____ _____ 兔, 蹦蹦 _____.

_____ _____ tù, bèng bèng _____

Little   white   rabbit, hop, hop, jump.

_____ _____ 萝卜, 他 _____ _____.

_____ _____ luóbo,   tā _____ .

Vegetables,   raddish,   he doesn't want.

_____ _____ _____ , 一口咬.

_____ _____ , yī kǒu yǎo.

Give   (a)   banana,   (he) snatches a bite.

你 _____, 好笑 _____ _____ _____?

Ni3 _____, hǎo xiào _____ _____ _____?

Say, (is it) funny (or) not   funny?

12. Motions

Following are a number of verbs that normally do not take an object. These are actions you can take without involving someone else.

来	**lái**	**come, arrive, coming up**

快来!
Come quickly!
Kuài lái!

你要不要来我家?
Would you like to come to my home?
Nǐ yào bú yào lái wǒ jiā?

人们<u>来</u>来<u>去</u>去.
People are coming and going.
Rénmén láilái-qùqù.

去	**qù**	**go, leave, remove, away (adv.)**

你要不要去加拿大?
Would you like to go to Canada?
Nǐ yào bú yào qù Jiānádà?

他<u>去世</u>了.
He died. (He left the world.)
Tā qùshì le.

他<u>出去</u>了.
He went out.
Tā chūqù le.

走	**zǒu**	**walk, go, leave, leak, lose original shape/flavor**

她走了.
She is gone.
Tā zǒu le.

你为什么**走来走去**? Why are you pacing back and forth?
Nǐ wèishénme zǒu lái zǒu qù?

回 **huí** **return, go back, reply**

我要**回家**. I'd like to go home.
Wǒ yào huíjiā.

他**回**到家了. He has arrived at home.
Tā huí dào jiā le.

我**回来**了. I'm back. (I have come back.)
Wǒ huílái le.

他们**回去**了. They have left for their place.
Tāmen huíqù le.

他来来回回走了半天. He walked back and forth for half a
Tā láilái-huíhuí zǒu le bàntiān. day (quite a while).

跳 **tiào** **jump, leap, bounce, skip, skip over**

她**跳上跳下**. She jumped up and down.
Tā tiào shàng tiào xià. (naughty, can't stay still)

你会不会**跳舞**? Do you know how to dance?
Nǐ huìbúhuì tiàowǔ?

请**跳到**第十九页. Please skip to page 19.
Qǐng tiào dào dì shíjiǔ yè.

飞   **fēi**   **fly, flit, flutter**

小鸟<u>飞</u>来<u>飞</u>去.   The dickeybirds fly to and fro.
Xiǎoniǎo fēi lái fēi qù.

他向我<u>飞眼</u>.   He makes eyes at me.
Tā xiàng wǒ fēiyǎn.

动   **dòng**   **move, stir, arouse, motion (n.), activity (n.)**

不要<u>动</u>那东西.   Don't touch (move) that thing.
Búyào dòng nà dōngxi.

有人在花园<u>走动</u>.   Someone is walking around
Yǒu rén zài huāyuán zǒudòng.   in the garden.

我<u>跑</u>不<u>动</u>了.   I can't run any more
Wǒ pǎo bú dòng le.   (because I'm tired).

今天有什么<u>活动</u>?   What activities are there today?
Jīntiān yǒu shénme huódòng?

运动   **yùndòng**   **exercise, campaign, sports (n.)**

我每天<u>运动</u>.   I exercise every day.
Wǒ měitiān yùndòng.

我天天<u>跑步</u>.   I jog each day.
Wǒ tiāntiān pǎobù.

我们不敢<u>溜冰</u>.   We don't dare to skate.
Wǒmen bùgǎn liūbīng.

他在太平洋里<u>游泳</u>.   He swims in the Pacific Ocean.
Tā zài Tàipíngyáng lǐ yóuyǒng.

爸爸在公园散步.
Bàba zài gōngyuán sànbù.

Dad is strolling in the park.

今晚我们在这儿露营.
Jīnwǎn wǒmen zài zhèr lùyíng.

Tonight we're camping here.

步行也是很好的运动.
Bùxíng yě shì hěn hǎo de yùndòng.

Walking is also a good exercise.

浮   **fú**   **float, superficial (adj.), flighty (adj.)**

小船浮在水上.
Xiǎo chuán fú zài shuǐ shàng.

The small boat floats on the water.

云浮在天上
Yún fú zài tiānshàng.

The cloud is floating in the sky.

球浮起來了.
Qiú fú qǐlái le.

The ball has floated up.

站   **zhàn**   **stand, take a stand, stop, a station (n.)**

他站在那儿.
Tā zhàn zài nàr.

He is standing there.

他在车站等你.
Tā zài chēzhàn děng nǐ.

He is waiting for you at the station.

站住!
Zhànzhù!

Freeze!
(Stop and stay right there!).

起   **chǐ**   **get up, rise, raise, set up, up (adv.), a start (n.)**

天亮了; 起床吧!   The day has broken; arise from bed!
Tiān liàng le; qǐchuáng ba!

你的飞机几点起飞?   What time does your plane take off?
Nǐ de fēijī jǐ diǎn qǐfēi?

躺   **tǎng**   **lie down, recline**

他躺在床上.   He is lying in bed.
Tā tǎng zài chuáng shàng.

请躺下.   Please lie down.
Qǐng tǎng xià.

倒   **dǎo**   **fall, topple, collapse, go out of business**

老先生倒在地上.   The old gentleman fell on the ground.
Lǎo xiānshēng dǎo zài dì shàng.

他的公司倒了.   His company went under.
Tā de gōngsī dǎo le.

跌倒 (diédǎo), 跌跤 (diéjiāo), and 摔跤 (shuāijiāo) are synonymous. They all mean "to fall over" or "to take a tumble". 昏倒 (hūndào) is to fall in a faint .

进   **jìn**   **enter, move forward, advance**

请进来.   *or*   请进.   Please come in.
Qǐng jìnlái.   Qǐng jìn.

她走进大门.
Tā zǒu jìn dàmén.

She entered (through) the main door.
(She went into the building.)

大家向前进!
Dàjiā xiàng qián jìn!

Everybody forge ahead!

退   **tuì**   **recede, move backward, withdraw, return, cancel**

大家向后退!
Dà jiā xiànghòu tuì!

Everybody retreat!

那公司不退钱给我.
Nà gōngsī bú tuì qián gěi wǒ.

That company won't give me a refund.

他不退让.
Tā bú tuìràng.

He won't give in.

步 (bù) is a step. 进步 (jìnbù) means to make progress, and 退步 (tuìbù) means to regress or to lag behind.

出   **chū**   **exit, come out, go beyond, produce, expel**

他出去了.
Tā chūqù le.

He went out.

他出门了.
Tā chūmén le.

He went on a journey.

她出走了.
Tā chūzǒu le.

She ran away from home.

太阳出现了.
Tàiyáng chūxiàn le.

The sun has appeared.

大家一同出力.

Everyone put in some effort (pitch in).

Dà jiā yītóng chūlì.

口 (kǒu) means a mouth or an opening. 入 (rù to enter) is the formal word for 进 (jìn to enter). It looks slightly different from 人 (rén person). With the character 人 (rén person), the left downward stroke sticks out at the top, while with 入 (rù to enter), the right downward stroke sticks out more at the top. In the printed character for 入 (rù to enter), the beginning of the right downward stroke is exaggerated so it appears like an extra short horizontal stroke. There is actually not an extra stroke for this character, which only contains two strokes. When you see a sign with "入口 (rùkǒu)" on it, you will know that it marks the entrance. The "Exit" sign would show "出口 (chūkǒu)". Note, however, that 出口 (chūkǒu) also means "export"; and 说出口 (shuō chūkǒu) means "to speak out", or "to utter". By the way, 人口 (rénkǒu) means population (a count of people's mouths).

| 等 | **děng** | **wait, equal, until (prep.), a rank (n.)** |

她等了一小时.

She waited for one hour.

Tā děng le yī xiǎoshí.

她白等了一小时.

She waited for one hour in vain.

Tā bái děng le yī xiǎoshí.

(Here, 白 (bái) means "for nothing".)

请等一下.

One moment, please.

Qǐng děng yīxià.

(Please wait a moment.)

一加一等于二.

One plus one equals two.

Yī jiā yī děngyú èr.

The following girl-scout round was possibly started in late 1920 or early 1930. It depicts a scenario of eternal anticipation.

Lily of the Valley
铃兰
Línglán

小小银铃悬挂在细杆上；
Xiǎoxiǎo yínlíng xuánguà zài xì gàn shàng.
Little silver bells suspended from slender stems,
White coral bells upon the slender stalks,

可爱的铃兰开在园里小道旁.
Kěài de línglán kāi zài yuán lǐ xiǎodào páng.
Lovely lily of the valley blooming by the small path in the garden.
Lily of the valley deck my garden walk.

你可希望听它们响叮当？
Nǐ kě xīwàng tīng tāmen xiǎng dīngdāng?
Do you wish to hear them go dingdong?
Oh, don't you wish that you might hear them ring?

那要等到天上仙女齐歌唱.
Nà yào děngdào tiānshàng xiānnǚ qí gēchàng.
That will have to wait until the fairies in heaven sing in unison.
That will only happen when the fairies sing.

悬挂 (xuánguà) means "hanging from" or "suspending from". 开 (kāi) means "to open". Here, it refers to the flowers blooming.

希望 (xīwàng) is "to hope". 仙 (xiān) is an immortal or celestial being. 仙女 (xiānnǚ) is a fairy.

齐 (qí) means "even", "uniform", "in unison", or "together". 歌唱 (gēchàng sing) and 唱歌 (chànggē sing) can be used interchangeably.

变   **biàn**   **become, transform, a turn of events (n.)**

天变亮了.
Tiān biàn liàng le.

The sky has turned bright.
(The day has dawned.)

那青蛙变成了王子.
Nà qīngwā biànchéng le wángzǐ.

The frog transformed into a prince.

去年有个<u>政变</u>.
Qùnián yǒu ge zhèngbiàn.

There was a coup d'état last year.

工作   **gōngzuò**   **to work, a job (n.)**

我们大家要努力<u>工作</u>.
Wǒmen dàjiā yào nǔlì gōngzuò.

We all must work hard.

吉米有一个好<u>工作</u>.
Jímǐ yǒu yī ge hǎo gōngzuò

Jimmy has a good job.

干活   **gànhuó**   **to work** (used in China, not usually in Taiwan)

我们<u>干活</u>去.
Wǒmen gànhuó qù.

Let's go to work.

休息   **xiūxī**   **rest**

工作完了要<u>休息</u>.
Gōngzuò wán le yào xiūxī.

After work, you should take a rest.

他躺在床上<u>休息</u>.
Tā tǎng zài chuáng shàng xiūxī.

He lies in bed to rest.

The following song is a parody of an aria titled "Caro Nome (Dearest Name)" from Verdi's opera, "Rigoletto". Don't be surprised if you catch yourself yawning while singing these lines slowly and repeatedly. It is all right to take a nap now before you move on to the next lesson. Besides, there is scientific evidence that it is during sleep that the information in the short-term memory area of the brain gets processed and sorted then filed away as long-term memory.

Yawning
打呵欠
Dǎhēqiàn

我整天都打呵欠.
Wǒ zhěngtiān dōu dǎhēqiàn.

I keep yawning all day long.

啊！啊！啊！啊！啊！啊！啊！
Ā! Ā! Ā! Ā! Ā! Ā! Ā! Ā!

Ah, ah, ah, ah, ah, ah, ah.

打了一遍又一遍.
Dǎ le yī biàn yòu yī biàn.

Yawning non-stop on and on.
(Doing it time and again.)

啊！啊！啊！啊！啊！啊！啊！
Ā! Ā! Ā! Ā! Ā! Ā! Ā! Ā!

Ah, ah, ah, ah, ah, ah, ah.

整天 (zhěngtiān) means the whole day. As you know, 都 (dōu) as an adverb means "all together", and is used with an action word for a group of people or things, as in "他们都走了. (Tāmen dōu zǒu le. They have all gone away.)". In "我整天都打呵欠. (Wǒ zhěngtiān dōu dǎhēqiàn.)", 都 (dōu) is used to indicate the entire duration of a time period. Here it can be translated as "all through".

一遍 (yī biàn) means "one time" or "once". 又 (yòu) means "again". Therefore, the phrase, 一遍又一遍 (yī biàn yòu yī biàn), means "time and again".

13. Love Me or Not?

In this chapter you will see some of the commonly used action words that normally take an object. The first word that comes to mind is, of course, "love". This is the very subject of the traditional American folk song, titled "Down in the Valley" or "Birmingham Jail". Shown below is a shortened version, which only includes two stanzas, along with their respective refrains.

Down in the Valley
在那山谷里
Zài Nà Shāngǔ Lǐ

在那山谷里，
Zài nà shāngǔ lǐ,

Down in the valley,
Down in the valley,

山路遥遥.
Shānlù yáoyáo.

Valley so low.
With long, winding roads.

把头探出去，
Bǎ tóu tàn chūqù,

Hang your head over,
Stick your head way out,

听风呼啸.
Tīng fēng hūxiào.

Hear the wind blow.
Hear the wind howl.

听那风呼啸.
Tīng nà fēng hūxiào.

Hear the wind blow, dear.
Hear that wind howling.

听风呼啸.
Tīng fēng hūxiào.

Hear the wind blow.
Hear the wind howl.

把头探出去，
Bǎ tóu tàn chūqù,

Hang your head over,
Stick your head way out,

听风呼啸.
Tīng fēng hūxiào.

Hear the wind blow.
Hear the wind howl.

给我写封信；
Gěi wǒ xiě fēng xìn;

Write me a letter;
Write me a letter;

快快寄来.
Kuài kuài jì lái.

Send it on time.
Send it out fast.

等你的回音 -
Děng nǐ de huíyīn -

Answer my question -
Awaiting your answer -

爱我不爱?
Ài wǒ bú ài?

Will you be mine?
Love me or not?

你爱我不爱?
Nǐ ài wǒ bú ài?

Will you be mine, dear?
You love me or not?

爱我不爱?
Ài wǒ bú ài?

Will you be mine?
Love me or not?

等你的回音 -
Děng nǐ de huíyīn -

Answer my question -
Awaiting your answer -

爱我不爱?
Ài wǒ bú ài?

Will you be mine?
Love me or not?

As you know, 山 (shān) is a mountain. 山谷 (shāngǔ) is a valley, and 山路 (shānlù) is a mountain path.

遥遥 (yiáoyiáo) is poetic parlance. In ordinary speech, you would say 遥远 (yáoyuǎn) for "far away".

探 (tàn) means to find out, explore, spy, visit, or stick out.

风 (fēng) is wind, and 呼啸 (hūxiào) is to scream or to howl.

写 (xiě) means to write. 写信 (xiěxìn) means writing a letter. 写信 (xiěxìn) and 写封信 (xiě fēng xìn) are common abbreviations for 写一封信 (xiě yī fēng xìn to write a letter).

寄 (jì) means to send out or to entrust to someone. "我去寄信. (Wǒ qù jì xìn.)" means: "I'm going out to mail a letter."

You know that 回 (huí) means to return. Therefore, 回音 (huíyīn), or "returned sound", is a response. 回信 (huíxìn) means "a letter in reply". It can also be used as a verb when you want to say, "to write a letter in reply". On the other hand, 退信 (tuì xìn) means to return a letter to the sender.

爱 (ài) is love. It works both as a noun and a verb. It is also included in such adjectives as 亲爱的 (qīnài de dear, beloved) and 心爱的 (xīnài de treasured in the heart). You probably already know that "我爱你. (Wǒ ài nǐ.)" means: "I love you." "你爱我不爱? (Nǐ ài wǒ bú ài?)" and "你爱不爱我? (Nǐ ài bú ài wǒ?)" both mean, "Do you love me or not?"

喜欢 (xǐhuān) is a verb that means: "to like", which is less intense than "to love".

想 (xiǎng) means to think. It also means to want to, to feel like doing something, to covet, to long for, or to miss somebody.

愿意 (yuànyì) means to be willing to. 意愿 (yìyuàn) is a wish or an intention.

Now you know a few ways of expressing your desire to do something - 爱 (ài) is to love, 喜欢 (xǐhuān) is to like, 要 (yào) and 想 (xiǎng) both mean to want, and 愿意 (yuànyì) means to be willing to.

In the following exercise, please fill each blank on the left side with an expression of your choice from the right side.

我要 _____.

Wǒ yào _____.

散步 to take a walk

sànbù

你要 _____嗎?

Nǐ yào _____ ma?

唱歌 to sing

chànggē

你要不要_____?

Nǐ yào bú yào _____?

吃三明治 to eat a sandwich

chī sānmíngzhì

他想 _____.

Tā xiǎng _____.

吃面 to eat noodles/pasta

chī miàn

我不想 _____.

Wǒ bù xiǎng _____.

坐火车 to travel by train

zuò huǒchē

你爱 _____嗎?

Nǐ ài _____ ma?

看电视 to watch TV

kàn diànshì

你爱不爱_____?

Nǐ ài bú ài _____?

看电影 to watch movies

kàn diànyǐng

我們喜欢_____.

Wǒmen xǐhuān _____.

运动 to do physical exercise

yùndòng

他喜欢 _____嗎?

Tā xǐhuān _____ ma?

学中文 to learn Chinese

xué zhōngwén

他們喜不喜欢_____?

Tāmen xǐ bù xǐhuān _____?

喝汽水 to drink soda

hē qìshuǐ

她不愿意_____.

Tā bù yuànyì _____.

跳舞 to dance

tiàowǔ

Here are a few more examples to show you how to use the word 想 (xiǎng).

想	xiǎng	think, consider, wish, want, long for, miss

我想, 你应该回家.
Wǒ xiǎng, nǐ yīnggāi huíjiā.

I think, you should go home.

想不到, 他赢了.
Xiǎngbúdào tā yíng le.

Unexpectedly, he won.

让我想一想.
Ràng wǒ xiǎngyīxiǎng.

Let me think about it a while

我想要看电视.
Wǒ xiǎng yào kàn diànshì.

I'd like to watch TV.

他不想上学.
Tā bù xiǎng shàngxué.

He doesn't want to go to school.

想得美!
Xiǎng dé měi!

Wishful thinking!
(It's not likely to happen.)

你想不想她?
Nǐ xiǎng bù xiǎng tā?

Do you miss her?

我很想她.
Wǒ hěn xiǎng tā.

I miss her very much.

想念 (xiǎngniàn) also mean to miss or to yearn for.

怀念 (huáiniàn) is to reminisce. It also works as a noun - reminiscence. 念 (niàn) is to think of. As a verb, 怀 (huái) means to embrace or to hold in one's bosom. As a noun it is the bosom. Remember the song, "Rock-a My Soul", we sang in a previous lesson?

回想 (huíxiǎn) means to think back or to recollect.

梦 (mèng) is to dream. When used as a noun, it means "a dream". 梦想 (mèngxiǎng) is a wish, or a fantasy. It also means to dream about something.

As a verb, 爱好 (àihào) means to love doing something. Note that in this expression, 好 (hào) is pronounced in the fourth tone rather than the third tone.

好 (hǎo) means good or nice, while 好 (hào) means to be fond of.

爱好 (àihào), 喜好 (xǐhào), and 喜爱 (xǐài) all mean to enjoy doing something. These words also work as nouns to represent a hobby or an interest in something. Following are some examples of hobbies.

| 他喜好弹吉他. | He likes playing the guitar. |
| Tā xǐhào tán jítā. | |

| 东尼喜欢写毛笔字. | Tony likes to do Chinese calligraphy. |
| Dōngní xǐhuān xiě máobǐ zì. | |

| 苏珊喜爱编织和画图. | Susan loves to knit and paint. |
| Sūshān xǐài biānzhī hé huàtú. | |

| 汤姆爱好吹笛. | Tom loves playing the flute. |
| Tāngmǔ àihào chuī dí. | |

| 丹尼喜欢弹钢琴. | Danny enjoys playing the piano. |
| Dānní xǐhuān tán gāngqín. | |

| 丽莎的喜好是种花. | Lisa's hobby is planting flowers. |
| Lìshā de xǐhào shì zhònghuā. | |

Please note that the word, 爱 (ài), also means to be apt to, or to be prone to. For example, "她爱头痛. (Tā ài tóutòng.)" means "She is prone to have headaches." No one in his or her right mind would love a headache!

I would also like to point out that when you want to say "to enjoy the benefit of", "to enjoy the pleasure of", or "a treat", the word to use is 享受 (xiǎngshòu).

她享受各种优待.
Tā xiǎngshòu gèzhǒng yōudài.

She enjoys all kinds of favors.

听音乐是一种享受.
Tīng yīnyuè shì yī zhǒng xiǎngshòu.

Listening to music is a pleasure.

As you have seen, 不 (bù) is a handy word that can be used with any adjective or any verb to form an antonym. For example, 不喜欢 (bù xǐhuān to dislike) is the opposite of 喜欢 (xǐhuān to like). The actual word for "to dislike" or "to be disgusted with" is: 讨厌 (tǎoyàn). Naturally, there are many other words that represent a range of negative feelings, as the following examples show.

我不欣赏这音乐.
Wǒ bù xīnshǎng zhè yīnyuè.

I don't appreciate this music.

我們不喜欢跑步.
Wǒmen bù xǐhuān pǎobù.

We don't care for jogging.

我們不愿跑步.
Wǒmen bú yuàn pǎobù.

We are unwilling to jog.

他嫌我不漂亮.
Tā xián wǒ bú piàoliàng.

He dismisses me as not being pretty.

我們讨厌跑步.
Wǒmen tǎoyàn pǎobù.

We don't like to jog.

他讨不讨厌吃水果?
Tā tǎo bù tǎoyàn chī shuǐguǒ?

Does he despise fruits or not?

我怕打针.
Wǒ pà dǎzhēn.

I'm scared of getting shots.

他厌恶懒汉.
Tā yànwù lǎnhàn.

He abhors lazybones.

我<u>恨</u>他.
Wǒ hèn tā.

I hate him.

我們<u>痛恨</u>坏人.
Wǒmen tònghèn huàirén.

We utterly hate bad guys.

Following are a few other things that our minds often do.

这件事必须好好<u>思考</u>.
Zhè jiàn shì bìxū hǎohǎo sīkǎo.

This matter needs to be mulled over good.

我<u>考虑</u>去巴黎.
Wǒ kǎolǜ qù Bālí.

I'm considering to go to Paris.

我們<u>计划</u>去巴黎度假.
Wǒmen jìhuà qù Bālí dùjià.

We plan to vacation in Paris.

<u>感谢</u>天, 他回来了.
Gǎnxiè tiān, tā huílái le.

Thank heavens, he has come back.

我<u>相信</u>你.
Wǒ xiāngxìn nǐ.

I believe you.

我<u>怀疑</u>他的话.
Wǒ huáiyí tā de huà.

I doubt his words.

我<u>猜</u>她不会去.
Wǒ cāi tā búhuì qù.

My guess is that she won't go.

他<u>嫉妒</u>丹尼的成功.
Tā jídù Dānní de chénggōng.

He is jealous of Danny's success.

我<u>记得</u>她爱吃面.
Wǒ jìde tā ài chī miàn.

I remember she loves noodles.

13. Love Me or Not?

不要忘记打电话给她.   Don't forget to call her.
Búyào wàngjì dǎdiànhuà gěi tā.

她担心亚当不来.   She worries that Adam won't come.
Tā dānxīn Yàdāng bù lái.

他抱怨小狗不听话.   He complains the puppy is naughty.
Tā bàoyuàn xiǎo gòu bù tīnghua.

请原谅他.   Please forgive him.
Qǐng yuánliàng tā.

饶 (ráo) is to have mercy on someone or to let someone off. It is more intense than 原谅 (yuánliàng to forgive). For example:

求求你, 再饶我一回.   I beg you to forgive me once more.
Qiú qiú nǐ, zài ráo wǒ yīhuí.

求 (qiú) is to beg or to plead.

再 (zài) means "again". 回 (huí to return), when used as a noun, means "one time" or "one bout".

So, when you have offended someone, you might try to appease his/her anger.

讨好   **tǎohǎo**   **to please, curry favor with, win appreciation**

她生气了, 快去讨好她.   She is angry, go butter her up.
Tā shēngqì le, kuài qù tǎohǎo tā.

这事不好做, 又不讨好.   This task is hard to do, and the
Zhè shì bù hǎo zuò, yòu bù tǎohǎo.   efforts aren't appreciated.

Here is another word for currying favor with someone. 巴结 (bājié) has more of a distasteful sense to it than 讨好 (tǎohǎo).

巴结　　　**bājie**　　　**fawn on, curry favor with, toady to**

他巴结他的老板.
Tā bājie tā de lǎobǎn.

He toadies to his boss.

他买花巴结他的女友.
Tā mǎi huā bājie tā de nǚyǒu.

He bought some flowers to flatter his girlfriend.

When someone apologizes to you, you might 接受 (jiēshòu accept) or 拒绝 (jùjué refuse) the apology.

她拒绝接受我的道歉.
Tā jùjué jiēshòu wǒ de dàoqiàn.

She refuses to accept my apology.

她拒绝我的帮助.
Tā jùjué wǒ de bāngzhù.

She refuses my help.

她接受了我的邀请.
Tā jiēshòu le wǒ de yāoqǐng.

She accepted my invitation.

Can you find the four verbs in the following tongue twister?

Purple Spiders

紫蜘蛛, 紫蜘蛛.
  Zǐ zhīzhū, zǐ zhīzhū.
                     Purple spiders, purple spiders.

找着数只紫蜘蛛.
Zhǎo zháo shù zhī zǐ zhīzhū.
                     I've found several purple spiders.

数数蜘蛛是十只.
Shǔ shǔ zhīzhū shì shí zhī.
                     Count the spiders; there are ten.

十只蜘蛛知不知?
Shí zhī zhīzhū zhī bù zhī?
                     As for the spiders, is it in their ken?

找 (zhǎo) means "to search for", whereas 找着 (zhǎo zháo) means to have found.

As a verb, 数 (shǔ) means to count. For example, 数数看 (shǔ shǔ kàn) means to take a count and see how many there are. As an adjective, 数 (shù) takes on the fourth tone and means "several" or "a few", such as in 数只 (shù zhī several), 大多数 (dàduōshù most, a majority of), and 少数 (shǎoshù few, a minority of).
As a noun, 数 (shù) means a number, such as in 数量 (shùliàng quantity), 小数 (xiǎoshù decimal), and 人数 (rénshù the number of people).

是 (shì) is the "be" verb. 知 (zhī) stands for 知道 (zhīdào to know).

你知道天上有多少星星吗?
Nǐ zhīdào tiānshàng yǒu duōshǎo xīngxīng ma?
Do you know how many stars there are in the sky?

抱歉, 我不知道.
Bàoqiàn, wǒ bù zhīdào.
Sorry, I don't know.

To Have or Not to Have

The plain fact about talents, 天分 (tiānfèn), and money, 钱 (qián), is that some people have it and some don't. That's life. However, if we are willing, we can always make friends, 朋友 (péngyǒu).

有   **yǒu**   **have, there is, there exists**

我有许多朋友.
Wǒ yǒu xǔduō péngyǒu.

     I have many friends.

他们很有钱.
Tāmen hěn yǒuqián.

     They have a lot of money.

他们是<u>有钱人</u>.
Tāmen shì yǒuqiánrén.

     They are rich people.

我们<u>没有</u>钱.
Wǒmen méiyǒu qián.

     We don't have money.

我们是<u>穷人</u>.
Wǒmen shì qióngrén.

     We are poor people.

In the following exercise, please pair up each term on the left side with each term on the right side:

我有 Wǒ yǒu	I have	两件外套 liǎng jiàn wàitào	two jackets
他有 Tā yǒu	He has	一个手机 yī ge shǒujī	a cell phone
李先生有 Lǐ xiānsheng yǒu	Mr. Lee has	一双手套 yī shuāng shǒutào	a pair of gloves

有 (yǒu) can also be used to indicate the existence of someone or something.

有多少人？　　　　　How many people are there?
Yǒu duōshǎo rén?

有八个人要来.　　　There will be eight persons coming.
Yǒu bā ge rén yào lài.

只有八个人要来.　　Only eight persons are coming.
Zhǐyǒu bā ge rén yào lài.

We have seen that many common descriptive phrases can be formed by combining 有 (yǒu) with a noun. Here are a three more examples: 有可能 (yǒukě'néng possible), 有毒 (yǒudú poisonous), and 有利 (yǒulì advantageous).

拥有 (yōngyǒu) just means to own or to possess, as in:

她拥有一块田地.　　She owns a farmland.
Tā yōngyǒu yī kuài tiándì.

无 (wú without) is the opposite of 有 (yǒu to have). It is usually used in expressions that serve as adjectives or adverbs. Some examples are:

无心　　　　wúxīn　　　　not be in the mood for, inadvertently

无比　　　　wúbǐ　　　　incomparable, unparalleled, matchless

无法　　　　wúfǎ　　　　no way to, unable to, incapable of

无法忍受　　wúfǎ rěnshòu　　intolerable (no way to tolerate)

忍 (rěn) means to tolerate, to endure or to put up with someone or something. No wonder this character features a dagger on a heart.

Seeing Is Believing

There are several Chinese characters that stand for looking and seeing in various ways. Many of them share the radical, 目 (mù), which was derived from the pictograph of an eye with the upper and lower eyelids. 目 (mù) is the formal word for eyes. In modern Chinese, you would say 眼 (yǎn) or 眼睛 (yǎnjing).

看   **kàn**   **look at, see, read, think, regard, watch, look after**

让我<u>看看</u>.
Ràng wǒ kàn kàn.
Let me take a look.

我<u>看</u>了才相信.
Wǒ kàn le cái xiāngxìn.
I'll be convinced only after I see it.

<u>我看</u>, 他不是美国人.
Wǒ kàn, tā búshì Měiguórén.
I think he is not an American.

她<u>看</u>不起我.
Tā kànbùqǐ wǒ.
She looks down upon me.

他带孩子去<u>看医生</u>.
Tā dài háizi qù kàn yīshēng.
He took his kid to see the doctor.

我<u>看出</u>她很高兴.
Wǒ kànchū tā hěn gāoxìng.
I can tell she is quite happy.

他<u>看上</u>那栋大房子.
Tā kànshàng nà dòng dà fángzi.
He has his eyes on that large house.

他们有不同的<u>看法</u>.
Tāmen yǒu bùtóng de kànfǎ.
They have a different point of view.

来看电视吧!
Lái kàn diànshì ba!

Come watch TV.

看来, 他不爱你.
Kànlái, tā bú ài nǐ.

It seems he does not love you.

In the last two examples above, notice how the word order for 来 (lái come) and 看 (kàn look) makes a difference in the meaning of the resulting sentence.

When 看 (kān) is used in the sense of watching over something or looking after someone, it is pronounced in the first tone, as in the following examples. However, if you pronounce it in the fourth tone, people will still be able to understand you.

狗会看门.
Gǒu huì kānmén.

Dogs can watch the house door.

她请了一位看护.
Tā qǐng le yī wèi kānhù.

She hired a nurse.

见   **jiàn**   **see, regard, meet, opinion (n.)**

我在街上看见他.
Wǒ zài jiē shàng kànjiàn tā.

I saw him on the streets.

我看不见.
Wǒ kàn bújiàn.

I can't see. I can't see it.

好久不见.
Hǎo jiǔ bújiàn.

It's been a while since I saw you.
("Long time no see.")

不见了.
Bújiàn le.

It has disappeared.

你有什么意见?
Nǐ yǒu shénme yìjiàn?

Do you have any opinion?
(What's your opinion?)

观   **guān**   **watch, look at, sight (n.), view (n), concept (n.)**

她喜欢参观博物馆.   She likes to tour museums.
Tā xǐhuān cānguān bówùguǎn.

这观念很好.   This is a great idea.
Zhè guānniàn hěn hǎo.   (This concept is great.)

望   **wàng**   **gaze ahead, see, visit, hope, reputation (n.)**

我在街上望见他.   I saw him on the streets.
Wǒ zài jiē shàng wàngjiàn tā.

他回去看望他的母亲.   He went back to visit his mother.
Tā huíqù kànwàng tā de mǔqīn.

我希望你能来.   I hope you can come.
Wǒ xīwàng nǐ néng lái.

他有一台望远镜.   He has a telescope.
Tā yǒu yī tái wàngyuǎnjìng.

Please note the fine distinction in meaning among the following words:
希望 (xīwàng to hope, a hope), 期望 (qíwàng to hope for, an expectation),
渴望 (kěwàng to thirst for, a yearning), 盼望 (pànwàng to look forward to, an anticipation).

视 (shì vision) is the formal word for looking at or watching. In everyday speech, it usually used in a polysyllable word, such as 近视 (jìnshì near-sighted, near-sightedness), 远视 (yuǎnshì far-sighted, far-sightedness), and 电视 (diànshì television).

Now, there are other ways of eying someone. 眯 (mī to squint) is to look with narrowed eyes, as an older person, a near-sighted person, or someone smiling might do. This is a friendly look. 瞪 (dèng), on the other hand, is to glower at someone, or to stare dumb-struck. For example: "他瞪了我一眼. (Tā dèng le wǒ yī yǎn.)" means: "He glowered at me." 瞄 (miáo) usually means to cast a sideways glance grudgingly, in disdain, or for a quick evaluation. 盯 (dīng) is to fix one's gaze or to keep a close watch on something or someone. For example, "盯住他. (Dīng zhù tā.)" means to keep an eye on him (and not let him run away or do something undesirable).

13. Love Me or Not?

14. Work, Work, Work

Just as there are a few ways of saying "doing something" in English, there are a number of Chinese words that represent the verb "to do". Following are a few that are regularly used in everyday speech.

| 做 | zuò | do, act, perform, make, produce, prepare |

做什么?
Zuò shénme?

Yes, what? (What do you want me to do?)

我要做一个玩具.
Wǒ yào zuò yī ge wánjù.

I plan to make a toy.

我做好了.
Wǒ zuò hǎo le.

I'm done. (I have finished doing it.)

我不爱做工.
Wǒ bú ài zuògōng.

I don't like to do manual labor.

他在图书馆做事.
Tā zài túshūguǎn zuòshì.

He works at the library.

他说到做到.
Tā shuōdàozuòdào.

He does what he says.
(He lives up to his words.)

她会做人.
Tā huì zuòrén.

She knows how to act decently
(or make herself look good).

我不欣赏她的做法.
Wǒ bù xīnshǎng tā de zuòfǎ.

I don't like her way of doing things.

我常常做梦.
Wǒ chángcháng zuòmèng.

I often dream.

他很会<u>做菜</u>.　　　　　　He knows how to cook well.
Tā hěn huì zuòcài.

Beware that there is another word that is pronounced exactly the same as 做 (zuò) and that has a similar meaning. If you look up the word 作 (zuò) in a dictionary, you will probably get the idea that it is synonymous with 做 (zuò). However, although there are a few instances where the two words are used interchangeably, generally, there is a fine distinction between these two words that dictates their proper usage. Whereas 做 (zuò) mostly refers to performing a physical action or producing a physical item, 作 (zuò) refers to composing a piece of literature, art or music, or bringing about a change or an effect.

作　　　　**zuò**　　　　**make, compose, bring about, act (n.), work (n.)**

我常常<u>作梦</u>.　　　　　　I often dream.
Wǒ chángcháng zuòmèng.

她会<u>作曲</u>.　　　　　　　She knows how to compose music.
Tā huì zuòqǔ.

这事由你<u>作主</u>.　　　　　This matter is for you to decide.
Zhè shì yóu nǐ zuòzhǔ.　　(You have the final say.)

我想同你<u>合作</u>.　　　　　I would like to collaborate with you.
Wǒ xiǎng tóng nǐ hézuò.

他常同我<u>作对</u>.　　　　　He often sets himself against me.
Tā cháng tóng wǒ zuòduì.

你不要<u>装聋作哑</u>.　　　　Don't feign ignorance.
Nǐ bú yào zhuāngnóngzuòyǎ.　(Don't pretend to be deaf and dumb.)

他在我家作客.
Tā zài wǒ jiā zuòkè.

He is staying at my house as a guest.

她喜欢这份工作.
Tā xǐhuān zhè fèn gōngzuò.

She likes this job.

我喜欢他的作品.
Wǒ xǐhuān tā de zuòpǐn.

I like his work (of art or literature).

干　　　　gàn　　　　**do, act, get rid of, ability, a main trunk (n.)**

干吗?
Gàn má?

What now? What on earth for? (colloquial)

我不爱干活.
Wǒ bú ài gànhuó.

I don't like to work.

他的工作被干掉了.
Tā de gōngzuò bèi gàn diào le.

His job has been eliminated.

The people in Taiwan say 做工 (zuògōng) or 做事 (zuòshì) when referring to working for a living or doing a job. On the other hand, someone from China would most likely say 干活 (gànhuó) instead.

弄 (nòng) and 搞 (gǎo) are two other informal ways of saying "to do" or "to cause to happen". For example, 弄坏了 (nònghuài le) and 搞坏了 (gǎohuài le) both mean to have damaged something. 弄错了 (nòngcuò le) and 搞错了 (gǎocuò le) both mean to be mistaken or to have misunderstood.

打	dǎ	hit, strike, attack, do, forge, a dozen (n.)

他打了一只苍蝇.
Tā dǎ le yī zhī cāngying.

He swatted a fly.
(In Taiwan, say "cāngyíng" for flies.)

请你打听他住哪儿.
Qǐng nǐ dǎtīng tā zhù nǎr.

Please find out where he lives..

他向我打招呼.
Tā xiàng wǒ dǎzhāohū.

He beckoned to me.

她常打喷嚏.
Tā cháng dǎpēntì.

She sneezes often.

你打算怎么办?
Nǐ dǎsuàn zěnme bàn?

What do you plan to do about it?

打 (dǎ hit) can be used instead of 玩 (wán play) when we talk about sports or games that involve the hands.

我弟弟爱玩篮球.
Wǒ dìdi ài wán lánqiú.

My brother loves to play basketball.

我弟弟爱打篮球.
Wǒ dìdi ài dǎ lánqiú.

My brother loves to play basketball.

她爱打乒乓球.
Tā ài dǎ pīngpāngqiú.

She loves playing ping-pong.

我不会打橄榄球.
Wǒ búhuì dǎ gǎnlǎnqiú.

I don't know how to play football.

他爱打冰上曲棍球.　　　　　　　He loves to play ice hockey.
Tā ài dǎ bīng shàng qūgùnqiú.

她教我打排球.　　　　　　　　　She taught me to play volleyball.
Tā jiāo wǒ dǎ páiqiú.

打麻将要四个人.　　　　　　　　It takes four persons to play mahjong.
Dǎ májiàng yào sì ge rén.

他打扑克输了钱.　　　　　　　　He lost money playing poker.
Tā dǎ pūkè shū le qián.

As for playing the game of soccer, you would say 踢 (tī) for kicking.

他很会踢足球.　　　　　　　　　He is very good at soccer.
Tā hěn huì tī zúqiú.　　　　　　　(He is good at kicking soccer ball.)

她踢了我一下.　　　　　　　　　She gave me a kick.
Tā tī le wǒ yīxià.　　　　　　　　(She kicked me one time.)

篮 (lán) is a basket. Therefore, 篮球 (lánqiú basketball) is a no-brainer.

橄榄 (gǎnlǎn) is a Chinese olive. Doesn't the football look kind of like a huge olive?

足 (zú) is the formal word for the foot. As you have seen before, it is the radical found in many Chinese action words that involve the feet. Do you remember the following two words? If not, please look for them in the chapter, titled "Let's Get into Action" then fill in the blanks below.

_____ to run　　　　　_____ to jump
_____ (pinyin)　　　　_____ (pinyin)

Following is a Chinese children's rhyme that doubles as a riddle.

Riddle
谜题
Mítí

脸皮绷绷. Liǎnpí bēng bēng.	Its face is pulled tight,
肚子空空. Dùzi kōng kōng.	And its belly's hollow.
打它三棍子. Dǎ tā sān gùnzi.	Whack it three times,
它叫: "痛, 痛, 痛." Tā jiào: "Tòng, tòng, tòng."	And "Pain, pain, pain," it whines.

解答 Solution
Jiědá

鼓 **gǔ**   the drum

脸皮 (liǎnpí) refers to the skin on the face. 绷 (bēng) means being taut or stretched tight.

肚子 (dùzi) is the belly. 空 (kōng) means being empty or hollow.

棍子 (gùnzi) is a rod or a stick. Here, 三棍子 (sān gùnzi) does not mean three rods. Rather, it indicates the number of times the rod is brought down.

In the following traditional Chinese nursery rhyme, a young blacksmith apprentice has forged a nice pair of scissors for his married sister who lives a distance away. He delivers it to her.

The Blacksmith
铁匠
Tiějiàng

张打铁, 李打铁.

Chāng dǎtiě, Lǐ dǎtiě.
Hammering left and hammering right,
(Zhang is forging iron, and Lee is forging iron.
- Everyone is busy hammering away.)

打把剪刀送姊姊.

Dǎ bǎ jiǎndāo sòng jiějie.
Scissors for Sis that are sharp and tight.
(I'm making a pair of scissors to give to Sister.)

姊姊留我歇; 我不歇.

Jiějie liú wǒ xiē; wǒ bù xiē.
Sis says to stay over, but I won't.

我要回家打夜铁.

Wǒ yào huíjiā dǎ yè tiě.
I must go home and work through the night.
(I must go home to do the night shift of forging.)

Handling Things

Like the word 打 (dǎ hit), many of the Chinese characters representing actions that involve the hands contain the radical 手 (shǒu hand) or a reduced form thereof. For example, the lower half of the character 拿 (ná take) shows the character 手 (shǒu hand). On the other hand, the radical on the left side of the word 打 (dǎ hit) is a reduced form of 手 (shǒu hand).

拿	ná	take, hold, capture, have a grasp of

她<u>拿著</u>一本书.
Tā ná zhe yī běn shū.

She is holding a book.

我<u>拿到</u>了护照.
Wǒ ná dào le hùzhào.

I've obtained my passport.

你<u>拿得到</u>吗?
Nǐ ná dé dào ma?

Can you reach? Can you grasp it?

请把那东西<u>拿走</u>.
Qǐng bǎ nà dōngxī ná zǒu.

Please take that thing away.

小费太少; <u>拿不出手</u>.
Xiǎofèi tài shǎo; nábùchūshǒu.

The tip is too small;
it's not presentable.

这个给你. <u>拿去</u>吧!
Zhège gěi nǐ. Ná qù ba!

This is for you. Go ahead and take it.

请把上衣<u>拿来</u>给我.
Qǐng bǎ shàngyī ná lái gěi wǒ.

Please fetch the shirt for me.

汤姆吹笛很<u>拿手</u>.
Tāngmǔ chuī dí hěn náshǒu.

Tom is skilled at playing the flute.

推　　　tuī　　　**push, push aside, shove, promote**

他<u>推</u>著脚踏车.　　　He is pushing his bicycle.
Tā tuī zhe jiǎotàchē.

她<u>推开</u>我.　　　She pushed me aside.
Tā tuī kāi wǒ.

她<u>推出</u>一本新书.　　　She releases a new book.
Tā tuīchū yī běn xīn shū.

拉　　　lā　　　**pull, draw, drag, lift, empty the bowels**

牛会<u>拉车</u>.　　　Oxen can pull carts.
Niú huì lā chē.

不要<u>拖拖拉拉</u>.　　　Don't drag your heels.
Búyào tuōtuō-lālā.

我<u>拉肚子</u>.　　　I have diarrhea (runny bowels).
Wǒ lādùzi.

The word for pulling out something is 拔 (bá). For example,

他<u>拔</u>了一颗牙.　　　He had a tooth pulled out.
Tā bá le yī kē yá.

放　　　fàng　　　**let go, set free, put, let out, release**

<u>放开</u>他.　　　Release him. (Let him go.)
Fàngkāi tā.

把铅笔<u>放下</u>.　　　Put the pencil down.
Bǎ qiānbǐ fàngxià.

请<u>放心</u>.　　　　　　　　Please don't worry. Rest assured.
Qǐng fàngxīn.　　　　　　　(Set your heart at ease.)

提　　　**tí**　　　**carry, lift, promote, bring up (mention)**

她<u>提著</u>菜篮.　　　　　　She is carrying a grocery basket.
Tā tí zhe zàilán.

咖啡可以<u>提神</u>.　　　　　Coffee can perk you up.
Kāfēi kěyǐ tíshén.

我有个<u>手提</u>包.　　　　　I have a handbag.
Wǒ yǒu ge shǒutíbāo.

他有没有<u>提起我</u>?　　　　Did he mention me?
Tā yǒu méiyǒu tíqǐ wǒ?

招　　　**zhāo**　　　**beckon, incur, enlist, attract, own up**

他们向我<u>招手</u>.　　　　　They wave at me.
Tāmen xiàng wǒ zhāoshǒu.

这会<u>招来</u>麻烦.　　　　　This will invite trouble.
Zhè huì zhāo lái máfán.

他们会<u>招待</u>你.　　　　　They will receive and entertain you.
Tāmen huì zhāodài nǐ.

他<u>不打自招</u>.　　　　　　He confessed on his own, without duress.
Tā bùdǎzìzhāo.

By the way, 握手 (wòshǒu) means to shake hands with someone.

188　　　　　14. Work, Work Work

Opening and Closing

In Chinese, opening, 开 (kāi), and closing, 关 (guān) also stand for turning on and turning off, respectively. These two characters are found in a host of other words and expressions. Please pay attention to the following examples to see the various ways in which these words are used.

| 开 | **kāi** | **open, turn on, operate, start boiling, away (adv.)** |

砰!砰!砰! 请开门!
Pēng! Pēng! Pēng! Qǐng kāimén!

Knock, knock, knock. Please open up!

谁呀? 是谁呀?
Shéi yā? Shì shéi yā?

Who? Who's there?
(familiar form)

哪一位呀?
Nǎ yī wèi yā?

Who is it?
(polite form)

请问, 是哪一位?
Qǐngwèn, shì nǎ yī wèi?

Who is it, please?
(most polite form)

他把电灯打开了.
Tā bǎ diàndēng dǎkāi le

He turned on the lamp (light).

你开心吗?
Nǐ kāixīn ma?

Are you happy?

他明天开刀.
Tā míngtiān kāidāo.

He will have the surgery tomorrow.

大家开始唱吧!
Dàjiā kāishǐ chàng ba!

Let's start singing!

枚瑰花开了.
Méigui huā kāi le.

The roses have bloomed.

水煮开了吗?
Shuǐ zhǔ kāi le ma?

Has the water boiled?

他明天开车去加州.
Tā míngtiān kāichē qù Jiāzhōu.

He will drive to California tomorrow.

开車 (kāichē) or 开汽車 (kāi qìchē) means to drive a car. 驾驶 (jiàshǐ) is the formal way of saying "to drive a car".

他明天一早要开會.
Tā míngtiān yīzǎo yào kāihuì.

He needs to attend a meeting early tomorrow morning.

我不想离开你.
Wǒ bù xiǎng líkāi nǐ.

I don't want to leave you.

他們分开了.
Tāmen fēnkāi le.

They have separated.

关   **guān**   **close, turn off, shut in, be concerned with**

他把门关上了.
Tā bǎ mén guān shàng le.

He closed the door.

请你把电灯关掉.
Qǐng nǐ bǎ diàndēng guān diào.

Please turn off the lamp (light).

警察把坏人关闭起来.
Jǐngchá bǎ huàirén guānbì qǐ lái.

The police locked up the bad guy(s).

他很关心你.
Tā hěn guānxīn nǐ.

He cares about you a lot.

这事有关大家.
Zhè shì yǒuguān dàjiā.

This matter involves all of us.

这不关你的事.
Zhè bù guān nǐ de shì.

This is none of your business.
(This does not concern you.)

没关系.
Méiguānxi.

It doesn't matter. That's all right.

Buying and Selling

The two characters, 买 (mǎi buy) and 卖 (mài sell), look quite similar. Take care not to mix them up.

买   **mǎi**   **buy, purchase**

你要买什么东西?
Nǐ yào mǎi shénme dōngxi?

What (thing) would you like to buy?

我要买些米.
Wǒ yào mǎi xiē mǐ.

I would like to buy some rice.

他买了一件新衬衫.
Tā mǎi le yī jiàn xīn chènshān.

He bought a new shirt.

他被收买了.
Tā bèi shōumǎi le.

He was bribed (bought over).

卖   **mài**   **sell, betray, show off**

卖菜哟!
Mài cài yō!

Vegetables for sale!

这些花要卖到外国.
Zhèxiē huā yào mài dào wàiguó.

These flowers will be sold to
foreign countries.

我们<u>卖力</u>地工作.   We work with all our efforts.
Wǒmen màilì de gōngzuò.   (We endeavor to work.)

他被<u>出卖</u>了.   He was betrayed (sold out).
Tā bèi chūmài le.

他爱<u>卖弄</u>小聪明.   He likes to show off petty smarts.
Tā ài màinòng xiǎocōngmíng.

Making Use of Things

使用 (shǐyòng) means "to make use of". For short, people just say "用 (yòng)".

利用 (lìyòng) means to utilize something or someone to one's own advantage.

费用 (fèiyòng) is a noun that means expenses.

用   **yòng**   **use, apply, utilize, the polite form of eating/drinking**

她用刀切开西瓜.   She uses a knife to cut open
Tā yòng dāo qiēkāi xīgua.   the watermelon.

他们<u>用心</u>做事.   They apply their mind to their work.
Tāmen yòngxīn zuòshì.

请<u>用力</u>一点.   Please do it a little harder.
Qǐng yònglì yīdiǎn.   (Please apply more force.)

<u>请用</u>.   Please partake of the food.
Qǐng yòng.   (Bon appétit!)

他在<u>利用</u>你.   He is using you.
Tā zài lìyòng nǐ.

可以<u>借用</u>电话吗?　　　May I borrow the phone?
Kěr yǐ jièyòng diànhuà ma?

不用　　　**búyòng**　　　**not to use, no need to do (something)**

您要喝茶吗?　　　Would you like to drink some tea?
Nín yào hēchá ma?

<u>不用</u>, 谢谢.　　　No, thanks.
Búyòng, xièxiè.

你<u>不用</u>担心.　　　You don't need to worry.
Nǐ búyòng dānxīn.

<u>不用</u>脱鞋.　　　No need to take off the shoes.
Búyòng tuō xié.

<u>不用</u>穿大衣.　　　No need to put on an overcoat.
Búyòng chuān dàyī.

Please note that 拖鞋 (tuō xié slippers) and 脱鞋 (tuō xié to take off the shoes) sound exactly the same. 拖 (tuō) means to procrastinate, drag on, or to drag across the floor, while 脱 (tuō) means to take off a garment, to shed (hair, skin, etc.), or to free oneself from something.

Exercises:

Here are a few personal hygiene routines and some relevant items. Please use the word 用 (yòng) to form sentences like the following example:

我用梳子梳头发.   I use a comb to comb the hair.
Wǒ yòng shūzi shū tóufà.

洗发精 xǐfàjīng	shampoo	洗头发 xǐ tóufà	to wash the hair
浴缸 yùgāng	bathtub	洗澡 xǐzǎo	to bathe
肥皂 féizào	soap	洗手 xǐshǒu	to wash the hands
毛巾 máojīn	towel	擦脸 cā liǎn	to wipe the face
牙膏 yágāo	toothpaste	刷牙 shuāyá	to brush the teeth
牙签 yáqiān	toothpick	剔牙 tī yá	to pick between the teeth
剪刀 jiǎndāo	scissors	剪指甲 jiǎn zhǐjiǎ	to trim the fingernails
剪刀 jiǎndāo	scissors	剪头发 jiǎn tóufà	to cut the hair
剃刀 tìdāo	razor	刮胡子 guā húzi	to shave the beard

By the way, the restroom is called 洗手间 (xǐshǒujiān). Some people refer to it obliquely as "Room # 1", or 一号 (yīhào). 厕所 (cèsuǒ) means lavatory or toilet. So, 男厕所 (náncèsuǒ) is the men's room, and 女厕所 (nǚcèsuǒ) is the ladies' room.

Now, we should also take care of housekeeping. Please use the word 用 (yòng) to match each task listed below with the relevant tool or item. In the following example, note that in the noun, 扫把 (sàobǎ broom), the word 扫 (sào) is pronounced in the fourth tone. On the other hand, in the verb, 扫地 (sǎodì sweep), the word 扫 (sǎo) is pronounced in the third tone.

他用扫把扫地

He uses a broom to sweep the floor.

Tā yòng sàobǎ sǎodì.

抹布	rags	擦桌面	to wipe the desktop
mābù		cā zhuōmiàn	
吸尘器	vacuum cleaner	吸地毯	to vacuum the carpet
xīchéngqì		xī dìtǎn	
拖把	the mop	擦地板	to mop the floor
tuōbǎ		cā dìbǎn	
洗碗机	dishwasher	洗碗	to clean the dishes
xǐwǎnjī		xǐ wǎn	
洗衣粉	detergent	洗衣服	to wash the clothes
xǐyīfěn		xǐ yīfu	
熨斗	the iron	烫衬衫	to iron the shirts
yùndǒu		tàng chènshān	
衣架	clothes hanger	挂衣服	to hang up the clothes
yījià		guà yīfu	
垃圾桶	garbage can	装拉圾	to hold the garbage
lājī tǒng		zhuāng lājī	
割草机	mower	割草	to cut the grass
gē cǎo jī		gē cǎo	(to mow the lawn)

In Taiwan, 抹布 (mābù) is pronounced as "mǒbù", and 垃圾 (lājī garbage) is pronounced as "lèsè".

14. Work, Work Work

15. Past, Present, and Future

In English, the verb usually changes form to indicate whether an action is taking place in the present, or it took place some time in the past. For example, the word "eat" changes to "ate" when it is used to talk about a past action.

In Chinese, the past, present and future tenses are indicated by mentioning the time of occurrence of the action, or with the help of an auxiliary word. The verb itself generally remains the same. As you can see from the examples below, the verb 下雨 (xiàyǔ to rain) does not change at all when going from one tense to another.

昨天没有下雨.   It did not rain yesterday.
Zuótiān méiyǒu xiàyǔ.

今天下雨.   It rains today.
Jīntiān xiàyǔ.

明天会下雨吗?   Will it rain tomorrow?
Míngtiān huì xiàyǔ ma?

In the following example, the verb, 是 (shì to be), is only implied.

昨天我很开心.   Yesterday I was very happy.
Zuótiān wǒ hěn kāixīn.

今天我很开心.   Today I am very happy.
Jīn tiān wǒ hěn kāixīn.

明天我会很开心.   Tomorrow I will be very happy.
Míngtiān wǒ huì hěn kāixīn.

Obviously, there is no way to change a word that is not written out. Since you cannot determine the time from the verb itself, you will need to rely on other clues.

For example, when reading a story about a past event, you would assume that everything transpired in the past. On the other hand, when you say, "再见. (Zàijiàn. See you again.)", the future tense is clearly understood. And, in the above sample sentences, there is no ambiguity because the time of occurrence is explicitly stated.

In a sentence, the time of occurrence generally comes before the verb. It may be placed before or after the subject.

我昨天很开心.   I was very happy yesterday.
Wǒ zuótiān hěn kāixīn.

我今天很开心.   I am very happy today.
Wǒ jīntiān hěn kāixīn.

以前 (**yǐqián**) means "in the past" or "previously", clearly pointing out the past tense.

她以前不爱跳舞.   She did not like to dance before.
Tā yǐqián bú ài tiàowǔ.

现在 (**xiànzài**) means "now" or "at present". 目前 (**mùqián**) means "presently" or "at this time". For example:

现在几点钟?   What time is it now?
Xiànzài jǐ diǎn zhōng?

她目前不想找工作.   She does not want to look for a job
Tā mùqián bù xiǎng zhǎo gōngzuò.   at this time.

将来 (**jiānglái**) means "future" or "in the future". As an example:

他将来要当兵.   He wants to become a soldier
Tā jiānglái yào dāngbīng.   in the future.

In the absence of any time indicator or helping words, the present tense is assumed.

我很开心.　　　　　　　　I am very happy.
Wǒ hěn kāixīn.

他爱打猎.　　　　　　　　He likes to hunt.
Tā ài dǎliè.

The words, 会 (**huì**) and 将 (**jiāng**), are both used as auxiliary verbs to indicate the future tense, with some nuances in meaning.

会 (huì) implies that something is likely to happen or you think it will certainly happen. For example:

我会很开心.　　　　　　　I will surely be very happy.
Wǒ huì hěn kāixīn.

When you want to state a plain fact about a future happening then you would use the auxiliary verb 将 (jiāng). In this case, no assessment is made about the likeliness of the future event happening or not. 将 (jiāng) is simply used to indicate the future tense. For example:

他明年将上大学.　　　　　He will go to college next year.
Tā míngnián jiāng shàng dàxué.

Please fill in the appropriate words to indicate the tense of the verbs below.

他_____ _____不来.　　　He will not come tomorrow.
Tā _____ bù lái.

我_____ _____二十六岁.　I am 26 years old now.
Wǒ _____ èrshíliù suì.

你＿＿＿后悔.　　　　　　　　You will surely regret it.

Nǐ ＿＿＿＿ hòuhuǐ.

The Perfect Tense

In Chinese, the perfect tense is indicated with the help of a few auxiliary words. The same expression in perfect tense applies whether we are talking about the present perfect tense or the past perfect tense. The following words are commonly used to show that an action has been completed.

了 **(le)** is a particle that is attached to the end of a verb to indicate that the action has taken place. Often the division between the past tense and the perfect tense is blurred in Chinese. Anything that happened in the past is considered completed.

他来了.　　　　　　　　　He has come.

Tā lái le.

昨天下了雨.　　　　　　　It rained yesterday.

Zuó tiān xià le yǔ.

已经 **(yǐjīng)** is the adverb that means "already". It is often added to the sentence to emphasize the completion of the action. For example:

他已经来了.　　　　　　　He has already come.

Tā yǐjīng lái le.

完 **(wán)** means whole, completed or finished. 完了 **(wán le)** is an expression that indicates the completion of an action. As shown below, if the action word takes an object, then the particle, 了 (le), may be placed either before or after the object.

我吃完饭了.　　　　　　　I have finished eating the meal.

Wǒ chī wán fàn le.

我已经吃完了饭.   I have already finished eating the meal.
Wǒ yǐ jīng chī wán le fàn.

你看完那本书了吗?   Have you finished reading that book?
Nǐ kàn wán nà běn shū le ma?

好 (**hǎo**) means good or well. When 好了 (**hǎo le**) is attached to a verb, it indicates that an action has been completed, usually satisfactorily. For example:

你做好了吗?   Have you finished it?
Nǐ zuò hǎo le ma?

她写好信了.   She has finished writing the letter.
Tā xiě hǎo xìn le.

过 (**guò**) means to cross, to pass, or the past. It is attached to a verb to form the perfect tense. For example:

我去过英国.   I have been to England.
Wǒ qù guò Yīngguó.

他们来过.   They have been here.
Tāmen lái guò.

从来没 . . . 过 (**cónglái méi . . . . guò**) means to have never done something.

他从来没去过.   He has never been there before.
Tā cónglái méi qù guò.

还没 (**hái méi**) means "to have not yet".

他怎么还没回来?   Why has he not yet returned?
Tā zěnme hái méi huílái?

Exercise:

When using 好 (hǎo), 完 (wán) or 过 (guò) to form the perfect tense of a "verb + object" combination, you would insert the word between the verb and the object. For example, the perfect tense for 写信 (xiěxìn to write a letter) is: 写好信 (xiě hǎo xìn to have finished writing the letter). Similarly, the perfect tense for 看见他 (kànjiàn tā) is 看见过他 (kàn jiàn guò tā to have seen him before).

Please use the above model to form the perfect tense for the following actions.

梳头	shūtóu	to comb the hair
洗脸	xǐliǎn	to wash the face
刷牙	shuāyá	to brush the teeth
煮饭	zhǔfàn	to cook the meal
看电视	kàn diànshì	to watch TV
打电话	dǎ diànhuà	to make a phone call
打篮球	dǎ lánqiú	to play basket ball

Answer:

好, 完 and 过 can all be used with each of the verbs, with some nuances in meaning. Optionally, you may add the particle 了 (le) to the expressions.

梳好头	shū hǎo tóu	to have finished combing the hair, or to have combed the hair neatly
梳好了头	shū hǎo le tóu	to have finished combing the hair, or to have combed the hair neatly
洗好脸	xǐ hǎo liǎn	to have finished washing the face, or to have washed the face cleanly
刷过牙	shuā guò yá	to have brushed the teeth
煮好饭	zhǔ hǎo fàn	to have finished cooking the meal
看完电视	kàn wán diànshì	to have finished watching the TV
打过篮球	dǎ guò lánqiú	to have finished playing basket ball, or to have played basket ball before
打完电话	dǎ wán diànhuà	to have finished telephoning

Please note that when starting a phone call, you would say,

喂? 我是 xxx. Wéi? Wǒ shì xxx.　　Hello ! I am so and so.

However, when hollering for a taxi, you would pronounce "喂 (wèi)" in the fourth tone.

喂! 计程车! Wèi! Jìchéngchē!　　Hey! Taxi!

The Progressive Tense

In Chapter 2, you learned that 在 (zài to be at) is a linking verb that connects a noun with a place or location. For instance, "他在公园里. (Tā zài gōngyuán lǐ.)" translates to: "He is in the park."

在 (zài) is also an auxiliary verb that helps to indicate the progressive tense of a verb. In this sense, it can be interpreted as "to be doing some task". For example, "我在工作. (Wǒ zài gōngzuò.)" means: "I am working." Practice this usage by pairing up any term listed below on the left side with any term listed on the right side.

你在 Nǐ zài	看书 kànshū	reading a book
他在 Tā zài	吃饭 chīfàn	having a meal
我们在 Wǒmen zài	喝水 hēshuǐ	drinking water
他们在 Tāmen zài	打字 dǎzì	typing
我不在 Wǒ bú zài	笑 xiào	laughing
你不在 Nǐ bú zài	哭 kū	weeping
她不在 Tā bú zài	唱歌 chànggē	singing
他也在 Tā yě zài	睡觉 shuìjiào	sleeping

正在 (zhèngzài) means to be in the process of doing something, as shown in the following sentences:

他正在打电话.　　　　　He is talking on the phone right now.
Tā zhèngzài dǎdiànhuà

请等一下. 他正在吃饭.　　Please wait a little while. He is
Qǐng děng yīxià. Tā zhèngzài chīfàn.　having a meal.

Another word that helps indicate an action in progress is 著 (zhe). You can attach this suffix to any action word to indicate the progressive tense. For example:

妹妹背著洋娃娃.　　　　Little sister is carrying a doll on
Mèimei bēi zhe yángwāwa.　her back.

我们喝著水.　　　　　　We are drinking water.
Wǒmen hē zhe shuǐ.

她唱著歌.　　　　　　　She is singing.
Tā chàng zhe gē.

他拿著一杯咖啡.　　　　He is holding a cup of coffee.
Tā ná zhe yī bēi kāfēi.

And, of course, the progressive tense can be indicated by the context of a sentence:

宝宝睡觉时不哭闹.
Bǎobao shuìjiào shí bù kūnào.
While sleeping, the baby does not cry and make noises.

我吃饭的时候, 喜欢听音乐.
Wǒ chīfàn de shíhòu, xǐhuān tīng yīnyuè.
While eating, I like to listen to music.

Here is an English folk song that expresses tender loving feelings through a charming riddle, 谜 (mí). The last stanza contains a few verbs in the progressive tense.

The Riddle Song
谜
Mí

我给你一颗樱桃, 它没子核.
Wǒ gěi nǐ yī kē yīngtáo, tā méi zǐ hé.
I gave my love a cherry that has no stone.

我给你一只小鸡, 它没骨骼.
Wǒ gěi nǐ yī zhī xiǎo jī, tā méi gǔgé.
I gave my love a chicken that has no bone.

我给你说个故事, 它说不完.
Wǒ gěi nǐ shuō ge gùshì, tā shuō bù wán.
I told my love a story that has no end.

我给你一个宝宝, 它不哭喊.
Wǒ gěi nǐ yī ge bǎobao, tā bù kū hǎn.
I gave my love a baby with no crying.

啊! 哪儿有这样的樱桃, 它没子核?
Ā! Nǎr yǒu zhèyàng de yīngtáo, tā méi zǐ hé?
How can there be a cherry that has no stone?

啊! 哪儿有这样的小鸡, 它没骨骼?
Ā! Nǎr yǒu zhèyàng de xiǎo jī, tā méi gǔgé?
How can there be a chicken that has no bone?

而哪儿有这样的故事, 它说不完?

Ér nǎr yǒu zhèyàng de gùshì, tā shuō bù wán?

How can there be a story that has no end?

啊! 哪儿有这样的宝宝, 它不哭喊?

Ā! Nǎr yǒu zhèyàng de bǎobao, tā bù kū hǎn?

How can there be a baby with no crying?

那开花时的樱桃, 它没子核.

Nà kāihuā shí de yīngtáo, tā méi zǐ hé.

A cherry that is blooming, it has no stone.

那孵育时的小鸡, 它没骨骼.

Nà fū yù shí de xiǎo jī, tā méi gǔgé.

A chicken that is pipping, it has no bone.

而我爱你的故事, 它说不完.

Ér wǒ ài nǐ de gùshì, tā shuō bù wán.

The story that I love you, it has no end.

那熟睡时的宝宝, 它不哭喊.

Nà shúshuì shí de bǎobao, tā bù kū hǎn.

A baby that is sleeping has no crying.

樱桃 (yīngtáo) are cherries. Their stones or pits are called 子 (zǐ seeds), 核 (hé pit, stone, nucleus), or 子核 (zǐ hé seeds).

鸡 (jī) means chicken. 小鸡 (xiǎo jī) is a small chicken or a baby chick.

Bones are called 骨(gǔ) or 骨头 (gǔtóu). 骨骼 (gǔgé) is the frame of bones, or the skeleton.

故事 (gùshì) are stories. To tell a story is to 讲故事 (jiǎng gùshì) or 说故事 (shuō gùshì). You know that 完 (wán) means finished. Therefore, 说不完 (shuō bù wán) means that the story is so long that you cannot get to its end to finish it.

宝 (bǎo) means treasured or a treasure. Many parents call their babies by the pet name 宝宝 (bǎobao). 宝宝 (bǎobao) is also a general term that refers to any baby. Babies tend to do a lot of crying, 哭 (kū), and screaming, 喊 (hǎn).

The expression "哪儿有 (nǎr yǒu)..." starts the legitimate question, "Where can I find...?" On the other hand, 哪儿有这样的 (nǎr yǒu zhèyàng de) translates to: "how can there possibly be such a..." This phrase is commonly used to express doubts and skepticism.

开花时 (kāihuā shí at the time it is blooming), 孵育时 (fū yù shí while hatching) and 熟睡时 (shúshuì shí while sleeping soundly) are all actions in progress.

Now, some ambiguity could well arise in the interpretation of 我爱你的故事 (wǒ ài nǐ de gùshì). In this song, it is clear that 我爱你 (wǒ ài nǐ I love you) is the 故事 (gùshì story) that is being told. Nevertheless, if taken out of context, this sentence could have been construed as 我爱 (wǒ ài) + 你的故事 (nǐ de gùshì), which translates to: "I love your story."

16. Yes, I Can

At this point, when someone asks you:

您会说中国话吗?　　　　Can you speak Chinese?
Nín huì shuō Zhōngguóhuà ma?

You should feel comfortable answering:

会一点儿.　　　　I can, a little bit.
Huì yīdiǎnr.

In the above response, the main verb 说 (shuō speak) is customarily omitted, in the same way as the English word "speak" is omitted when you answer, "I can."

Auxiliary verbs, such as "can", "may" and "must", are words that support and add to the meaning of the main verb. Some auxiliary verbs, such as "will" and "have" serve to indicate the tense of the main verb. We have seen in the previous chapter how to use the words 会 (huì) and 将 (jiāng) in forming the future tense.

As an auxiliary verb, 会 (huì) means to be able to, to be capable of, to be good at something, to be likely to, or to be surely to. As a noun it means a meeting, a get-together, a chief city, or an occasion or opportunity, 机会 (jīhuì). As a verb, it means to meet or get together, as in 会面 (huìmiàn).

The word 将 (jiāng) also has other meanings. When used as a noun, it means "a general", "commander-in-chief", or the principal piece in Chinese chess. The Chinese word for a general is 将军 (jiāngjūn). When you are in a position to checkmate in a game of Chinese chess, you would exclaim, "将 (jiàng)!" In this case, the word is pronounced in the fourth tone.

In this chapter, we will focus on the use of these words as auxiliary verbs. A few other common auxiliary verbs are listed below.

能 néng	can, may, be capable of	你能帮我一个忙吗? Nǐ néng bāng wǒ yī ge máng ma? Could you do me a favor?
不能 bùnéng	cannot, may not, unable to	他牙疼, 不能吃饭. Tā yā téng, bùnéng chīfàn. He has a toothache, and cannot eat.
能够 nénggòu	can, be able to	他感冒, 不能够来. Tā gǎnmào, bù nénggòu lái. He has a cold, and cannot come.
应该 yìnggāi	ought to, must, should	你应该道歉. Nǐ yǐnggāi dàoqiàn. You should apologize.
必须 bìxū	must, have to	人必须吃东西才能活. Rén bìxū chī dōngxī cái néng huó. Man must eat in order to live.
得 děi	must, have to (informal)	我得回家. Wǒ děi huíjiā. I must go home.
无须 wúxū	need not	你无须担心. Nǐ wúxū dānxīn. You need not worry.
不用 búyòng	need not	你不用担心. Nǐ búyòng dānxīn. You don't need to worry.

可以	can, may	我可以进来吗?
kěyǐ		Wǒ kěyǐ jìnlái ma?
		May I come in?

不要	don't	不要吵他.
búyào		Búyào chǎo tā.
		Don't disturb him.

In general, you can turn a statement into a question by adding the particle "吗 (ma)" at the end of the sentence. For example, when people hear you say, "你来吗? (Nǐ lái ma? Are you coming?)", they know right away that you are asking a question rather than stating a fact.

Alternatively, you could combine the verb with its negative counterpart to form a query, as in "你来不来? (Nǐ lái bù lái? Are you coming or not?)" In this case, do not add the interrogative particle 吗 (ma). You may add the particle 呢 (ni or ne) to soften the tone of such a question, but this is entirely up to you.

When an auxiliary verb is used in a sentence, then the query is expressed through the auxiliary verb, and the main verb remains unchanged. For example:

他会不会来呢   Will he likely come or not?
Tā huìbúhuì lái ne?

你能不能小声一点?   Can you lower your voice or not?
Nǐ néngbùnéng xiǎoshēng yīdiǎn?   (The speaker is somewhat annoyed.)

我可不可以去?   May I go?
Wǒ kěbùkěyǐ qù?

Yet another way to form the query is to use 是不是 (shìbúshì whether) or 是否 (shìfǒu), 是否 (shìfǒu whether) being the formal form of 是不是 (shìbúshì). Then the previous sentences would become:

他<u>是不是</u>会来?   Is he likely to come or not?
Tā shìbúshì huì lái?

你<u>是否</u>能小声一点?   Can you lower your voice or not?
Nǐ shìfǒu néng xiǎoshēng yīdiǎn?   (The speaker is somewhat annoyed.)

我<u>是不是</u>可以去?   Is it all right or not for me to go?
Wǒ shìbúshì kěyǐ qù?

Did you notice that the word 否 (fǒu) is made up of the characters 不 (bù no, not) and 口 (kǒu mouth)? Not surprisingly, this word means to negate or to deny. It is the formal word for the negative reply of "不是 (búshì)".

Exercise:

Please fill each blank on the left side using an expression from the right side.

我会 _____.

Wǒ huì _____.

你会 _____ 吗?

Nǐ huì _____ ma?

你会不会 _____呢?

Nǐ huìbúhuì _____ ni?

他可以 _____.

Tā kěyǐ _____.

我可以 _____吗?

Wǒ kěyǐ _____ ma?

我可不可以 _____?

Wǒ kěbùkěyǐ _____?

他能 _____.

Tā néng _____.

我能 _____吗?

Wǒ néng _____ ma?

我能不能 _____?

Wǒ néngbùnéng _____?

洗衣   wash clothes
xǐyī   (do laundry)

进来   come in
jìnlái

作菜   cook
zuòcài

拍手   clap
pāishǒu

唱歌   sing
chànggē

吹口哨   whistle
chuī kǒushào

坐下   sit down
zuòxià

打电话   make a phone call
dǎdiànhuà

说中国话   speak Chinese
shuō Zhōngguóhuà

Following is a fun traditional song to sing. The Erie Canal is located in northern Pennsylvania. It seems the heavy work won't feel as onerous when you have a good companion like Sal.

The Erie Canal
伊利运河
Yīlì Yùnhé

我有匹骡儿，她名叫阿花.　　*I've got a mule, her name is Sal.*
Wǒ yǒu pī luór, tā míng jiào Āhuā.
(I have a mule, her name is A-Hua.)

十五里在那伊利运河.　　*Fifteen miles on the Erie Canal.*
Shíwǔ lǐ zài nà Yīlì Yùnhé.

我每天干活，不能没有她.　　*She's a good old worker,*
Wǒ měi tiān gànhuó, bùnéng méiyǒu tā.　　*she's a good old pal.*
(I work hard daily, and can't be without her.)

十五里在那伊利运河.　　*Fifteen miles on the Erie Canal.*
Shíwǔ lǐ zài nà Yīlì Yùnhé.

骡 (luó) is a mule. 骡儿 (luór) is a familiar way to refer to one's mule.

名叫 (míng jiào) means "to be named" or "to be called". 花 (huā flower) appears often in names for girls. It is customary to form a nickname for a child by adding the prefix 阿 (ā) to one of the characters in the given name or some other endearing name.

运 (yùn) means to move, to transport, or transportation. You already know that 河 (hé) is a river. Combine these two characters, and you'll get the word for canal.

不能 (bùnéng cannot) is an auxiliary verb that modifies "to be without".

Exercise:

Please fill in the blanks to complete the following sentences.

我有匹＿＿＿＿ ＿＿＿＿, 她名叫嫦娥.

Wǒ yǒu pī ＿＿＿＿＿＿＿, tā míng jiào Cháng'é.

I've got a mule; her name's Chang'e. (The apostrophe helps group the syllables.)

＿＿＿＿ ＿＿＿＿ ＿＿＿在那伊利运河.

＿＿＿＿ ＿＿＿＿ ＿＿＿ zài nà Yīlì Yùnhé.

Fifteen miles on the Erie Canal.

她很 ＿＿＿＿干活, 她也会＿＿＿ ＿＿＿.

Tā hěn ＿＿＿＿＿ gànhuó, tā yě huì ＿＿＿＿＿＿＿.

She's very good at working ; she also can sing.

十五里在那伊利 ＿＿＿＿ ＿＿＿.

Shíwǔ lǐ zài nà Yīlì ＿＿＿＿＿＿＿＿.

Fifteen miles on the Erie Canal.

Answer:

我有匹骡儿, 她名叫嫦娥.　　I've got a mule; her name's Chang'e.

Wǒ yǒu pī luór, tā míng jiào Cháng'é.

十五里在那伊利运河.　　Fifteen miles on the Erie Canal.

Shíwǔ lǐ zài nà Yīlì Yùnhé.

她很会干活, 她也会唱歌.　　She's very good at working;

Tā hěn huì gànhuó, tā yě huì chànggē.　　she also can sing.

十五里在那伊利运河.　　Fifteen miles on the Erie Canal.

Shí wǔ lǐ zài nà Yīlì Yùnhé.

Let's review the following three important little words: 是 (shì) is the linking verb, "to be". 在 (zài) means "to be at (a place)", or "to be doing (something)". In the first case, it is used as a linking verb. In the second case, it is used as an auxiliary verb. When used as an auxiliary verb, 会 (huì) means "can", "to be able to", or to be "good at (something)".

Exercise:

Please pick the appropriate word to fill in the blanks in the sentences below. Please note that some of these sentences have two correct answers.

我 _____ 吹口哨.
Wǒ _____ chuī kǒushào.
I _____ whistle.

他 _____ 火车上.
Tā _____ huǒchē shàng.
He _____ on the train.

他们 _____ 说中国话.
Tāmen _____ shuō Zhōngguóhuà.
They _____ speak Chinese.

你 _____ 好人.
Nǐ _____ hǎorén.
You _____ a good person.

他们 _____音乐家.
Tāmen _____ yīnyuèjiā.
They _____ musicians.

我们 _____ 家里.
Wǒmen _____ jiālǐ.
We _____ at home.

Answer:

我会吹口哨.
Wǒ huì chuī kǒushào.
I can whistle.

or 我在吹口哨.
Wǒ zài chuī kǒushào.
I'm whistling.

他在火车上.
Tā zài huǒchē shàng.
He is on the train.

他们会说中国话.
Tāmen huì shuō Zhōngguóhuà.
They can speak Chinese.

or 他们在说中国话.
Tāmen zài shuō Zhōngguóhuà.
They are speaking Chinese.

你是好人.
Nǐ shì hǎorén.
You are a good person.

他们是音乐家.
Tāmen shì yīnyuèjiā.
They are musicians.

我们在家里.
Wǒmen zài jiālǐ.
We are at home.

16. Yes, I Can

17. When? Where? How?

Everyone knows the world-famous nursery rhyme that tells of the collapse of the London Bridge. Thanks to the gravitational force, it must fall down and not upward. 垮 (kuǎ) means to collapse or fall. 下来 (xiàlái) points to the downward direction. It answers the question, "Which way is the bridge falling?" Words that state why, to whom, when, where or how an action takes place are called adverbs.

London Bridge is Falling Down
伦敦铁桥垮下来
Lúndun Tiě Qiáo Kuǎ Xiàlái

伦敦铁桥垮下来，
Lúndūn Tiě Qiáo kuǎ xiàlái,

London Bridge is falling down,

垮下来，垮下来.
Kuǎ xiàlái, kuǎ xiàlái.

Falling down, falling down.

伦敦铁桥垮下来，
Lúndūn Tiě Qiáo kuǎ xiàlái,

London Bridge is falling down,

美丽的小姐.
Měilì de xiǎojiě.

My fair lady.
(Pretty young lady.)

Words that modify an adjective are also called adverbs. In the above line, 美丽 (měilì beautiful, pretty) is an adjective that describes the young lady. You could add the adverb 很 (hěn very) to make her very pretty, or 很美丽 (hěn měilì). Finally, adverbs can also be used to modify other adverbs. A simple example is: 他跑得很快 (Tā pǎo de hěn kuài. He runs very fast). Here, 快 (kuài fast) is the adverb that describes how the person runs; and 很 (hěn) is the adverb that tells us just how fast he runs.

Words that Modify Action Words

There are many words and phrases you can use to tell about the location, position, time or date of an action, the reason for the action, or the manner in which the action is performed. Based on the type of questions they address, these adverbs and adverbial phrases can be sorted into the following groups.

1. Why? To whom? 为什么? Wèishénme? 向谁? Xiàng shéi?

The adverbial phrase answering this type of questions is placed before the verb. For example:

他为生活写作.
Tā wèi shēnghuó xiězuò.

He writes to earn a livelihood.

他为妳來.
Tā wèi nǐ lái.

He came for your sake.

我们都为他拍手.
Wǒmen dōu wèi tā pāishǒu.

We all clapped for him.

她向我们招手.
Tā xiàng wǒmen zhāoshǒu.

She waved at us.

我对她说了.
Wǒ duì tā shuō le.

I have spoken to her about it.
(I have told her.)

2. When? 在什么时候? Zài shénme shíhòu?

Generally, the adverb indicating the time of occurrence is placed before the verb in a sentence. You already know such words as: 今天 (jīntiān today), 明天

(míngtiān tomorrow), 今年 (jīnnián this year), 明年 (míngnián next year) and 现在 (xiànzài now). For example, in "明天见. (Míngtiān jiàn. See you tomorrow.)", 明天 (míngtiān tomorrow) prescribes the time of occurrence of the verb 见 (jiàn to see).

Following are a number of other useful time-related adverbs. It will be worth your while to learn a few of them by heart.

他马上来. Tā mǎshàng lái.	He will come immediately.
他一会儿来. Tā yīhuǐr lái.	He will come in a moment.
他等一下来. Tā děng yīxià lái.	He will come after a short while.
他还没来. Tā hái méi lái.	He still has not come.
他已经来了. Tā yǐjīng lái le.	He has already come.
她忽然来了. Tā hūrán lái le.	She suddenly came.
她突然生病了. Tā tūrán shēngbìng le.	She unexpectedly fell ill.
我先走了. Wǒ xiān zǒu le.	I'm leaving now. I'm going ahead.
到时再说. Dào shí zài shuō.	Let's deal with it when the time comes. Let's wait and see.

他早来十分钟.
Tā zǎo lái shí fēnzhōng.

He came ten minutes early.

他晚到十分钟.
Tā wǎn dào shí fēnzhōng.

He arrived ten minutes late.

抱歉, 我迟到了.
Bàoqiàn, wǒ chídào le.

Sorry, I'm late.

3. Where?　在什么地方? Zài shénme dìfāng?

The adverbs that answer this type of questions may indicate a location or a direction of motion. They are usually placed **after** the verbs they modify.

这里 (zhèlǐ) and 这儿 (zhèr) both mean "here". 那里 (nàlǐ) and 那儿 (nàr) both mean "there". A few other adverbs that indicate locations are also shown in the examples below.

放这里.
Fàng zhèlǐ.

Put (it) over here.

她坐那儿.
Tā zuò nàr.

She sits over there.

她站旁边.
Tā zhàn pángbiān.

She stands by the side.

她坐左边.
Tā zuò zuǒbiān.

She sits on the left side.

我在右边.
Wǒ zài yòubiān.

I am on the right side.

Following are some examples of adverbs that indicate the direction of motion.

她走进房间.
Tā zǒu jìn fángjiān.

She walks into the room.

她走出房间.
Tā zǒu chū fángjiān

She walks out of the room.

她骑上马.
Tā qí shàng mǎ.

She gets on the horse to ride it.

他喝下三杯水.
Tā hē xià sān bēi shuǐ.

He gulps down three cups of water.

那小孩跳上跳下.
Nà xiǎohái tiào shàng tiào xià.

That kid jumps up and down.

他拿起一本书.
Tā ná qǐ yī běn shū.

He a picks up a book.

他把书放下.
Tā bǎ shū fàngxià.

He put the book down.

靠近我一点.
Kào jìn wǒ yīdiǎn.

Get closer to me a bit.

她走远了.
Tā zǒu yuǎn le.

She has gone away a distance.

走开!
Zǒukāi!

Go away!

You know that 来 (lái) and 去 (qù) are action words that mean "to come" and "to go", respectively. These two words are also used as adverbs to indicate the direction of motion. 来 (lái) means moving toward you, while 去 (qù) means moving away from you. For example, 走來 (zǒu lái) means "to walk over here". Similarly, 走去 (zǒu qù) means "to walk over there". The phrase 走来走去 **(zǒu lái zǒu qù)** means "walking to and fro" or "walking back and forth". Following are a few more examples using 来 (lái) and 去 (qù) as adverbs.

那个男人<u>跑来跑去</u>.   That man runs to and fro.
Nàge nánrén pǎo lái bǎo qù.

他把我拉<u>上去</u>.   He pulled me up there.
Tā bǎ wǒ lā shàngqù.

把书放<u>下来</u>.   Put the book down.
Bǎ shū fàng xiàlái.

不要走<u>出去</u>.   Don't go out there.
Búyào zǒu chūqù.

You can easily form an adverbial phrase by combining a preposition with a noun. Some common prepositions that take a position or direction as the object are: 在 (zài at, in, or on), 向 (xiàng to, toward), 往 (wǎng toward), 从 (cóng from), and 到 (dào to).

An adverbial phrase containing 从 (cóng from) must come **before** the verb, while an adverbial phrase containing 到 (dào to) must come **after** the verb.

她<u>从</u>伦敦飞<u>到</u>巴黎.   She flies from London to Paris.
Tā cóng Lúndūn fēi dào Bālí.

他走<u>到</u>店里去.   He goes into the store.
Tā zǒu dào diàn lǐ qù.

In most cases, the other adverbial phrases may be placed either **before or after** the verbs they modify, as shown in the following examples.

他坐<u>在中间</u>.　　He sits in the middle.
Tā zŏu zài zhōngjiān.

他走<u>在前面</u>.　　He walks ahead.
Tā zŏu zài qiánmiàn.　　(He leads.)

我跟<u>在后面</u>.　　I follow behind.
Wŏ gēn zài hòumiàn.　　(I follow.)

我留<u>在外面</u>.　　I stay outside.
Wŏ liú zài wàimiàn.

他住<u>在家里</u>.　　He lives at home.
Tā zhù zài jiālĭ.

野雁<u>向南方</u>飞.　　The wild geese fly south.
Yěyàn xiàng nánfāng fēi.

请你<u>往前</u>走.　　Please move forward.
Qǐng nǐ wăng qián zŏu.

4. How? 如何? **Rúhé?** 怎样? **Zěnyàng?**

There are as many adverbs that answer this type of questions as there are ways to describe an action. An adverb that specifically indicates the manner in which an action is performed is usually placed **before** the verb it modifies. However, there are exceptions, as shown by the last two of the following group of examples.

<u>用力</u>拉!　　Pull hard!
Yònglì lā!

他<u>努力</u>工作.　　He works hard.
Tā nŭlì gōngzuò.

他们<u>一起</u>吃饭.　　They eat together.
Tàmen yīqĭ chīfàn.

他们<u>各自</u>回家.　　　　The went home separately.
Tāmen gèzì huíjiā.

请<u>各别</u>包装.　　　　　Please wrap separately, or individually.
Qǐng gèbié bāozhuāng.

机器<u>自动</u>停了.　　　　The machine automatically stopped.
Jīqì zìdòng tíng le.

不要<u>乱</u>说.　　　　　　Don't say nonsense.
Búyào luànshuō.

大家<u>快</u>来呀!　　　　　Everyone come over here quickly!
Dàjiā kuài lái yā!

请<u>慢慢</u>讲.　　　　　　Please speak slowly.
Qǐng mànmàn jiǎng.

请讲<u>慢</u>一点.　　　　　Please speak a bit slower.
Qǐng jiǎng màn yīdiǎn.

请走<u>快</u>一点.　　　　　Please walk a little faster.
Qǐng zǒu kuài yīdiǎn.

Many Chinese adjectives also function as adverbs. To make a distinction between the two in a written document, the particle 的 (de) at the end of the adjective is replaced with the particle 地 (di, or de) for the adverb. For example, 小心的人 (xiǎoxīn de rén) is a careful person, while 小心地走 (xiǎoxīn di zǒu) means to walk carefully. When used as a particle, the word 地 (dì earth, ground) can be pronounced either as "di" or "de". If you wish, you may simply pronounce the particle 地 (di) as "de", and the adjective and the adverb will sound exactly the same.

Following are a few more examples of words that are used both as adjectives and adverbs:

仔细的人	zǐxì de rén	detail-oriented person
仔细地做	zǐxì di zuò	do painstakingly
专心的学者	zhuānxīn de xuézhě	scholar engrossed in work
专心地跑	zhuānxīn di pǎo	run with concentration
耐心的人	nàixīn de rén	patient person
耐心地说	nàixīn di shuō	speak patiently
紧张的人	jǐnzhāng de rén	nervous person
紧张地看	jǐnzhāng di kàn	watch nervously
温柔的猫	wēnróu de māo	gentle cat
温柔地说	wēnróu di shuō	speak gently
安全的房子	ānquán de fángzi	safe house
安全地开车	ānquán di kāichē	drive safely
随便的人	suíbiàn de rén	slipshod person
随便地说	suíbiàn di shuō	say casually
有趣的故事	yǒuqù de gùshì	interesting story
有趣地说笑	yǒuqù di shuōxiào	laugh and chat amusingly
有效率的人	yǒuxiàolǜ de rén	efficient person
有效率地做	yǒuxiàolǜ di zuò	do cfficiently

Some adverbs indicate the result or effect of the action rather than describe the manner in which the action takes place. Such adverbs are usually placed **after** the verbs they modify. In many cases, they are combined with the verb to form a new action word. For example:

他打破了一个杯子.　　He broke a cup.
Tā dǎpò le yī ge bēizi.

别把电脑弄坏了.　　Don't damage the computer.
Bié bǎ diànnǎo nònghuài le.

把鞋带拉紧.　　Pull the shoelaces tight.
Bǎ xiédài lā jǐn.

Often, the particle 得 (de) is used to link a verb to an adverb that shows the result or effect of the action. In this case, the syntax is:

Verb + 得 **(de)** + **adverb**

老虎跑得快.　　Tigers run fast.
Lǎohǔ pǎo de kuài.

鹿跳得高.　　Deer jump high.
Lù tiào de gāo.

她说得对.　　She said it right. (She is right.)
Tā shuō de duì.

做得好!　　Well done!
Zuò de hǎo!

他穿得整齐.　　He is dressed neatly.
Tā chuān de zhěngqí.　　(He is dressed up.)

你唱得好.　　You sing well.
Nǐ chàng de hǎo.

她写得不清楚.　　She wrote unclearly.
Tā xiě de bù qīngchǔ.　　(She did not make it clear.)

Exercise:

Use the following list of words to practice making sentences. Form each sentence by selecting one word from each column.

她 Tā She	小心地 xiǎoxīn di carefully	走 zǒu walks, goes
他 Tā He	慢慢地 mànmàn di slowly	写字 xiězì writes
彼得 Bǐdé Peter	急忙 jímáng hastily	吃饭 chīfàn eats
保罗 Bǎoluó Paul	随便 suíbiàn casually, carelessly	把东西放下 bǎ dōngxī fàngxià puts the thing(s) down
爱迪生 Àidíshēng Edison	高兴地 gāoxìng di cheerfully	说话 shuōhuà speaks, talks
安妮 Ānní Annie	勉强地 miǎnqiǎng di reluctantly	回答 huídá replies

17. When? Where? How?

18. All Day, All Night

There are a number of adverbs that tell how long or how frequently an action is performed. Such adverbs are always placed **before** the verb they modify.

整天 (成天) zhěngtiān (chéngtiān)	all day	不時 bùshí	often, frequently
老是 lǎoshì	always	永远 yǒngyuǎn	forever
從來 cónglái	all along	一向 yīxiàng	all along
每天 měitiān	each day	每年 měinián	each year
一次 yīcì	once	一遍 yī biàn	one time, once
每次 měicì	each time	屢次 lǚcì	repeatedly
又, 再 yòu, zài	again, once more	很少 hěn shǎo	seldom
不斷 búduàn	constantly	一直 yīzhí	continually
常常, 时常 chángcháng, shícháng	frequently, often	不常 bù cháng	infrequently
从來不 (从不) cónglái bù (cóng bù)	has never	绝不 juébù	would never

Let's sing the following traditional song to cheer the tireless Mary-Ann.

Mary-Ann

成天, 成夜, 玛莉安,
Chéngtiān, chéngyè, Mǎlìān,
All day, all night, Mary-Ann,

老在那海滩上筛沙.
Lǎo zài nà hǎitān shàng shāi shā.
Always on the seashore sifting sand.
Down by the seashore sifting sand.

小朋友们都爱玛莉安,
Xiǎopéngyǒu men dōu ài Mǎlìān,
All the little children love Mary-Ann,

老在那海滩上筛沙.
Lǎo zài nà hǎitān shàng shāi shā.
Always on the seashore sifting sand.
Down by the seashore sifting sand.

海 (hǎi) means "sea", and 滩 (tān) means "beach" or "shoals". 海滩 (hǎitān) is a seashore or an ocean beach.

老 (lǎo), or 老是 (lǎoshì), is used colloquially as an adverb that means "always (doing something)". For example, "他老爱打喷嚏. (Tā lǎo ài dǎpēntì.)" means: "He sneezes regularly."

The entire expression 在那海滩上 (zài nà hǎitān shàng on the seashore) is an adverbial phrase.

筛 (shāi) means "to sift". 沙 (shā) is sand.

Exercise:

Use the following list of words to practice making sentences. Form each sentence by selecting one word from each column.

他
Tā (he)
He

整天
zhěngtiān
whole day

笑
xiào
laughs

張小姐
Zhāng xiǎojiě
Miss Zhang

每天
měitiān
every day

哭
kū
weeps

哥哥
Gēge
Elder Brother

常常
chángcháng
often

工作
gōngzuò
works

姊姊
Jiějie
Elder Sister

不常
bù cháng
seldom

看書
kànshū
reads books

弟弟
Dìdi
Younger Brother

很少
hěn shǎo
rarely

生氣
shēngqì
gets angry

妹妹
Mèimei
Younger Sister

從不
cóngbù
never

唱歌
chànggē
sings

那個人
Nàge rén
That person

一直
yīzhí
continuously

跳舞
tiàowǔ
dances

Adverbs that Indicate Likelihood

Words that indicate the probability or likelihood of an action occurring are always placed **before** the verb they modify.

你真的会去?
Nǐ zhēn de huì qù?

Are you **really** going?

我答应你, 一定去.
Wǒ dāyìng nǐ, yīdìng qù.

I promise you, I will **definitely** go.

我宁可不去.
Wǒ nìngkě bú qù.

I **would rather** not go.

他可能来吗?
Tā kěnéng lái ma?

Will he **probably** come?

他或许会来.
Tā huòxǔ huì lái.

Perhaps he will come.

他当然会来.
Tā dāngrán huì lái.

Of course, he will come.

你万万不要告诉她.
Nǐ wànwàn búyào gàosù tā.

Absolutely do not tell her.

她顶多有一万美元.
Tā dǐngduō yǒu yī wàn měiyuán.

She has **at most** ten thousand dollars.

Try substituting each of the above adverbs with one listed below that makes sense.

宁愿 (nìngyuàn)   would rather   也许 (yěxǔ)   perhaps

肯定 (kěndìng)   definitely   绝对 (juéduì)   absolutely

最好 (zuìhǎo)   had best   至少 (zhìshǎo)   at least

Words that Modify Adjectives

As you know, 是 (shì to be) is usually implied in linking a subject to an attribute.

For example, you don't see the word, 是 (shì), in "她累了. (Tā lèi le. She is tired.)" Instead, another word, such as: 很 (very), 好 (very), or 非常 (extremely), is often inserted to show the level of intensity of the attribute. As shown below, such an adverb always comes before the adjective.

她<u>很</u>累了.
Tā hěn lèi le.
She is very tired.

大家都<u>好</u>高兴.
Dàjiā dōu hǎu gāoxìng.
All are glad. (Everyone is happy.)

她<u>颇</u>高兴.
Tā pǒ gāoxìng.
She's quite happy.

我<u>太</u>满意了!
Wǒ tài mǎnyì le!
I'm too pleased.
(I'm totally pleased.)

这样<u>更</u>好.
Zhèyàng gènghǎo.
It's even better this way.

这样<u>最</u>好.
Zhèyàng zuìhǎo.
It's best this way.

那<u>绝对</u>不可能.
Nà juéduì bùkěnéng.
That's absolutely impossible.

那<u>完全</u>不可能.
Nà wánchuán bùkěnéng.
That's totally impossible.

那<u>根本</u>不可能.
Nà gēnběn bùkěnéng.
That's fundamentally impossible.

Words that Modify Adverbs

Words that modify adverbs are called adverbs as well. In fact the same set of adverbs that are commonly used to modify adjectives may also be used to modify some adverbs. Let's look at a few of the previous shown examples of adverbs that indicate the result or effect of an action.

老虎跑得＿＿＿＿快.　　　　　Tigers run fast.
Lǎohǔ pǎo de＿＿＿＿kuài.

她说得＿＿＿＿对.　　　　　She is right.
Tā shuō de ＿＿＿＿duì.

他穿得＿＿＿＿整齐.　　　　He is dressed neatly.
Tā chuān de ＿＿＿＿zhěngqí.　　(He is dressed up.)

她写得＿＿＿＿不清楚.　　　She wrote it unclearly.
Tā xiě de ＿＿＿＿bù qīngchǔ.　　(She did not make it clear.)

We could fill in the blanks with words that qualify the adverbs. For example:

老虎跑得<u>真快</u>.　　　　　Tigers run really fast.
Lǎohǔ pǎo de zhēn kuài.

她说得<u>很对</u>.　　　　　She is quite right.
Tā shuō de hěn duì.

他穿得<u>好整齐</u>.　　　　He is dressed very neatly.
Tā chuān de hǎo zhěngqí.

她写得<u>非常不清楚</u>.　　She wrote extremely unclearly.
Tā xiě de fēicháng bù qīngchǔ.　　(She did not make it clear at all.)

Try filling the blanks in the previous examples with some of the following adverbs:

颇 rather
pǒ

相当 fairly, rather
xiāngdāng

有些, 有点 a bit, somewhat
yǒuxiē, yǒudiǎn

多么 so very
duōme

这样, 这么 so, thus
zhèyàng, zhème

那样, 那么 so, to that extent
nàyàng, nàme

实在 truly, indeed
shízài

的确 really, indeed
díquè

更 more
gèng

比较 more so
bǐjiào

最 most
zuì

太 too
tài

极 extremely
jí

异常 extraordinarily
yìcháng

特别 especially
tèbié

格外 exceptionally, markedly
géwài

And, of course, you could also use an adverbial phrase to modify an adverb:

他跑得<u>像我一样</u>快.
Tā pǎo de xiàng wǒ yīyàng kuài.

He runs fast like I do.
(He runs as fast as I.)

他穿得<u>比昨天</u>整齐.
Tā chuān de bǐ zuótiān zhěngqí.

He is dressed more neatly than
he was yesterday.

她写得<u>一点儿也不</u>清楚.
Tā xiě de yīdiǎnr yě bù qīngchǔ.

She did not make it clear one bit.

Similar to "London Bridge is Falling Down", the Town Gate is a rhyme sung by Chinese children when picking sides for a game. It goes like this: Two children stand face-to-face, joining their hands together and holding them high to form an arch. The other children line up and walk in a circle, passing under the "town gate" while this rhyme is being recited. When the rhyme stops, the gate drops down and catches the person who is under the gate at that moment. That person gets to be on one of the teams, and the next person captured will be on the other team, and so on.

Town Gate
城门
Chéngmén

城门, 城门, 几尺高?
Chéngmén, chéngmén, jǐ chǐ gāo?
Town gate, town gate, how many feet tall?

三十六尺高.
Sān shí liù chǐ gāo.
36 feet tall.

骑白马, 带把刀,
Qí bái mǎ, dài bǎ dāo,
Riding a white horse, carrying a saber,

走近城门, 敲一敲.
Zǒu jìn chéngmén, qiāo yī qiāo.
Get (close) to the town gate; knock, knock.

Can you tell the difference between the following two terms? They sound exactly the same. In the above rhyme, the "knock, knock" gives away the fact that the person has not yet passed through the town gate, but is approaching it.

走近	zǒu jìn	Go near, or get close to
走進	zǒu jìn	Enter, or go into

19. Simple Sentences

In the previous chapters, you have sampled Chinese words from various groups that represent the major parts of speech in Chinese - nouns, pronouns, adjectives, verbs, adverbs, prepositions, conjunctions and interjections. These are the building blocks with which you can construct all kinds of sentences, or 句子 (jùzi). In fact, if you have been doing the exercises provided with the previous lessons, you have already made quite a few simple Chinese sentences.

In this chapter, you will review the various ways of embellishing a bare-bone simple sentence with adjectives, adverbs, prepositions, interjections, verbs in the infinitive form, and/or additional nouns to make it more informative or interesting. The emphasis here is on the sentence pattern and proper word order. Given a sentence pattern, you could make any number of new sentences by reaching into your vocabulary treasure chest and pulling out the proper words to replace the various parts of speech.

A simple sentence consists of a subject and one statement about the subject. The bare-bone pattern for a simple sentence is:

Subject + Verb

For example:

他想.   He wants. He thinks.
Tā xiǎng.

In the imperative mood, the subject of the sentence may be omitted. For example:

来!   Come!
Lái!

A sentence may be formulated in the active voice, as shown above. Or it can be formulated in the passive voice, as shown below:

他被咬了.   He was bitten.
Tā bèi yǎo le.

To give a verb the **passive voice**, simply place the word 被 (bèi) before it.

被 **(bèi) + Verb**

Following are a few ways to modify a simple sentence. I will use the above examples to illustrate the process.

1. Change the statement into a question.

You can do so by **adding the particle 吗 (ma) at the end of the sentence**, or by using the "**do + not do**" pattern.

他想吗?
Tā xiǎng ma?

Does he want to?

他想不想?
Tā xiǎng bù xiǎng?

Does he want to or not?

他被咬了吗?
Tā bèi yǎo le ma?

Was he bitten?

2. Change the statement into an interjection.

You could inject some energy into the sentence by adding the particle 啊 (ā ah), 噢 (ō oh), 呀 (yā ah), or 吧 (ba) at the end.

他想啊!
Tā xiǎng ā!

He does wish to!

来吧!
Lái ba!

Come!

他被咬了呀!
Tā bèi yǎo le yā!

He was bitten!

You could also add an independent interjection before the sentence:

对! 他想啊!   Right! He does wish to!
Duì! Tā xiǎng ā!

呀! 他被咬了.   Oh! He was bitten!
Yā! Tā bèi yǎo le!

3. Insert an infinitive.

This opens up a whole world of possibilities. In Chinese, the "to" is omitted from the infinitive. Therefore, the infinitive appears just like a verb.

他想<u>去</u>.   He wants to go.
Tā xiǎng qù.

他想<u>旅行</u>.   He wants to travel.
Tā xiǎng lǔxíng.

来<u>看</u>!   Come to see!
Lái kàn!

4. Change the singular person into multiple persons.

<u>苏珊和查理</u>都想去.   Susan and Charlie both want to go.
Sūshān hé Cháliě dōu xiǎng qù.

<u>她们</u>都想去.   They all want to go.
Tāmen dōu xiǎng qù.

<u>大家</u>都来!   Everybody comc!
Dàjiā dōu lái!

<u>他们</u>都被咬了.   They were all bitten.
Tāmen dōu bèi yǎo le.

5. Add a noun as the object of an action or a preposition.

他想苏珊.　　　　　　　　　He misses Susan.
Tā xiǎng Sūshān.

他想打开窗户.　　　　　　　He wants to open the window.
Tā xiǎng dǎkāi chuānghù.

他被狗咬了.　　　　　　　　He was bitten by a dog.
Tā bèi gǒu yǎo le.

In the above sentence in passive voice, the word 被 (bèi) corresponds to the English preposition "by". It takes the doer of the action, 狗 (gǒu dog), as its object. Notice that the word order is different from the corresponding English sentence. A verbatim translation would have yielded, "He was by a dog bitten."

6. Insert an adjective or adjective phrase to modify a noun.

Place the adjective immediately before the noun it describes, except in the case when it is referred to the noun by a linking verb.

他想打开楼上的窗户.　　　He wants to open the upstairs window.
Tā xiǎng dǎkāi lóushàng de chuānghù.

他被一只小黄狗咬了.　　　He was bitten by a small tan dog.
Tā bèi yī zhī xiǎo huáng gǒu yǎo le.

她的体力好.　　　　　　　　Her physical strength is sound.
Tā de tǐlì hǎo.　　　　　　　(She has stamina.)

7. Insert an adverb or adverbial phrase to modify a verb.

他不想去.　　　　　　　　　He does not want to go.
Tā bù xiǎng qù.

他想马上去.　　　　　　　　He wants to go immediately.
Tā xiǎng mǎshàng qù.

快来呀!　　　　　　　Come quickly!
Kuài lái yā!

明天再来.　　　　　　Come again tomorrow.
Míngtiān zài lái.

明天再来一次.　　　　Come once again tomorrow.
Míngtiān zài lái yīcì.

他想为苏珊开窗.　　　He wants to open the window for Susan.
Tā xiǎng wèi Sūshān kāi chuāng.

In the above sentence, 为苏珊 (wèi Sūshān for Susan) is the adverbial phrase that modifies the action of opening the window. The pattern used for forming this **adverbial phrase** is:

Preposition + Noun

Here are a few more examples containing adverbial phrases:

他想同苏珊去旅行.　　He wants to travel **with** Susan.
Tā xiǎng tóng Sūshān qù lǚxíng.

从这边来!　　　　　　Come **from** this side!
Cóng zhèbiān lái!

到那边去!　　　　　　Go **to** that side! Go over there!
Dào nàbiān qù!

8. Invert the order of the transitive verb and its object by using the preposition 把 (bǎ) or 将 (jiāng).

The word 把 (bǎ, or bà), when used as a noun, means "a handle", such as in 把手 (bǎshǒu a handle), or 门把 (ménbà a door knob).

把 (bǎ) is also used as a preposition in the following special syntax:

把 (bǎ) + Object + Verb

This word order places the focus on the object rather than on the action. It is a common expression that can be interpreted as: "Take the object and do the action to it." For example:

他想把窗户打开.　　　　He wants to open the window.
Tā xiǎng bǎ chuānghù dǎkāi.

他不想把门打开.　　　　He does not want to open the door.
Tā bù xiǎng bǎ mén dǎkāi.

So, you see that there are two ways of saying a sentence containing a transitive verb and an object.

把门打开. = 打开门.　　　Open the door.
bǎ mén dǎkāi　　dǎkāi mén

把灯关掉. = 关掉灯.　　　Turn off the lamp.
bǎ dēng guāndiào　　guān diào dēng

And, the following two sentences can be used interchangeably:

他把那本书弄丢了.　　　He lost that book.
Tā bǎ nà běn shū nòng diū le.

他弄丢了那本书.　　　　He lost that book.
Tā nòng diū le nà běn shū.

When used as a preposition, the word 将 (jiāng) serves the same purpose as 把 (bǎ). 把 (bǎ) is used in everyday speech, while 将 (jiāng) is mostly used in writings, poems and songs.

Here are two examples using 将 (jiāng) as the preposition:

他将门打开了.　　　　　He opened the door.
Tā jiāng mén dǎkāi le.

让我来将你摘下.　　　　Let me pluck you.
Ràng wǒ lái jiāng nǐ zhāi xià.

(The above line is from the Chinese folk song, "Jasmine Flower".)

Exercise:

Rewrite each of the following sentences by using 把 (bǎ) or 将 (jiāng).

1.　请　关　上　窗.　　　　Please shut the window.
　　Qǐng guān shàng chuāng.

　　———— ———— ———— ————

2.　她　吃　完　饭.　　　　She finished eating the meal.
　　Tā　chī　wán　fàn.

　　———— ———— ———— ————

3.　他　收　下　钱.　　　　He accepted the money.
　　Tā　shōu　xià　qián.

　　———— ———— ———— ————

4.　我　拿　起　锅.　　　　I lifted the wok up.
　　Wǒ　ná　qǐ　guō.

　　———— ———— ———— ————

Answer:

1. 请把窗关上.
   Qǐng bǎ chuāng guān shàng.

   Please close the window.

2. 她把饭吃完.
   Tā bǎ fàn chī wán.

   She finished eating the meal.

3. 他将钱收下.
   Tā jiān qián shōu xià.

   He accepted the money.

4. 我把锅拿起.
   Wǒ bǎ guō ná qǐ.

   I lifted up the wok.

You will get to sing a translated version of the traditional American folk song, titled "Study War No More". But first let's look at the two main lines in the song.

The first line employs the word 把 (bǎ) to place the object before the verb.

我要把我的剑和盾抛弃在大河边.
Wǒ yào bǎ wǒ de jiàn hé dùn pāoqì zài dà hé biān.
I will dump my sword and shield by the side of the big river.

剑 (jiàn sword) and 盾 (dùn shield) are ancient weapons of war. They are the objects of the preposition 把 (bǎ). 我的 (wǒ de my) functions as the adjective that qualifies the sword and the shield.

抛弃 (pāo qì) means to discard or throw away. It is the action word of this sentence. 河 (hé) is a river. 大河 (dà hé) is a large river. 边 (biān) means the side, the edge or the rim of something.

The adverbial phrase, 在 .... 边 (zài …….. biān), means "by the side of". Therefore, 在大河边 (zài dà hé biān) means by the side of the large river.

Similarly, 在这边 (zài zhèbiān) means over here, and 在那边 (zài nàbiān) means over there.

In the second line, the verb and object follow the normal word order.

我不要再研究战争.
Wǒ búyào zài yánjiù zhànzhēng.
I'm not going to study war anymore.

This 再 (zài) is an adverb that means "again", "once more" or "anymore".

Therefore, 不要再 (búyào zài) means "not any more" or "no more".

研究 (yánjiù) is to study or to do research. It can also be used as a noun.

战争 (zhànzhēng) means war or warfare. Peace is 和平 (hépíng).

Study War No More
不要再研究战争
Búyào Zài Yánjiù Zhànzhēng

我要把我的剑和盾 | Gonna lay down my sword and shield
Wǒ yào bǎ wǒ de jiàn hé dùn | (I will take my sword and shield,)
抛弃在大河边, | Down by the river side,
Pāoqì zài dà hé biān, | (And dump them by the river side.)
抛弃在大河边, | Down by the river side,
Pāoqì zài dà hé biān, | (Dump them by the river side.)
抛弃在大河边. | Down by the river side.
Pāoqì zài dà hé biān. | (Dump them by the river side.)
我要把我的剑和盾 | Gonna lay down my sword and shield
Wǒ yào bǎ wǒ de jiàn hé dùn | (I will take my sword and shield,)
抛弃在大河边, | Down by the river side,
Pāoqì zài dà hé biān, | (And dump them by the river side.)
抛弃在大河边. | Down by the river side,
Pāoqì zài dà hé biān. | (Dump them by the river side.)
我不要再研究战争, | I ain't gonna study war no more,
Wǒ búyào zài yánjiù zhànzhēng, |
再研究战争, | Study war no more,
Zài yánjiù zhànzhēng, |
再研究战争. | Study war no more.
Zài yánjiù zhànzhēng. |

我不要再研究战争, | I ain't gonna study war no more,
Wǒ búyào zài yánjiù zhànzhēng, |
再研究战争; | Study war no more,
Zài yánjiù zhànzhēng, |
不要再研究战争. | Ain't gonna study war no more.
Búyào zài yánjiù zhànzhēng. |

20. Grocery

In this chapter you will see the names of many different kinds of foods, which are called 食物 (shíwù) or 食品 (shípǐn). What would you buy when you go to the market? Why not make your next grocery list in Chinese? The little pigs in this cute 18th Century nursery rhyme will help get you started.

This Little Pig Went To The Market
小猪上菜场
Xǎo Zhū Shàng Càichǎng

这只小猪上菜场.
Zhè zhī xiǎo zhū shàng càichǎng.

This little pig went to the market.
This little pig went to the market.

这只小猪等在家.
Zhè zhī xiǎo zhū děng zài jiā.

This little pig stayed home.
This little pig waited at home.

这只小猪烤肉香.
Zhè zhī xiǎo zhū kǎoròu xiāng.

This little pig had roast beef.
This little pig roasted meat so sweet.

这只小猪空磨牙.
Zhè zhī xiǎo zhū kōng móyá.

This little pig had none.
This little pig just gritted its teeth.

这只小猪胡乱嚷;
Zhè zhī xiǎo zhū húluàn rǎng;

This little pig crie,d"Wee, wee, wee, wee!"
This little pig cried like crazy,

一路尖叫回到家.
Yīlù jiānjiào huí dào jiā.

All the way home.
Squealing all the way home.

菜场 (càichǎng) and 市場 (shìchǎng) both mean "market". Although 菜 (cài) means "vegetables", this word is also used to refer to foods in general. Therefore, 买菜 (mǎi cài) means grocery shopping, and not just shopping for vegetables.

超級市场 (chāojíshìchǎng) are modern supermarkets, which are available in larger cities in China and Taiwan. 商场 (shāngchǎng trading market) also translates to "market" but it usually refers to department stores.

烤肉 (kǎoròu) as a verb means "to roast meat", whereas 烤肉 (kǎoròu) as a noun refers to the roasted meat. In the latter case, it is the abbreviation of 烤的肉 (kǎo de ròu roasted meat) where 烤的 (kǎo de) is an adjective describing the meat.

香 (xiāng) means "smelling good", whether the good smell comes from a flower, a perfume or a roasted chicken. Therefore, you can use this word whenever you want to say: "fragrant", "aromatic", "sweet smelling", or "scented".

空 (kōng) as an adjective means "empty". 磨牙 (móyá) is "grinding teeth". In 空磨牙 (kōng móyá), 空 (kōng) becomes an adverb that modifies the action of grinding teeth, and it takes on the meaning of "in vain".

乱 (luàn) means "randomly" or "disorderly". 胡 (hú) refers to the tribes that lived to the north and west of the ancient self-centered Han Dynasty. Those people were considered uncultured and reckless. Words like 胡乱 (húluàn recklessly) and 胡说 (húshuō to talk nonsense) have become everyday expressions and have lost their original connotation of disrespect for the northern tribes.

嚷 (rǎng) and 叫 (jiào) both mean "yell" or "shout". They are often combined into one word, 叫嚷 (jiàorǎng clamor). As 尖 (jiān) means "sharp" or "pointed", you could have guessed that 尖叫 (jiānjiào) means to scream, to screech or to squeal.

一路 (yīlù) means "all the way" or "through the entire journey". For example, if you were taking a hike and sang songs along the way, you could report: "我们一路唱歌. (Wǒmen yīlù chànggē.)"

青菜 or 蔬菜 Vegetables
Qīngcài   Shūcài

白菜	báicài	Bokchoy (white cabbage)
大白菜	dàbáicài	Napa Cabbage, Chinese Cabbage
高丽菜	gāolìcài	Green Cabbage
芹菜	qíncài	Celery
菠菜	bōcài	Spinach
沙拉菜	shālācài	Lettuce (salad vegetable)
花椰菜	huāyécài	Broccoli
萝卜	luóbo	Radish (large, white radish)
胡萝卜	húluóbo	Carrot (foreign radish)
番茄	fānqié	Tomato (foreign eggplant)
黄瓜	huángguā	Cucumber
豆荚	dòujiá	Pea Pod
四季豆	sìjìdòu	Green Bean
番薯	fānshǔ	Yam (foreign tuber)
洋芋	yángyù	Potato (foreign taro)
洋葱	yángcōng	Onion (foreign scallion)
玉米	yùmǐ	Corn

水果 *or* 生果 **Fruits**

Shuǐguǒ   Shēngguǒ

苹果	píngguǒ	Apple
梨子	lízi	Pear
桔子 *or* 橘子	júzi	Orange
香蕉	xiāngjiāo	Banana
桃子	táozi	Peach
李子	lǐzi	Prune
梅子	méizi	Plum
樱桃	yīngtáo	Cherry
葡萄	pútáo	Grape
草莓	cǎoméi	Strawberry
杨莓	yángméi	Raspberry
香瓜	xiāngguā	Muskmelon (Cantaloupe)
西瓜	xīguā	Watermelon
木瓜	mùguā	Papaya
凤梨	fènglí	Pineapple
芒果	mángguǒ	Mango
石榴	shíliǔ	Pomegranate

| 番石榴 | fānshíliŭ | Guava (foreign pomegranate) |
| 无花果 | wúhuāguŏ | Fig |

肉类及海鲜 Meats and Seafood
Ròu Lèi jí Hăixiān

鸡肉	jīròu	Chicken Meat
鸡翅	jī chì	Chicken Wings
鸡腿	jī tuĭ	Chicken Drumstick
火鸡腿	huŏjī tuĭ	Turkey Drumstick
鸭肉	yāròu	Duck Meat
牛肉	niúròu	Beef
牛排	niúpái	Beefsteak
牛尾	niúwĕi	Oxtail
羊肉	yángròu	Mutton
猪肉	zhūròu	Pork
猪排	zhūpái	Pork Chop
火腿	huŏtuĭ	Ham
香肠	xiāngcháng	Sausage
鱼肉	yúròu	Fish (flesh of fish)
鳟鱼	zūnyú	Trout

虾	xiā	Shrimp
龙虾	lúngxiā	Lobster
螃蟹	pángxiè	Crab
蛤蜊 *or* 蚌	gélì *or* bàng	Clam

奶制品 Dairy Products
Nǎi Zhì Pǐn

牛乳	niúrǔ	Milk
牛奶	niúnǎi	Milk
奶油	nǎiyóu	Butter
牛酪	niúlào	Cheese
酸奶	suānnǎi	Yogurt

零食及点心 Snacks and Desserts
Língshí jí Diǎnxīn

糖果	tángguǒ	Candies
巧克力糖	qiǎokèlì táng	Chocolates
洋芋片	yángyù piàn	Potato Chips
果干, 干果	guǒgān, gānguǒ	Dried Fruits
葡萄干	pútáogān	Raisins

堅果	jiānguǒ	Nuts
牛肉干	niúròugān	Beef Jerk
饼干	bǐnggān	Cookies
蛋糕	dàngāo	Cake
冰淇淋	bīngqílín	Ice cream, Sherbet
霜淇淋	shuāngqílín	Soft ice cream, Sundae

"Dim-sum" is the Cantonese pronunciation of 点心 (diǎnxīn refreshment). The Cantonese particularly like to have a variety of dim-sums with tea for brunch.

谷类及豆类 Grains and Legumes
Gǔ Lèi jí Dòu Lèi

米	mǐ	Rice (uncooked)
糯米	nuòmǐ	Glutinous Rice (Sweet Rice)
饭	fàn	Cooked Rice
小麦	xiǎomài	Wheat
大麦	dàmài	Barley
面粉	miànfěn	Flour
面包	miànbāo	Bread
面, 面条	miàn, miàntiáo	Pasta, Noodles
燕麦	yènmài	Oat

麦片	màipiàn	Oatmeal (rolled oat)
米粉	mǐfěn	Rice Noodles ("pho")
粉条	fěntiáo	Broad Rice Noodles ("fun")
粉丝	fěnsī	Vermicelli (made of mung bean starch)
豌豆	wāndòu	Pea
干白豆	gān báidòu	Navy Bean
绿豆	lǜdòu	Mung Bean
黄豆	huángdòu	Soy Bean
红豆	hóngdòu	Red Bean
红豆汤	hóngdòu tāng	Sweetened Red Bean Soup

Wheat and barley are the main sources of carbohydrates for the people in the colder northern provinces of China. That's why people from northern China are generally good at making steamed buns and cooked dumplings. On the other hand, rice is the staple in most of the remaining parts of China. It is customary at lunch and dinner to eat a bowl of plain cooked white rice (饭 fàn, 米饭 mǐfàn, or 白米饭 bái mǐfàn) along with some other foods. The term "吃饭 (chīfàn)" refers to having a meal rather than just eating cooked rice. For breakfast, the rice is watered down to make a gruel, or porridge, called 稀饭 (xīfàn diluted rice) or 粥 (zhōu porridge).

When you water down the gruel even further, you get diluted porridge, or 稀粥 (xī zhōu), which is something that you might feed a sick person whose digestive function has been compromised. This is how the very poor would prepare their meals to make their supply of rice grains last longer.

During the Anti-Japanese war that took place in China between 1938 and 1945, food shortage was widespread. Consequently, the college cafeterias served the students soupy, thin gruel instead of the usual plump and fluffy white rice. On the thin gruel, the students got hungry much sooner between meals. One day, in the mess hall of the National Southwest Associated University in the Yunnan Province, a group of students protested. They rapped their plates with their chopsticks and spoons, and chanted loudly in unison to the diatonic scale:

多 来 米 饭, 少 来 稀 粥. Bring us more rice; give us less gruel!
Duō lái mǐ fàn, shǎo lái xī zhōu.
(do re mi fa sol la ti do)

(The name of the student who initiated this clever parody is unknown.)

作料及添加剂 Condiments and Additives
Zuóliào jí Tiānjiājì

糖	táng	Sugar
盐	yán	Salt
麻油 *or* 香油	máyóu, xiāngyóu	Sesame Seed Oil
菜油	càiyóu	Vegetable oil
沙拉油	shālāyóu	Salad oil
料酒	liàojiǔ	Cooking Wine
酱油	jiàngyóu	Soy Sauce
甜面酱	tiánmiànjiàng	Sweet Flour Paste
胡椒	hújiāo	Pepper
辣椒	làjiāo	Hot Pepper
花椒	huājiāo	Chinese Prickly Ash

五香粉	wǔxiāng fěn	Five-spice Powder
八角	bājiǎo	Star Anise
咖喱粉	gālǐ fěn	Curry Powder
苏打粉	sūdǎ fěn	Baking Soda
发粉	fāfěn	Baking Powder
香草精	xiāngcǎo jīng	Vanilla Extract
杏仁精	xìngrén jīng	Almond Extract
葱	cōng	Green Onion
姜	jiāng	Ginger
桂皮	guìpí	Cinnamon

饮料 Beverages
Yǐnliào

开水	kāishuǐ	boiled water*
白开水	báikāishuǐ	plain boiled water*
茶	chá	Tea
柠檬水	níngméng shuǐ	Lemonade
咖啡	kāfēi	Coffee
巧克力饮料	qiǎokèlì yǐnliào	Chocolate Drink
乳酸饮料	rǔsuān yǐnliào	Yogurt Drink
苏打水	sūdǎ shuǐ	Soda Drink

汽水	qìshuǐ	Carbonated Drink
果汁	guǒzhī	Fruit Juice
苹果汁	píngguǒ zhī	Apple Juice
葡萄酒	pútáojiǔ	Grape Wine
啤酒	píjiǔ	Beer
威士忌	wēishìjì	Whisky
白兰地	báilándì	Brandy
加冰块	jiā bīngkuài	with ice cubes added

Please fill in the Chinese characters and/or pinyin for the following juices:

_____ _____ _____   grape juice
_____ _____ _____

_____ _____ _____   orange juice
_____ _____

_____ _____ _____   tomato juice
_____ _____

---

* In many countries outside of USA, tap water is unsafe to drink. In China and Taiwan, people boil the water before drinking it plain or making tea.

20. Grocery

21. Chinese Foods

Chinese Foods, or 中国菜 (zhōngguó cài), encompasses a great variety of dishes from the various Chinese provinces and localities. Generally, the people in the northern provinces make tasty steamed buns and dumplings, the Sichuan Province, 四川 (Sìchuān), is known for its spicy dishes, the Cantonese, 广东人 (Guǎngdōng rén), turn out mouthwatering fried noodles and dim-sums, and, of course, Beijing is famous for its Peking Duck. The Chinese culinary art has evolved through ages and attained a level of unparalleled sophistication. As is often the case, you would not be able to recognize the food by simply looking at a dish. Take 炒粉 (chǎo fěn) for example. It looks and tastes much like noodles. However, it is made of rice. And you may be surprised to find out that those plump white balls floating in a delicately flavored chicken soup are actually made from fish. The people from the Hubei Province, 湖北 (Húběi), like their fish balls super tender, almost melting in the mouth. On the other hand, most Taiwanese would insist that fish balls must be firm and bouncy.

We owe the many delicious Chinese dishes to the generations of emperors, generals, warlords and other rich and powerful gourmands who demanded nothing but the very best from their chefs. For example, Kung-Pao Chicken, or 宫保鸡丁 (gōngbǎo jī dīng) was named after a late Qing Dynasty official from Sichuan, whose formal title was 宫保 (gōngbǎo palatial guardian).

Fancy names are often given to the dishes to make the guests feel they are being honored with special treats. For instance, chicken wings might be referred to as phoenix wings. 芙蓉蛋 (fúróng dàn hibiscus eggs) is a dish prepared with scrambled eggs, and 狮子头 (shīzi tóu lion's head) is an extra large fried meatball braised with Chinese cabbage. Then there is a soup, named 佛跳墙 (Fó tiào qiáng Budha jumps over the wall). It contains all sorts of delicious ingredients and tastes so good that the great Budha would invite himself to it.

Guess what the following refers to?

金香白玉板,　　　　　　　　Golden savory slabs of white jade
Jīn xiāng bái yù bǎn,

红嘴绿鹦哥.　　　　　　　　with red-beaked green parrot.
Hóng zuǐ lǜ yīnggē.

The answer is: Pan-fried tofu with spinach.

Following are a few Chinese dishes that have become popular in western countries.
More often than not, these dishes have been adjusted to please the western palate.

蛋花汤	dàn huā tāng	Egg Flower Soup
馄饨汤	húntún tāng	Won-ton Soup
酸辣汤	suān là tāng	Spicy hot soup
春卷	chūnjuǎn	Spring Rolls
包子	bāozi	Steamed Stuffed Buns
饺子	jiǎozi	Dumplings
水饺	shuǐjiǎo	Dumplings (boiled)
锅贴	guōtiē	Pot-stickers (pan-fried)
炒饭	chǎo fàn	Fried Rice
炒粉	chǎo fěn	Fried Rice Noodles
炒面	chǎo miàn	Fried Noodles
宫保鸡丁	gōngbǎo jī dīng	Kung-Pao Chicken (spicy)

柠檬鸡	níngméng jī	Lemon Chicken
北京烤鸭	běijīng kǎoyā	Peking Duck
虾仁炒雪豆	xiārén chǎo xuědòu	Shrimp with Snowpeas
椒盐虾	jiāo yán xiā	Seasoned Deep-fried Shrimp
叉烧肉	chā shāo ròu	Barbecued Pork
糖醋排骨	tángcù páigǔ	Sweet and Sour Pork
猪肉炒雪豆	zhūròu chǎo xuědòu	Pork stir-fried with Snow Peas
麻婆豆腐	má pó dòufǔ	Grandma's Tofu (spicy)
蒙古烤肉	Měnggǔ kǎoròu	Mongolian Beef
蚝油牛肉	háo yóu niúròu	Beef with Oyster Sauce
牛肉炒芹菜	niúròu chǎo qíncài	Beef stir-fried with Celery

You could also try other combinations of stir-fried meats and vegetables, such as:

牛肉炒花椰菜 niúròu chǎo huāyécài Beef stir-fried with Broccoli

Hot cross buns are not generally available in China and Taiwan, but you may still be able to see vendors pedaling around in a village, hawking hot steamed buns. For this traditional children's song, I have substituted the hot cross buns with the hot steamed buns. To be fair, I added a second stanza so the little girl also gets a chance to eat the hot steamed bun. Feel free to substitute the word 馒头 (mántóu steamed buns) with another food that has a two-syllable name.

Hot Cross Buns

卖馒头

Mài Mántóu

卖馒头哟,
Mài mántóu yō,

Hot cross buns!
Selling steamed buns!

卖馒头!
Mài mántóu!

Hot cross buns.
Selling steamed buns!

一个馒头, 两个馒头,
Yī ge mántóu, liǎng ge mántóu,

One a penny, two a penny,
One steamed bun, two steamed buns,

卖馒头!
Mài mántóu!

Hot cross buns.
Selling steamed buns!

要是没有丫头儿,
Yàoshì méiyǒu yātóur,

If you haven't a daughter,

买给小毛头.
Mǎi gěi xiǎo máotóu.

Give it to your sons.
Buy for your little boy.

一个馒头, 两个馒头,
Yī ge mántóu, liǎng ge mántóu

One a penny, two a penny,
One steamed bun, two steamed buns,

卖馒头!
Mài mántóu!

Hot cross buns.
Selling steamed buns!

卖馒头哟，
Mài mántóu yō,

Selling steamed buns!

卖馒头！
Mài mántóu!

Selling steamed buns!

吃了馒头, 无忧无愁.
Chī le mántóu, wú yōu wú chóu.

Eat a steamed bun; no more worries.

卖馒头！
Mài mántóu!

Selling steamed buns!

要是没有毛头儿，
Yàoshì méi yǒu máotóur,

If you haven't a young son,

买给小丫头.
Mǎi gěi xiǎo yātóu.

Buy for your little girl.

吃了馒头, 无忧无愁.
Chī le mán tóu, wú yōu wú chóu.

Eat a steamed bun; no more worries.

卖馒头！
Mài mántóu!

Selling steamed buns!

要是 (yàoshì) is one way of saying "if". I will talk about other alternatives in a later chapter on making longer sentences.

丫头 (yātóu) refers to the traditional hairstyle of little girls in China. With a little bun sticking out on each side, the head takes the forked shape of a "Y".

小毛头 (xiǎo máotóu) refers to the traditional hairstyle of little boys in China. Typically, the boy just has one small tuft of hair at the top of his head.

馒头 (mántóu) are plain steamed buns. Steamed buns that are stuffed with meat or vegetables are called 包子 (bāozi). 包 (bāo) means to wrap or bag up something.

包括 (bāokuò) means to include something or someone.

Cooking

The Chinese word for culinary art is 烹饪 (pēngrèn). A cooking pot or pan is called 锅 (guō). 电锅 (diànguō) is an electric cooker that takes the guesswork out of making steamed rice. Many Chinese families eat rice on a daily basis, and the 电锅 (diànguō) has become a standard appliance in their kitchens.

方便 (fāngbiàn) means convenient or easy to use. You could also say 好用 (hǎoyòng easy to use).

煮 (zhǔ) means cooking, typically in water, in soup or in a sauce. 煮饭 (zhǔfàn) is cooking rice, and 煮面 (zhǔ miàn) is cooking noodles. 煮菜 (zhǔcài), 烧菜 (shāocài) and 作菜 (zuòcài) all refer to cooking foods in general, regardless of the method of cooking and the type of food cooked. Always watch what you are cooking so the food does not get burnt (烧焦 shāo jiāo).

炒菜锅 (chǎocàiguō) is a pan for stir-frying, commonly known as "wok". 炒菜 (chǎocài) refers to stir-frying foods in general, not just the vegetables. 炒面 (chǎo miàn) as an activity means to stir-fry noodles. As an object, it refers to stir-fried noodles. Similarly, 炒虾仁 (chǎo xiārén) can be construed as the activity of stir-frying shrimp meat, or a dish of stir-fried shrimp meat.

油炸 (yóu zhà) is deep-frying, while 煎 (jiān) is pan-frying.

烤 (kǎo) refers to baking, roasting or barbecuing. The oven is called 烤箱 (kǎoxiāng).

刀叉 (dāochā) refers to the knife and the fork, 筷子 (kuàizi) are chopsticks, and 汤匙 (tāngchí) are tablespoons. The Chinese word for cutting is 切 (qiè cut).

Please study the following sentences, then substitute the words in brackets with suitable words of your choice. For example, the adverb, 很 (hěn very, quite), in the first sentence could be substituted with the adverb, 非常 (fēicháng extremely).

用电锅煮饭<很>方便.
Yòng diànguō zhǔfàn hěn fāngbiàn.

It is quite convenient to use
an electric cooker to cook rice.

煮面要用<不少>水.
Zhǔ miàn yào yòng bùshǎo shuǐ.

It takes a fair amount of water
to cook the noodles.

<油炸>时要小心.
Yóu zhà shí yào xiǎoxīn.

Be careful when deep-frying.

她用炒菜锅炒<虾仁>.
Tā yòng chǎocàiguō chǎo xiārén.

She uses a stir-frying pan to
stir-fry the shrimp meat.

查理把<牛肉>烧焦了.
Chálǐ bǎ niúròu shāo jiāo le.

Charlie burnt the beef.

理查会<炒面>.
Lǐchá huì chǎo miàn.

Richard knows how to
stir-fry noodles.

乔治喜欢吃煎<鳟鱼>.
Qiáozhì xǐhuān chī jiān zūnyú.

George likes pan-fried trout.

<我们>都爱吃煎饼.
Wǒmen dōu ài chī jiānbǐng.

We all love to eat pancakes.

达尔文用刀叉吃<火鸡>.
Dárwén yòng dāochā chī huǒjī.

Darwin uses the knife and fork
to eat the turkey.

露西烤的<蛋糕>最好吃.
Lùxī kǎo de dàngāo zuì hǎochī.

The cake baked by Lucy
tastes the best.

吉米想学用<筷子>.
Jímǐ xiǎng xué yòng kuàizi.

Jimmy wants to learn how to
use the chopsticks.

Wendy, who comes from Taiwan, is meeting up for lunch at a Chinese restaurant with her American friends, Susan, Charlie and Nick, who have learned to speak some Chinese. You can pick the person you want to be, and play his or her part in the following conversation.

At the Restaurant
在餐厅
Zài Cāntīng

文蒂: 你好.
Wéndì: Nǐ hǎo.
Wendy: Good day.

服务员: 您好. 您说中国话吗?
fúwùyuán: Nín hǎo. Nín shuō Zhōngguóhuà ma?
Waiter: Good day. You speak Chinese?

文蒂: 是的.
Wéndì: Shì de.
Wendy: Yes.

     我的朋友们也都会说中国话.
     Wǒ de péngyǒu mén yě dōu huì shuō Zhōngguóhuà.
     My friends all speak Chinese, too.

服务员: 今天点些什么?
fúwùyuán: Jīntiān diǎn xiē shénme?
Waiter: What are you ordering today?

文蒂: 我点牛肉炒面.
Wéndì: Wǒ diǎn niúròu chǎomiàn.
Wendy: I'm ordering beef with fried noodles.

苏珊: 我要锅贴.
Sūshān::   Wǒ yào guǒtiē.
Susan: I'd like to have pot-stickers.

查理:　　　我要宫保鸡丁, 但是不要太辣.
Chálǐ:　　Wǒ yào gōngbǎo jī dīng, dànshì búyào tài là.
Charlie:　I'd like to have kung-pao chicken, but not too spicy.

尼克:　　我喜欢海鲜.
Níkè:　　Wǒ xǐhuān hǎixiān.
Nick:　　I like seafood.

　　　　来一盘虾仁炒雪豆吧.
　　　　Lái yī pán xiārén chǎo xuědòu ba.
　　　　Bring me a plate of shrimp with snowpeas.

服务员:　　要炒饭, 还是白饭?
fúwùyuán:　Yào chǎo fàn, háishì báifàn?
Waiter:　　Would you like stir-fried rice, or plain rice?

苏珊:　　各一半好了. 谢谢.
Sūshān:　Gè yībàn hǎo le. Xièxiè.
Susan:　　Half of each, please. Thanks.

服务员:　　好的. 谢谢. 菜马上就来.
fúwùyuán:　Hǎo de. Xièxiè. Cài mǎshàng jiù lái.
Waiter:　　Okay. Thanks. The food will be served shortly.

There are a number of ways of saying "a restaurant" in Chinese.

餐厅	restaurant, dining room	速食餐厅	fast-food restaurant
cāntīng		sùshí cāntīng	(not a Sushi restaurant ☺)
餐馆	restaurant	小吃店	snackbar, small eatery
cānguǎn		xiǎochīdiàn	
饭店	restaurant, hotel	馆子	small eating house
fàndiàn		guǎnzi	
饭馆	restaurant	咖啡馆	café
fànguǎn		kāfēiguǎn	

Most local small eateries in China and Taiwan do not have a tipping system. However, the modern restaurants do expect you to leave a tip (小费 xiǎofèi).

中国话 (Zhōngguóhuà) is spoken Chinese. Some people call it 汉语 (Hànyǔ the Han language), or 普通话 (pǔtōnghuà common language, Mandarin). 中文 (Zhōngwén Chinese language) usually refers to the written Chinese language. It's easy to write the character 中 (zhōng), which means "middle" or "center". Simply make a rectangle then put a vertical stroke through it.

点 (diǎn) as a verb means "point to", "make a dot", or "choose from". 点菜 (diǎncài) or 订菜 (dìng cài) means to order from a menu at a restaurant.

来一盘 (lái yī pán) is a casual way of saying, "Bring me a dish of something".

各一半好了 (gè yībàn hǎo le) is the same as 各一半吧 (gè yībàn ba). It sort of says: "All right, let's have half of each." Here, 好了 (hǎo le) is simply an expression that serves to soften the tone. As the following sentences show, you must interpret 好了 (hǎo le) based on the context in which it is used.

你帮我做好了. **All right**, you do it for me.
Nǐ bāng wǒ zuò hǎo le.

她已經帮我做好了. She has already helped me **finish** the task.
Tā yǐjīng bāng wǒ zuò hǎo le.

22. *Weather Conditions*

Here are a few common terms that will be useful to know about the weather.

天气	weather	气象	weather conditions
tiānqì		qìxiàng	
气象学	meteorology	气象预报	weather forecast
qìxiàngxué		qìxiàng yùbào	
天晴	sunny	晴天	sunny day
tiān qíng		qíngtiān	
大晴天	bright sunny day	大热天	very hot day
dà qíngtiān		dà rètiān	
阴天	overcast day	雨天	rainy day
yīntiān		yǔ tiān	
下雨	raining	下大雨	raining hard
xiàyǔ		xià dàyǔ	
打雷	thundering	闪电	lightning
dǎléi		shǎndiàn	
多云	cloudy	刮风	windy
duō yún		guā fēng	
台风	typhoon	飓风	hurricane
táifēng		jùfēng	
下雪	snowing	龙卷风	tornado
xià xuě		lóngjuǎnfēng	
大风雨	big storm	大风雪	snowstorm
dà fēngyǔ		dà fēng xuě	
雾天	foggy day	露点	dew point
wù tiān		lùdiǎn	
薄霜	light frost	结冰	to ice up (freeze)
bó shuāng		jiébīng	

In a casual conversation you would probably want to avoid discussing politics and religion. However, it's usually safe to comment on the weather.

今天天气很好.
Jīntiān tiānqì hěn hǎo.

It's a nice day today.

希望明天也是晴天.
Xīwàng míngtiān yě shì qíngtiān

I hope it'll also be sunny tomorrow.

今天出大太阳. 好热!
Jīntiān chū dà tàiyáng. Hǎo rè!

The sun shines bright today.
It's quite hot!

还好, 我带了阳伞.
Hái hǎo, wǒ dài le yángsǎn.

Fortunately, I brought the parasol.

今天是阴天.
Jīn tiān shì yīntiān.

It's cloudy today (with overcast sky).

明天可能会下雨.
Míngtiān kěnéng huì xiàyǔ.

It may rain tomorrow.

带件雨衣吧.
Dài jiàn yǔyī ba.

Take a raincoat along.

变天了.
Biàntiān le .

The weather has changed
(for the worse).

雾天开车要当心.
Wù tiān kāichē yào dāngxīn.

On foggy days, one must
drive carefully.

现在风速每小时八哩.
Xiànzài fēngsù měi xiǎoshí bā lǐ.

Currently, wind velocity is 8 mph.
(miles per hour)

龙卷风很可怕.
Lóngjuǎnfēng hěn kěpà.

Tornadoes are terrifying.

温 (wēn) means lukewarm or temperate. 度 (dù) denotes the degree of intensity. It is also used a unit of measure for angles, 角度 (jiǎodù), and temperatures, 温度 (wēndù). 身体 (shēntǐ) is the body. Therefore, 体温 (tǐwēn) is body temperature. Similarly, 空气 (kōngqì), or 大气 (dàqì), is the atmosphere or the air. Therefore, 气温 (qìwēn) is the air temperature. Fahrenheit is translated into 华氏 (Huáshì), and Celsius is translated as 摄氏 (Shèshì), where 氏 (shì), or 姓氏 (xìngshì), means family name.

湿 (shī) means wet, damp or humid. Therefore, 湿度 (shīdù) is the degree of humidity. 压力 (yālì) means pressure. 气压 (qìyā) is the air pressure, or atmospheric pressure.

If you are inclined to talk about the air temperature or pressure, here are a few examples:

今天 气温很低.
Jīntiān xìwēn hěn dī.
The temperatures are low today.

今天湿度很高
Jīntiān shīdù hěn gāo.
It's very humid today.

室温差不多是摄氏二十度.
Shìwēn chàbuduō shì Shèshì èrshí dù.
Room temperature is about 20 degrees Celsius.

华氏三十二度等于摄氏零度. (冰点)
Huáshì sānshíèr dù děngyú Shèshì líng dù. (bīng diǎn)
32 degrees Fahrenheit equals 0 degrees Celsius. (ice point)

华氏零下四十度等于摄氏零下四十度.
Huáshì língxià sìshí dù děngyú Shèshì língxià sìshí dù.
40 degrees below zero Fahrenheit equals 40 degrees below zero Celsius.

Sun and moon, and clouds, and stars. Those are what many poets like to write about.

Let's look at a short poem written by the famous ancient Chinese poet, 李白 (Lǐ Bái). Classical Chinese poems are typically terse, carefully constructed verses that follow rigorous rhyming rules and contain well-placed allusions to other classical literary works. They are meant to be chewed on, studied and admired. In contrast, the poems of 李白 (Lǐ Bái) are unassuming and easy to understand. The beautiful verses go directly to the reader's heart. In China and Taiwan, if you stop an elementary school student on the street, chances are that he or she will be able to recite the following piece for you.

Homesick on a Moonlit Night
月夜思乡
Yuè Yè Sī Xiāng

床前明月光;	The moonshine on my pillow,
Chuáng qián míng yuèguāng;	(The moonlight in front of my bed,)
疑是地上霜.	I mistook it for frost.
Yí shì dì shàng shuāng.	(I thought it was the frost on the ground.)
抬头望明月,	My heart is filled with sorrow
Táitóu wàng míng yuè,	(I look up to see the bright moon.)
低头思故乡.	For the homeland I have lost.
Dītóu sī gùxiāng.	(I look down and long for my homeland.)

疑 (yí), or 怀疑 (huáiyí), means to suspect or to doubt. It also works as a noun to represent suspicion or doubt.

抬 (tái) is to lift or to carry. 抬头 (táitóu) means to raise one's head.

低 (dī) means low. In 低头 (dītóu lower one's head), it serves as a verb.

Here is a little song I wrote to celebrate friendship. Indeed, friendship is like sunshine that warms our hearts and helps sustain us through the cloudy days and occasional storms in life.

Happy Friends
快乐的朋友
Kuàilè de Péngyǒu

我有个朋友, 那就是你.
Wǒ yǒu ge péngyǒu, nà jiù shì nǐ.
I have a good friend, and that is you.

我们手牵手, 每天笑嘻嘻.
Wǒmen shǒu qiān shǒu, měitiān xiàoxīxī.
We walk hand in hand, always in good mood.

不管晴天, 雨天, 都是好天气,
Bùguǎn qíngtiān, yǔ tiān, dōu shì hǎo tiānqì,
Sunshine is welcome; rain is okay, too,
(No matter sunny or rainy, it's good weather to me,)

只要我们能够永远在一起.
Zhǐyào wǒmen nénggòu yǒngyuǎn zài yīqǐ.
As long as I can always be with you.
(As long as we can always be together.)

牵 (qiān) means to lead someone or something along or to involve someone.

管 (guǎn) as a verb means to manage, to discipline or to mind. As expected, 不管 (bùguǎn) means not to care, regardless, or no matter. As a noun, 管 (guǎn) means a tube, a pipe, or a wind instrument.

You could substitute the second line with:

我们一同读书, 也一同游戏.

Wǒmen yītóng dúshū, yě yītóng yóuxì.

We study together, and play together, too.

读书 (dúshū to read a book out loud) usually refers to studying at school. 游戏 (yóuxì) is to play and have fun. As a noun, 游戏 (yóuxì) means a game.

Now do the following exercises then try your hand at making rhymes by fitting some other pairs of action words into this song.

Exercise 1:

Fill in the blanks with the appropriate words.

我有个＿＿＿ ＿＿＿, 那就是你.

Wǒ yǒu ge ＿＿＿＿＿＿, nà jiù shì nǐ.

I have a good friend, and that is you.

你不会＿＿＿ ＿＿＿, 也不会＿＿＿ ＿＿＿.

Nǐ búhuì ＿＿＿＿＿＿, yě búhuì ＿＿＿＿＿＿.

You're never jealous, and never lose your cool (get angry).

不管晴天, 雨天, 都是 ＿＿＿ ＿＿＿ ＿＿,

Bùguǎn qíngtiān, yǔ tiān, dōu shì ＿＿＿ ＿＿＿＿,

No matter sunny or rainy, it's good weather to me,

只要我们能够 ＿＿＿ ＿＿＿ 在一起.

Zhǐyào wǒmen nénggòu ＿＿＿＿＿＿ zài yīqǐ.

So long as I can always be with you.

(So long as we can always be together.)

Exercise 2:

Fill in the blanks with the appropriate words.

我有个朋友, 那 _____ _____ 你.

Wǒ yǒu ge péngyǒu, nà _____ _____ nǐ.

I have a good friend, and that is you.

我们一同 _____ _____, 也一同休息.

Wǒmen yītóng _____, yě yītóng xiūxī.

We work together, and unwind when we should.

不管 _____ _____, 雨天,都是好天气,

Bùguǎn _____, yǔ tiān, dōu shì hǎo tiānqì,

No matter sunny or rainy, it's good weather to me,

只要我们能够 _____ _____ 不分离.

Zhǐyào wǒmen nénggòu _____ bù fénlí.

So long as I will never part with you.

(So long as we will always not get separated.)

Answers:

我有个朋友, 那就是你.

Wǒ yǒu ge péngyǒu, nà jiù shì nǐ.
I have a good friend, and that is you.

你不会嫉妒, 也不会生气.

Nǐ búhuì jídù, yě búhuì shēngqì.
You're never jealous, and never lose your cool (get angry).

不管晴天雨天, 都是好天气,

Bùguǎn qíngtiān yǔ tiān, dōu shì hǎo tiānqì.
No matter sunny or rainy, it's good weather to me,

只要我们能够永远在一起.

Zhǐyào wǒmen nénggòu yǒngyuǎn zài yīqǐ.
So long as I can always be with you.
(So long as we can always be together.)

我有个朋友, 那就是你.

Wǒ yǒu ge péngyǒu, nà jiù shì nǐ.
I have a good friend, and that is you.

我们一同工作, 也一同休息.

Wǒmen yītóng gōngzuò, yě yītóng xiūxī.
We work together, and unwind when we should.

不管晴天雨天, 都是好天气,

Bùguǎn qíngtiān yǔ tiān, dōu shì hǎo tiānqì,
No matter sunny or rainy, it's good weather to me,

只要我们能够永远不分离.

Zhǐyào wǒmen nénggòu yǒngyuǎn bù fēnlí.
So long as I will never part with you.
(So long as we will always not get separated.)

23. The Four Seasons

In most parts of China, there are four distinct seasons, referred to as 四季 (sìjì). The Chinese have designated a representative flower for each season. The graceful grass orchid in the spring, 春天 (chūntiān), the lively bamboo in the summer, 夏天 (xiàtiān), the charming chrysanthemum in the autumn, 秋天 (qiūtiān), and the hardy plum blossom in the winter, 冬天 (dōngtiān), are all favorite subjects in Chinese brush paintings. They are also featured on four of the tiles used in the game of mahjong.

春兰
chūn lán
spring orchid

夏竹
xià zhú
summer bamboo

秋菊
qiū jú
autumn mum

冬梅
dōng méi
winter plum

春兰 (chūn lán spring orchid) and 秋菊 (qiū jú autumn mum) are popular Chinese names for girls. There are also many Chinese names that contain the word 梅 (méi plum).

In Northern China, the winter is bitter cold, while in some parts of Southern China the summer can be unbearably hot. 昆明 (Kūnmíng) is the capital of the Yunnan Province (云南省 Yúnnán shěng) in the southwestern part of China. It is balmy year-round and fondly touted by the Chinese as: 四季如春 (Sìjì rú chūn. All four seasons are like spring.)

Following is a popular Chinese slapstick rhyme that makes fun of students who always have an excuse not to study hard.

Spring, Summer, Fall and Winter

春天不是读书天.
Chūntiān bú shì dúshū tiān.

Spring days are not for studying.

夏日炎炎, 正好眠.
Xià rì yányán, zhèng hǎo mián.

The hot summer makes you sleep.
(Summer is hot; just right for sleeping.)

等到秋来, 冬又至.
Děng dào qiū lái, dōng yòu zhì.

When fall arrives, winter heels.

收拾书包, 好过年.
Shōushi shūbāo, hǎo guònián.

Time to pack up for New Year's leave.
(Put the book bag away for New Year.)

读书 (dúshū) means to read a book or to study.

睡 (shuì), 睡觉 (shuìjiào), 眠 (mián) and 睡眠 (shuìmián) all mean "sleep" (verb or noun). The word for insomnia is 失眠 (shīmián losing sleep). 醒 (xǐng) is to wake up, sober up, to come to, to be awake, or to be clear of mind.

The word, 炎 (yán), has one 火 (huǒ fire) on top of another. It represents "scorching hot". It also refers to an inflammation. 炎炎 (yányán) and 炎热 (yánrè) both mean "blazing hot". 炎炎 (yányán) is mostly used in poems and songs. 炎热 (yánrè) is what you would say in everyday speech.

收 (shōu) means to receive, accept or put away. 拾 (shí) means to pick up. 收拾 (shōushi) means to tidy up, or gather together and pack up. For example: 我把房间收拾好了. (Wǒ bǎ fángjiān shōushi hǎo le. I have tidied up the room.) 收拾书包 (shōushi shūbāo) is to gather the books into the satchel.

至 (zhì arrive, to, until, to the extreme) is the formal form of 到 (dào arrive, to, until). It is found in many expressions in spoken Chinese, but mostly in the sense of "to the extent" or "to the extreme", as shown in the following sentences.

至于停留一星期, 那不可能.
Zhìyú tíngliú yī xīngqī, nà bù kěnéng.
As for staying one week, that's not possible.

他很担忧, 甚至连饭都吃不下.
Tā hěn dānyōu, shèngzhì lián fàn dōu chī bú xià.
He was so worried, he couldn't **even** eat.

他至少吃了三个包子.
Tā zhìshǎo chī le sān ge bāozi.
He ate **at least** three meat buns.

国王有至上的权力.
Guówáng yǒu zhìshàng de quánlì.
The king has **the utmost** authority.

In everyday speech, the word to use for "arrive", "until", and "to" is: 到 (dào).

到家了.
Dào jiā le.
We have **arrived home**.

到今天她还是不知道.
Dào jīntiān tā háishì bù zhīdào.
Until today, she still does not know.

我說到哪兒了?
Wǒ shuō dào nǎr le?
What was I **speaking of**? (Where was I?)

我收到一件有趣的礼物.
Wǒ shōudào yī jiàn yǒuqù de lǐwù.
I received an interesting gift.

Here is a simple rhyme to help you memorize the names of the seasons. You can sing it to the tune of the hilarious song, named "Delaware", which was composed by Irving Gordon in 1959. Please try it with each of the four seasons: 春天 (chūntiān), 夏天 (xiàtiān), 秋天 (qiūtiān), and 冬天 (dōngtiān). The two characters, 我 (wǒ) and 的 (de) should be sung quickly to fit to the same note.

The Autumn Days Are Here

秋天已经来啦!
Qiūtiān yǐjīng lái lā!

The autumn days are here, hey,

秋天已来到.
Qiūtiān yǐ láidào.

The autumn days are here.

秋天已经来啦!
Qiūtiān yǐjīng lái lā!

The autumn days are here, hey,

秋天已来到.
Qiūtiān yǐ láidào.

The autumn days are here.

秋天已经来啦!
Qiūtiān yǐjīng lái lā!

The autumn days are here, hey,

秋天已来到.
Qiūtiān yǐ láidào.

The autumn days are here.

你可知道?
Nǐ kě zhīdào?

Are you aware?

我的好朋友,
Wǒ de hǎo péngyǒu,

My good old friend,

秋天已来到!
Qiūtiān yǐ láidào!

The autumn days are here!

已 (yǐ) is the short form of the adverb 已经 (yǐjīng already). It is used mostly in written documents. In everyday speech, people say: 已经 (yǐjīng).

The word, 可 (kě), has many different uses. In the following two sentences, it means "can" or "may":

我<u>可以</u>接受.　　　　　　I can accept (this).
Wǒ kěyǐ jiēshòu.

我<u>可以</u>了解.　　　　　　I can understand (this).
Wǒ kěyǐ liǎojiě.

你<u>可以</u>回家了.　　　　　You may go home (now).
Nǐ kěyǐ huíjiā le.

可以 (kěyǐ) also means to be fine or to be worth doing.

他做得<u>还可以</u>.　　　　　He did the job okay.
Tā zuò de hǎi kěyǐ.　　　　　(His work is passable.)

这生意<u>可以</u>做.　　　　　This business is worth doing.
Zhè shēngyì kěyǐ zuò.

In the following, 可 (kě) can be interpreted as "perhaps", "after all", or "however".

你<u>可</u>了解我的心情?　　　Do you perhaps understand how I feel?
Nǐ kě liǎojiě wǒ de xīnqíng?

你<u>可</u>知道我不想去?　　　Are you aware that I don't wish to go?
Nǐ kě zhīdào wǒ bù xiǎng qù?

现在你<u>可</u>知道了.　　　　Now you know after all.
Xiànzài nǐ kě zhīdào le.

我<u>可</u>不想去.　　　　　　I, however, am not interested in going.
Wǒ kě bùxiǎng qù.

"Sakura" is probably the most widely known Japanese folk song in the world. The delicate cherry blossoms have given inspiration to many Japanese poets, artists and photographers. The Japanese especially love to watch the cherry petals drift down in a gentle breeze.

Sakura (Cherry Blossoms)
樱花
Yīnghuā

樱花开, 樱花开.
Yīnghuā kāi, yīnghuā kāi.

Cherry blooms, cherry blooms,

开在丘陵和山间;
Kài zài qiūlíng hé shān jiān:

Up on hills and mountain side,

花海一片又一片.
Huā hǎi yī piàn yòu yī piàn.

Seas of flowers, no end in sight.

那是烟雾, 还是云?
Nà shì yiānwù, háishì yún?

Are these mists? Or, are these clouds?

花香一阵又一阵.
Huā xiāng yī zhèn yòu yī zhèn.

Waves of fragrance wafting out.

樱花开, 樱花开.
Yīnghuā kāi, yīnghuā kāi.

Cherry blooms, cherry blooms,

好花正盛开.
Hǎo huā zhèng shèng kāi.

Flowers in full bloom.

樱花开, 樱花开.
Yīnghuā kāi, yīnghuā kāi.

Cherry blooms, cherry blooms,

开在美丽的春天.
Kāi zài mèilì de chūntiān.

In the balmy, clear spring sky,

花海一片又一片.
Huā hǎi yī piàn yòu yī piàn.

Seas of flowers, no end in sight.

看似烟雾, 也似云.
Kàn sì yiānwù, yě sì yún.

Seem like mists, and seem like clouds,

花香一阵又一阵.
Huā xiāng yī zhèn yòu yī zhèn.

Waves of fragrance wafting out.

快快来! 快快来!
Kuài kuài lái! Kuài kuài lái!

Come along! Come along!

好花不长开.
Hǎo huā bù cháng kāi.

Fair blooms won't last long.

Please note the difference between the following two statements:

好花不<u>长</u>开.
Hǎo huā bù cháng kāi.

Beautiful flowers don't bloom long.

好花不<u>常</u>开.
Hǎo huā bù cháng kāi.

Beautiful flowers don't bloom often.

"好花不长开. (Hǎo huā bù cháng kāi.)" is a Chinese cliché expressing the regret that good things don't last.

The Chinese like to use 山 (shān, mountain) and 海 (hǎi sea, ocean) to represent greatness, hugeness or vastness. 花海 (huā hǎi) is a sea of flowers. 人山人海 (rénshānrénhǎi a mountain and a sea of people) is a common expression that means "huge crowds of people".

In 一片又一片 (yī piàn yòu yī piàn one expanse following another) and
一阵又一阵 (yī zhèn yòu yī zhèn one draft after another), there is a pattern that
you can use to form other common phrases, such as:

我說了<u>一遍又一遍</u>.   I said (that) time and again.
Wǒ shuō le yī biàn yòu yī biàn.

他吃了<u>一口又一口</u>.   He took one bite after another.
Tā chī le yī kǒu yòu yī kǒu.

盛 (shèng) means flourishing, prosperous, abundant, or magnificent, as in:

<u>盛大</u>的宴会   magnificent banquet
shèngdà de yànhuì

那些树长得很<u>茂盛</u>.   Those trees are flourishing
Nàxiē shù zhǎng de hěn màoshèng.   (or growing well).

Note that, when used in the sense of "long", the word "长" is pronounced as
"cháng". When it is used as the verb, "to grow", "长" is pronounced as "zhǎng".

似 (sì) and 像 (xiàng) both mean "seem like, look like, appear to be". 似 (sì) is
the formal word, while 像 (xiàng) is the familiar form used in conversations.

似乎 (sìhu) and 好像 (hǎoxiàng) both mean "to seem like" or "to look like".
They are used interchangeably in daily speech.

看来 (kànlái) is a common expression that means "It seems . . .". It can also be
used as an adverb that means "seemingly". 看似 (kàn sì) is the abbreviation for
看来似乎 (kànlái sìhu) or 看来好像 (kànlái hǎoxiàng), which means "to
look as if" or "to appear to look like something".

Exercise:

Please fill in the blank for each of the following sentences:

一年之中, 我最喜欢的是 _____ 季.

Yī nián zhī zhōng, wǒ zuì xǐhuān de shì _____ jì.

Within the year, my favorite is the _____ season.

夏天天 _____ ; 要多喝 _____.

Xiàtiān tiān _____ ; yào duō hē _____.

It's hot in the summer; it's advisable to drink plenty of water.

_____ 天到了, 桃花开.

_____ tiān dào le, táohuā kāi.

Spring is here, and the peach flowers bloom.

秋天里, 许多树叶都变 _____ 色.

Qiūtiān lǐ, xǔduō shùyè dōu biàn _____ sè.

In autumn many leaves turn red.

冬天天 _____ ; 要穿 _____ _____.

Dōngtiān tiān _____ ; yào chuān _____.

It's cold in the winter; it's advisable to wear jackets.

你是我 _____ _____ 的 _____ _____,

Nǐ shì wuǒ _____ de _____,

You are my (bright) sun in the winter,

_____ _____ 的 ___ . ___ ___.

_____ de _____.

my ice cream in the summer.

Answer:

一年之中，我最喜欢的是夏季.
Yī nián zhī zhōng, wǒ zuì xǐhuān de shì xiàjì.
Within the year my favorite is the summer season.

For this sentence, you may fill in any of the four seasons. Take an extra credit if you came up with: 橄榄球季 (gǎnlǎnqiú jì football season).

夏天天热; 要多喝水.
Xiàtiān tiān rè; yào duō hē shuǐ.
It's hot in the summer; it's advisable to drink plenty of water.

春天到了, 桃花开.
Chūntiān dào le, táohuā kāi.
Spring is here, and the peach flowers bloom.

秋天里, 许多树叶都变红色.
Qiūtiān lǐ, xǔduō shùyè dōu biàn hóngsè.
In autumn many leaves turn red.

冬天天冷; 要穿外套.
Dōngtiān tiān lěng; yào chuān wàitào.
It's cold in the winter; it's advisable to wear a jacket.

你是我冬天的太阳,
Nǐ shì wuǒ dōngtiān de tàiyáng,
You are my (bright) sun in the winter,

夏天的冰淇淋.
xiàtiān de bīngqílín.
my ice cream in the summer.

24. Holidays

Holidays, or 节日 (jiérì), are a time for reconnecting with family and friends to commemorate, to celebrate, or just to be together. It is through holidays that many interesting traditions are passed from generation to generation. Listed below are the major holidays celebrated by the Chinese people. I will talk a little about some of them in the following sections.

新年	xīnnián	New Year
春节	chūnjié	Chinese Lunar New Year
元宵	yuánxiāo	The 15th of the first lunar month; the Lantern Festival
清明节	qīngmíngjié	Day for commemorating ancestors
端午节	duānwǔjié	Mid-May Festival (Dragon Boat Festival)
国庆日	guóqìng rì	National Holiday
中秋节	zhōngqiūjié	Mid-Autumn Festival, Moon Festival
劳工节	láogōngjié	Labor Day
教师节	jiàoshījié	Teacher's Day (Confucius' Birthday)
圣诞节	shèngdànjié	Christmas

Spring Festival

The Chinese celebrate two New Year's holidays, one by the Gregorian calendar, the other by the lunar calendar. The Chinese Lunar New Year usually occurs in the early part of February on the Gregorian calendar. It is also referred to as the Spring Festival, 春节 (chūnjié). Whereas the workers get a couple days off for the New Year holiday, they have two weeks to celebrate the Spring Festival and visit their relatives.

Celebration of the Lunar New Year begins on the evening before. On New Year's Eve, 除夕 (chúxì), family members sit down together for a scrumptious feast to send off the old year. Traditionally, this is called "gathering around the hearth", or 围炉 (wéi lú). Many families make it a point to serve fish but not eat it. This is because fish, 鱼 (yú), sounds the same as 余 (yú), which means surplus or remainder, and is also a Chinese surname. Saving the fish symbolizes carrying this year's surplus of good fortune over to the next year.

On the first day of the Lunar New Year, firecrackers are let off everywhere to announce and welcome the new year. Family and friends visit each other, and grownups give children gifts of red envelopes containing cash. (Although not originally intended, this gifting system does away with the trouble of having to return unwanted gifts to the stores.) The red envelopes are called 红包 (hóng bāo).

On this day, many Chinese also eat 饺子 (jiǎozi filled dumplings). The belief is that the dumplings, being shaped like gold ingots, will help bring in good luck and riches.

鞭炮 (biānpào) is a string of firecrackers that is usually suspended from the end of a long pole or from a tall building alongside the street. When it is set off, the loud popping noises can last quite a while. The action of setting off a string of firecrackers is called 放鞭炮 (fàng biānpào).

On the streets, peddlers wheel around cartfuls of colorful sweets and hairpins adorned with artificial cherry blossoms. The pink man-made flowers add a sense of newness to the little girls wearing them, and effectively broadcast the joy of the

New Year to the onlookers. You will also hear people congratulate each other on the arrival of the New Year. They will make a bow with clasped hands, and holler joyfully:

恭禧, 新年好!   Congratulations, Happy New Year!
Gōngxǐ, xínnián hǎo!

A few other standard greetings on New Year's Day are:

新年好!   Happy New Year!
Xínnián hǎo!

新年快乐!   Happy New Year!
Xīnnián kuàilè!

恭禧发财!   Happy New Year and make a fortune!
Gōngxǐ fācái   (Happy New Year and get rich!)

In the Cantonese dialect, this is pronounced as: Kūng hěi fàt chói!

For fun, try adding the following characters to the season's greeting cards, 贺年卡 (hènián kǎ), you are sending out this year:

恭贺新禧!
Gōnghèxīnxǐ!

This standard salutation on Chinese season's greeting cards translates to:

Respectfully Congratulating You on New Year's Auspiciousness and Jubilation

As an exercise, try searching the Internet for "gong xi gong xi gong xi ni" to play a video featuring this joyful song with the lyrics displayed on the screen. You should know most of the words in the first two stanzas. This song was written by 陈歌辛 (Chén Gēxīn) in 1945 to celebrate the end of the second Sino-Japan war. Since then it has been adopted as the New Year song by his fans.

Lantern Festival

元宵 (yuánxiāo), the 15th day of the first lunar month, marks the end of the Lunar New Year celebration. It is also referred to as the Lantern Festival, 灯节 (dēngjié). At this festival, hand-made lanterns are displayed, glutinous-rice dumplings are served, and poets compete in making fun or insightful rhymes. The glutinous-rice dumplings, themselves referred to as 元宵 (yuánxiāo), are round balls made from glutinous rice flour, and are served in a soup. The filling can be sweet red bean paste, sweet sesame seed paste, shrimp, or meat with vegetables. If you get a chance to sample these glutinous rice dumplings, be sure to take small bites and chew well. They are tasty but can stick to your ribs, or even choke you.

At the festival, riddles are written on some of the lanterns for people to solve. A crowd would gather around a lantern and cheer the person who comes up with the correct answer. Would you like to give the following well-known lantern riddles a try?

Lantern Riddle
灯谜
Dēngmí

1. 猜一个字. Guess one word (from the clue provided).
   Cāi yī ge zì.

   一人一口.   Each person takes one bite.
   Yī rén yī kǒu.

   Answer: 合 (hé together)

2. 猜一个字. Guess one word (a Chinese surname).
   Cāi yī ge zì.

一点; 一横长;　　　　　One dot, one flat stroke;
Yī diǎn yī héng cháng ;

一撇到南洋.　　　　　Slant left to the South Seas.
Yī piē dào Nányáng

拐个弯; 一撇, 一撇.　　Make a turn; slant left, slant left.
Guǎi ge wān; yī piē, yī piē.

再拐个弯; 一撇, 一撇.　Turn again; slant left, slant left.
Zài guǎi ge wān; yī piē, yī piē.

左一撇, 右一撇.　　　　One left slant, one right slant.
Zuǒ yī piē, yòu yī piē.

一撇, 一撇, 又一撇.　　Slant left, slant left, and slant left.
Yī piē, yī piē, yòu yī piē.

拐弯 (guǎiwān) and 转弯 (zhuǎnwān) both mean "to turn a corner" or "to make a turn". 南洋 (Nányáng) is a general term for southern Asia.

点 (diǎn) means a point, a drop, a spot, to point out or to light up. It is also the dot stroke in Chinese characters. 横 (héng) means side-ways, traverse or flagrantly. It is also the horizontal stroke in Chinese characters. 撇 (piē) means to fling or cast aside. It is also the left-falling stroke in Chinese characters. 捺 (nà) means to press down or restrain. It is also the right-falling stroke in Chinese characters. Therefore, strictly speaking, in the above riddle, "右一撇 (yòu yī piē)" should be written as "右一捺 (yòu yī nà)", but then it would not flow as well with the other lines.

Answer: 廖 (liào a Chinese surname)

Dragon Festival

The Mid-May Festival, 端午节 (duānwǔjié), occurs in the middle of the 5th month on the Chinese lunar calendar. This day was designated for commemorating a Chinese poet, named Qu Yuan, 屈原 (Qū Yuán).

Qu Yuan served as an important government official. He was loyal to the Emperor and much loved by his constituents. The local people also admired his poetry. Unfortunately, he was framed by some other government officials and lost favor with the Emperor. Accused as a traitor, Qu Yuan wrote a long poem to reaffirm his loyalty to the country then threw himself into the Yantse River (the Long River). The sorrowful local people sent out boats to search for his body. They wrapped cooked sweet rice in large leaves and dumped those into the river to feed the fish so the latter would leave Qu Yuan's body alone. This ritual was kept up year after year and eventually evolved into a dragon boat race. That's why the Mid-May Festival is also referred to as the Dragon Boat Festival.

All Chinese kids know that the highlight of the Mid-May Festival is the dragon boat race. They have learned this line by heart:

端午节, 划龙船.   Race dragon boats for Mid-May Festival.
Duānwǔjié, huá lóngchuán.

划船 (huáchuán) is to row or paddle a boat.

龙船 (lóngchuán) is a dragon boat, one that is colorfully decorated to look like a dragon. 龙船 (lóngchuán) is also referred to as 龙舟 (lóngzhōu).

舟 (zhōu boat) is the formal word for 船 (chuán boat).

Moon Festival

The Mid-Autumn Festival, 中秋节 (zhōngqiūjié), is a time for family reunion. The moon appears to be fullest on this 15th day of the 8th month on the Chinese lunar calendar. The round moon signifies the complete family circle and perfect union. Therefore, this festival is also called the Moon Festival. You may think of the Moon Festival as the equivalent of Thanksgiving Day, 感恩节 (gǎn'ēnjié), in North America.

For the Moon Festival, people give to one another moon cakes as gifts. Moon cakes, 月饼 (yuèbǐng), are delicious, small round cakes, with an assortment of fillings - sweet bean paste, lotus seed paste, salted egg yolks, melon seeds, candied fruits, mincemeat, and so on.

In the evening of the Mid-Autumn Festival, family members gather to have a feast, eat the moon cakes, and admire the full, brilliant moon. 赏月亮 (shǎng yuèliàng) means to watch and admire the moon. The vague shadows on the moon are the source of many Chinese legends. One of the legend has it that, in ancient times, there were originally ten suns in the sky, and a famous but self-conceited archer 后羿 (Hòuyì) set about to shoot them down. His wife 嫦娥 (Cháng'é), a beautiful fairy, pleaded with him to no avail. Finally, when 后羿 (Hòuyì) shot down the ninth sun, 嫦娥 (Cháng'é), decided to leave him. She flew off to the moon and took her pet rabbit along. The remorseful 后羿 (Hòuyì) spared the last sun, but he was unable to get his wife back. All he could do was strain his eyes at the moon and try to make out her figure on the bright round disk.

Confucius Said

孔子 (Kǒngzǐ), or 孔夫子 (Kǒng fūzǐ) is regarded by the Chinese as the greatest teacher of all times. Here, 子 (zǐ) is the abbreviation for 夫子 (fūzǐ), which means "master" or "mentor". In the west, people refer to 孔夫子 (Kǒng fūzǐ) as Confucius. Confucius taught personal discipline and advocated for social order, stability and harmony. He traveled widely, and offered advice to many regional rulers. His disciples documented his teachings and compiled a book, titled 论语 (Lúnyǔ), The Analects of Confucius. Each section in that book starts with 子曰 (Zǐ yuē), which means "Confucius said". 曰 (yuē) is an ancient word for "say". It looks similar to the word 日 (rì day) but is sqattier. For example,

子曰: 己所不欲, 勿施於人.
Zǐ yuē: Jǐ suǒ bú yù, wù shī yú rén.

Confucius said, "What you do not want for yourself, do not impose on others." This is the equivalent of the Western maxim: "Do not do unto others what you would not have others do unto you."

The "Analects of Confucius" was written in terse classical Chinese. In the above line, 己 (jǐ) stands for 自己 (zìjǐ oneself). 所 (suǒ) is the relational pronoun, "what". 欲 (yù) means "desire" or "to want to do". 勿 (wù) is the formal word for 不要 (bú yào do not). 施 (shī) is to bestow, hand out, apply, impose on, or carry out. It is also a Chinese surname. 於 (yú) can be used as the preposition "at", "in", "to" or "onto".

To honor Confucius, September 28 was designated the Teacher's Day.

九月二十八日是教师节.
Jiǔ yuè èrshíbā rì shì jiàoshī jié.

25. Making Longer Sentences

Just as with English, there are also compound sentences, complex sentences and compound-complex sentences in Chinese. You have already encountered a number of compound and complex sentences in the previous lessons, but I did not point them out to you as such. In this chapter, you will learn some of the connective words that are essential for forming the compound and complex sentences. Once you know how to make these longer sentences, you can claim to know all types of sentences in Chinese. Remember, though, that practice makes master. All the lessons and songs in this book offer plenty of examples of various sentence patterns and word usage. Besides learning each sentence as is, also ask yourself how you could turn it into your own by substituting, perhaps, the noun, the verb, the adjective or the adverb in the sentence with what you want to say. Study all the chapters in this book to expand your vocabulary and learn the cultural bits. To speak Chinese well, it helps to think like a Chinese.

Compound Sentences

To put several independent statements in one sentence, you will need to join them together by using such conjunctives as "and", "but" and "then". The independent statements are called **co-ordinate clauses**, and the combined result is called a compound sentence.

Suppose you know that Sam is smart. In addition, you also know that he likes to play basketball. Then you could disclose these two separate facts in one sentence by saying:

他聪明, 而且他喜欢打篮球.
Tā cōngmíng, érqiě tā xǐhuān dǎ lánqiú.
He is smart, **and** he likes to play basketball.

Or, you could say:

他不但聪明, 而且他喜欢打篮球.
Tā búdàn cōngmíng, érqiě tā xǐhuān dǎ lánqiú.
Not only is he smart, **but also** he likes to play basketball.

Please note that 而且 (érqiě **and also**, **but also**) is usually used instead of 和 (hé and) as the conjunctive in compound sentences.

Pay attention to the conjunctives used in the following examples:

他来了, <u>但是</u>他的朋友走了.
Tā lái le, dànshì tā de péngyǒu zǒu le.
He has come, **but** his friend is gone.

他聪明. <u>然而</u>他身体不好.
Tā zōngmíng. Rán'ér tā shēntǐ bù hǎo.
He is smart. **However**, he has poor health.

我按他的意思做, 他<u>反而</u>不高兴.
Wǒ àn tā de yìsī zuò, tā fǎnér bù gāoxìng.
I did it according to his wish, (he should be pleased)
but on the contrary he was not pleased.

快点儿! <u>不然</u>我要先走了.
Kuài diǎnr! Bùrán wǒ yào xiān zǒu le.
Hurry up! **Otherwise** I'm going ahead (leaving without you).

快点儿! <u>否则</u>我要先走了.
Kuài diǎnr! Fǒuzé wǒ yào xiān zǒu le.
Hurry up! **Otherwise** I'm leaving without you.

但是 (dànshì) and 可是 (kěshì) both mean "but" or "however", and are used interchangeably. 然而 (rán'ér however) is typically used in written form. An apostrophe is inserted in the pinyin for this word to clarify the grouping of syllables.

Both 而且 (érqiě **and also**, **but also**) and 然而 (rán'ér **however**) are abbreviated as 而 (ér). Therefore, you will often see just the word, 而 (ér), used as the conjunctive in a sentence. This does not present a problem as it should be rather easy to determine the meaning of 而 (ér) from the context of the sentence.

Often, the conjunctive "and" is omitted from the sentence altogether. In this case, a semicolon is used to separate the two clauses. For example:

你爱唱歌; 我爱笑.
Nǐ ài chànggē; wǒ ài xiào.
You like to sing; I like to laugh.

Following are a few other conjunctives that are used in everyday speech:

他一边说故事, 一边弹钢琴.
Tā yībiān shuō gùshì, yībiān tán gāngqín.
While he was telling a story, he was playing the piano **at the same time**.

一方面她兴奋, 一方面她担心.
Yīfāngmiàn tā xìngfèn, yīfāngmiàn tā dānxīn.
On the one hand she is excited; **on the other hand** she is worried.

一会儿他说这样, 一会儿他说那样.
Yīhuǐr tā shuō zhèyàng, yīhuǐr tā shuō nàyàng.
One moment he said this, **the next moment** he said that.

Complex Sentences

A complex sentence consists of a main statement and one or more other statements that serve to explain, state a condition for, or to complement the main statement. The main statement is called the **main clause**, and the other statements are called the **subordinate clauses**. The subordinate clauses are typically joined to the main clause by such conjunctives as: "when", "how", "where", "why", "which", "that", "because", "if ", "whether", "since", "as long as", and "unless".

To make it easier for you to find the appropriate conjunctives to use when you want to make a complex sentence, I have grouped the following examples by the function of the various types of subordinate clauses. **The subordinate clause in each of the complex sentences is underlined.**

1. Adverbial clauses containing "when", "while", "since", "wait until", or "as soon as"

<u>当我们同在一起</u>, 其快乐无比.

Dāng wǒmen tóng zài yīqǐ, qí kuàilè wúbǐ.

When we get together, the happiness is unparalleled.

<u>我在看电视的时候</u>, 她来了.

Wǒ zài kàn diànshì de shíhòu, tā lái le.

While I was watching TV, she came.

The conjunctive 当 (dāng when, while) is implied in the above example.

<u>等他来了</u>, 我再走.

Děng tā lái le, wǒ zài zǒu.

Wait till he comes, **then** I'll go.

<u>他一不小心</u>, 就跌跤了.

Tā yī bù xiǎoxīn, jiù diéjiāo le.

The moment he did not pay attention, he fell down.

<u>我一叫</u>, 小狗就来了.

Wǒ yī jiào, xiǎo gǒu jiù lái le.

As soon as I called, (**then**) the puppy came.

In English, the conditional subordinate clause can be placed before or after the main clause. In Chinese, it usually precedes the main clause. A subordinate clause containing 当 (dāng when, while), 每当 (měidāng whenever), and 等 (děng when, wait until) **always** precedes the main clause.

You could say: <u>等他来了</u>, 我再走.

Děng tā lái le, wǒ zài zǒu.

When he comes, then I'll go.

but not: <u>我再走</u>, 等他来了.

Wǒ zài zǒu, děng tā lái le.

I'll go when he comes.

2. Adverbial clauses containing "if", "in case", "only if", "as long as", or "were it not that"

<u>如果他去</u>, 我也要去.

Rúguǒ tā qù, wǒ yě yào qù.

If he goes, I'll go, too.

<u>如果他去的话</u>, 我也要去.

Rúguǒ tā quù de huà, wǒ yě yào qù.

If he goes, I'll go, too. (If we are talking about his going, then I'll go, too.)

<u>万一下雨</u>, 我就不去.

Wànyī xiàyǔ, wǒ jiù bú qù.

In case (with a chance of one out of ten thousand) it rains, **then** I won't go.

<u>要不是真的很痛</u>, 我是不会哭的.

Yàobúshì zhēn de hěn tòng, wǒ shì búhuì kū de.

Were it not that it really hurt so much, I **would not** have cried.

<u>除非真的很痛</u>, 我是不会哭的.

Chúfēi zhēn de hěn tòng, wǒ shì búhuì kū de.

Unless it really hurts a lot, I **will not** cry.

<u>只要你答应留下</u>, 我就高兴.

Zhǐyào nǐ dāyìng liùxià, wǒ jiù gāoxìng.

As long as you agree to stay, I'll be happy.

假如 (jiǎrú), 假若 (jiǎruò) and 倘若 (tǎngruò) also mean "if", and can be used interchangeably with 如果 (rúguǒ). For example:

<u>假如那马车翻倒了</u>, 你还是最乖的小宝宝.

Jiǎrú nà mǎchē fān dǎo le, nǐ háishì zuì guāi de xiǎo bǎobao.

If that horse and cart falls down, you'll **still** be the sweetest baby (in town).

Sometimes, the conditional conjunctive in the subordinate clause is implied, and not explicitly stated. Following are some examples:

你答应留下, 我就高兴.

Nǐ dāyìng liùxià, wǒ jiù gāoxìng.

If you agree to stay, **then** I'll be happy.

他去的话, 我也要去.

Tā qù de huà, wǒ yě yào qù.

If he goes, I'll go, too.

他去, 我才去.

Tā qù, wǒ cái qù.

Only if he goes, **then** I'll go.

3. **Adverbial clauses containing "even if", "no matter", "regardless", or "nevertheless"**

即使他不来, 我还是要走.

Jíshǐ tā bù lái, wǒ háishì yào zǒu.

Even if he doesn't come, I will **still** go.

无论天气好坏, 我都要走.

Wúlùn tiānqì hǎo huài, wǒ dōu yào zǒu

No matter if the weather is good or bad, I will **still** leave.

不管天气好不好, 他都要去.

Bùguǎn tiānqì hǎo bùhǎo, tā dōu yào qù.

Regardless of the weather being good or not, he will **still** go.

他没来; 不过, 我还是要走.

Tā méi lái, búguò, wǒ háishì yào zǒu.

He did not come; **nevertheless** I'll **still** go.

4. **Adverbial clauses containing "because", "therefore", or "although"**

因为他们来了, 所以她走了.

Yīnwèi tāmen lái le, suǒyǐ tā zǒu le.

Because they came, therefore she left.

他们来了, 所以她走了.

Tāmen lái le, suǒyǐ tā zǒu le.
Because they came, **therefore** she left. ("Because" is implied.)

虽然才五点, 可是天已经亮了.

Suīrán cái wǔ diǎn, kěshì tiān yǐjīng liàng le.
Although it's only 5 o'clock, (**but**) the day has already broken.

In Chinese, if a sentence starts with 因为 (yīnwèi because), it is almost always paired with 所以 (suǒyǐ therefore) or 结果 (jiéguǒ as a result, consequently). However, you may omit 所以 (suǒyǐ therefore), and place the subordinate clause containing 因为 (yīnwèi because) after the main clause, as in:

她不想吃饭, 因为她不饿.

Tā bù xiǎng chīfàn, yīnwèi tā bú è.
She does not want to eat because she is not hungry.

5. Noun subordinate clauses containing an implied "that", "whether", "what", "which", "when", "where, "why", or "how"

我以为他喜欢喝茶.

Wǒ yǐwéi tā xǐhuān hē chá.
I thought (assumed) **that** he liked tea.

我知道她不会来.

Wǒ zhīdào tā búhuì lái.
I know **that** she won't come.

我不知道她是否会来.

Wǒ bù zhīdào tā shìfǒu huì lái.
I don't know **whether** she will come.

我不知道她喜欢什么.

Wǒ bù zhīdào tā xǐhuān shénme.
I don't know **what** she likes.

我不知道她比较喜欢哪个.

Wǒ bùzhī dào tā bǐjiào xǐhuān nǎge.

I don't know **which** one she likes better.

我不在乎他什么时候来.

Wǒ búzàihū tā shénme shíhòu lái.

I don't care **when** he comes.

我想知道她住哪儿.

Wǒ xiǎng zhīdào tā zhù nǎr.

I would like to know **where** she resides.

请告诉我他为什么没来.

Qǐng gàosù wǒ tā wèishénme méi lái.

Please tell me **why** he did not come.

请告诉我他是怎么受伤的.

Qǐng gàosù wǒ tā shì zěnme shòushāng de.

Please tell me **how** he incurred the injury.

6. **Adjective subordinate clauses containing an implied "that", "who", "which" or "why"**

我喜欢吃玛莉做的菜.

Wǒ xǐhuān chī Mǎlì zuò de cài.

I like to eat the foods **that** Mary prepares.

你看到那个戴著帽子的男人吗?

Nǐ kàndào nàge dài zhe màozi de nánrén ma?

Do you see that guy **who** is wearing a hat?

那栋他看中的房子已经卖给别人了.

Nà dòng tā kànzhòng de fángzi yǐjīng mài gěi biérén le.

The house, **which** he had his eyes on, has been sold to someone else.

Compound-Complex Sentences

A compound complex sentence has two or more independent co-ordinate clauses and one or more dependent clauses. It may be viewed as having a compound sentence component nested in a complex sentence platform, or having a complex sentence component nested in a compound sentence platform. The great physicist, Albert Einstein, once said, "Everything should be made as simple as possible, but not simpler." Therefore, you may wish to keep life simple and not wear out your brains and bewilder your listener by making super complicated sentences. You can always break down a compound-complex sentence into two or more shorter sentences. I will not drill you on constructing compound-complex sentences. I will just illustrate the structure of such sentences with a couple of examples.

1. "The phone rang while she was putting on her coat and the little boy was crying."

在她穿大衣而小男孩啼哭时, 电话响了.
Zài tā chuān dàyī ér xiǎo nánhái tíkū shí, diànhuà xiǎng le.

The platform is that of a complex sentence, with "电话响了 (diànhuà xiǎng le the phone rang)" as the main clause. "她穿大衣 (tā chuān dàyī she put on her coat)" and "小男孩啼哭 (xiǎo nánhái tíkū the little boy cried)" are two independent clauses that are joined together in a compound sentence structure. This is the subordinate component that tells us when the phone rang.

2. "He wanted me to stay, but I went home after eating the meal."

他要我留下, 但我吃完饭就回家去了.
Tā yào wǒ liúxià, dàn wǒ chī wán fàn jiù huíjiā qù le.

Here, the platform is that of a compound sentence, using 但 (dàn but) to join the two independent components. "他要我留下 (tā yào wǒ liúxià he wanted me to stay)" is a simple independent clause. The second independent component contains a complex structure in it. "我吃完饭 (wǒ chī wán fàn after I have eaten the meal)" is a subordinate clause that specifies the time for the action "回家去了 (huíjiā qù le went home)" in the main clause.

Exercise:

1. Please write down one simple sentence.

_____

_____ (pinyin)

2. Please complete the following two compound sentences.

_____ _____ 来了, 而且许多花都 _____ 了.

_____ lái le, érqiě xǔduō huā dōu _____le.

Spring has come, and many flowers are blooming.

菜 _____ _____ _____ , _____ _____ 我吃不下了.

Cài _____ _____, _____ wǒ chī bú xià le.

The food tastes very good, but I can't eat any more. (I'm full.)

3. Complete the following complex sentences.

_____ _____ _____ _____, 我就不去了.

_____ _____, wǒ jiù bú qù le.

If it rains, I won't go.

我 _____ _____ _____ 为什么她没有来.

Wǒ _____ _____ wèishénme tā méiyǒu lái.

I don't know why she did not come.

_____ _____ 她 _____ _____ 了, 所以她没有来.

_____ tā _____ le, suǒyǐ tā méiyǒu lái.

Because she was ill, therefore she did not come.

_____ _____他邀请我, 我是不会去的.

_____ tā yāoqǐng wǒ, wǒ shì búhuì qù de.

Unless he invites me, I won't be going.

他一 _____ _____, 就骂人.

Tā yī _____ , jiù mà rén.

Whenever he gets angry, he scolds people.

Answer:

1. Please write down one simple sentence.

我在写信.　　　I'm writing a letter.
Wǒ zài xiěxìn.

2. Please complete the following two compound sentences.

春天来了, <u>而且</u>许多花都开了.
Chūntiān lái le, érqiě xǔduō huā dōu kāi le.
Spring has come, and many flowers are blooming.

菜很好吃, <u>但是</u>我吃不下了.
Cài hěn hǎochī, dànshì wǒ chī bú xià le.
The food tastes very good, but I can't eat any more. (I'm full.)

3. Complete the following complex sentences.

<u>如果</u>下雨, 我<u>就</u>不去了.
Rúguǒ xiàyǔ, wǒ jiù bú qù le.
If it rains, I won't go.

我不知道<u>为什么</u>她没有来.
Wǒ bù zhīdào wèishénme tā méiyǒu lái.
I don't know why she did not come.

<u>因为</u>她生病了, <u>所以</u>她没有来.
Yīnwèi tā shēngbìng le, suǒ yǐ tā méiyǒu lái.
Because she got ill, therefore she did not come.

<u>除非</u>他邀请我, 我是<u>不会去的</u>.
Chúfēi tā yāoqǐng wǒ, wǒ shì búhuì qù de.
Unless he invites me, I will not be going.

他<u>一</u>生气, <u>就</u>骂人.
Tā yī shēngqì, jiù mà rén.
Whenever he gets angry, he scolds people.

25. Making Longer Sentences　　　307

Worried Man Blues (Traditional Song)

啊!每当我烦恼,
Ā! Měidāng wǒ fánnǎo,

我就唱这条歌呀.
Wǒ jiù chàng zhè tiáo gē ya.

每当我烦恼,
Měidāng wǒ fánnǎo,

我就唱这条歌.
Wǒ jiù chàng zhè tiáo gē.

啊!每当我烦恼,
Ā! Měidāng wǒ fánnǎo,

我就唱这条歌.
Wǒ jiù chàng zhè tiáo gē.

我一开口,
Wǒ yī kāi kǒu,

那烦恼就消失了.
Nà fánnǎo jiù xiāoshī liǎo.

It takes a worried man
(Ah, whenever I'm worried,)

To sing a worried song.
(I'd sing this song.)

It takes a worried man
(Whenever I'm worried,)

To sing a worried song.
(I'd sing this song.)

It takes a worried man
(Ah, whenever I'm worried,)

To sing a worried song.
(I'd sing this song.)

I'm worried now,
(As soon as I open my mouth,)

But I won't be worried long.
(That worry disappears.)

烦恼 (fánnǎo) will work both as an adjective and as a noun. 条 (tiáo strip), 支 (zhī branch), and 首 (shǒu head, chief) can all be used as a unit for songs.

这条歌
zhè tiáo gē
this song

这支歌
zhè zhi gē
this song

那首儿歌
nà shǒu érgē
that children's song (nursery rhyme)

一条歌
yī tiáo gē
one song

两支民谣
liǎng zhi mínyáo
two folk songs

三首摇滚乐曲
sān shǒu yáogǔn yuèqǔ
three pieces of rock'n'roll music

26. Punctuation

The correct placement of punctuation marks helps to clarify the meaning of a sentence. Use a period mark (.) to end each statement. Use a comma (,) to separate the clauses within a compound sentence or a complex sentence. A comma is also used to separate the items in a set of nouns, verbs, adjectives or adverbs. Use a semicolon (;) to separate two co-ordinate sentences. A question mark (?) denotes a question. Use the exclamation point (!) with interjections and for emphasis.

The following anecdote about a famous artist in ancient China underscores the importance of the proper use of the punctuation marks. Before his career took off, this artist often freeloaded at a relative's house and overstayed his welcome. One rainy evening, the artist came for dinner and clearly intended to stay overnight. His relative had had enough. To show class, this unwilling host did not confront the unwelcome houseguest. Instead, he hastily wrote a line in large characters on the wall of the living room when the artist went to the washroom. Then he went into another room, hoping that the artist would leave after seeing the note that read:

下雨天 留客 天留 我不留

Xiàyǔ tiān liú kè. Tiān liú, wǒ bù liú.
Hosting guest on a rainy day. The sky is willing, but not I.

When the hapless man returned to his living room, what did he see but the artist smiling at him and thanking him for his hospitality. Puzzled, he looked at the wall, and found that the artist had added punctuation marks to the note, turning it into a totally different message:

下雨天, 留客天. 留我不? 留.

Xiàyǔ tiān, liú kè tiān. Liú wǒ bù? Liú.
Rainy day, a day to host a guest. Keep me? Yes (Keep).

As an intransitive verb, 留 (liú) means to stay or remain at a place. For example, 留在家裡 (liú zài jiālǐ) means to stay at home. In the above story, 留 (liú) is used as a transitive verb in the sense of keeping someone or saving something. 留客 (liú kè) means to keep a guest at one's house. 留胡子 (liú húzi) means to grow and save a beard.

Please take note of the punctuation marks used in the following well-known Chinese story. In Chinese, a colon (:) is used instead of a comma before a direct quote.

矛盾 **Contradiction**
Máodùn

有一个人在街上卖兵器.
Yǒu yī ge rén zài jiē shàng mài bīngqì.
A peddler was selling hand weapons on the street (market).

他拿起一枝矛, 向路人说:
Tā ná qǐ yī zhī máo, xiàng lùrén shuō:
He picked up a spear and said to the passerby,

"我的矛最尖锐, 可以刺破任何盾."
"Wǒ de máo zuì jiānruì, kěyǐ cì pò rènhé dùn."
"My spears are the sharpest. They can pierce through any shield."

然后, 他放下矛, 拿起一个盾, 向路人说:
Ránhòu, tā fàng xià máo, ná qǐ yī ge dùn, xiàng lùrén shuō:
Then he put down the spear, picked up a shield and said to the passerby,

"我的盾最坚固, 可以阻挡任何矛."
"Wǒ de dùn zuì jiāngù, kěyǐ zǔdǎng rènhé máo."
"My shields are the sturdiest. They can stop any spear."

路人问:
Lùrén wèn:
The passerby asked,

"如果用你的矛刺你的盾, 会怎样?"
"Rúguǒ yòng nǐ de máo cì nǐ de dùn, huì zěnyàng?"
"What happens if you hurtle your spear against your shield?"

街 (jiē) is a street, and 路 (lù) or 马路 (mǎlù) is a road. 在街上 (zài jiē shàng) means on the street, and 在路上 (zài lù shàng) means on the road. 巷 (xiàng) means a lane or an alley. 在巷子里 (zài xiàngzi lǐ) means in a small alley.

Pedestrians are called 路人 (lùrén), 路上的人 (lù shàng de rén), 街上的人 (jiě shàng de rén), or 行人 (xíngrén a walking person).

兵器 (bīngqì) are weapons of war.

In ancient times, people used 矛 (máo spears) and 盾 (dùn shields) as weapons of war.

尖锐 (jiānruì) means pointed and sharp, acute or incisive. It can be used to describe an instrument or a piercing remark.

刺破 (zì pò) is to pierce through. 破 (pò) means broken or damaged.

任何 (rènhé) means any or whatever. 任何人 (rènhé rén) means anybody, and 任何事 (rènhé shì) means any matter or anything.

坚固 (jiāngù) means firm and sturdy. 坚固的信念 (jiāngù de xìnniàn) is a firm belief or conviction.

阻挡 (zǔdǎng) means to stop or to obstruct. Both 阻 (zǔ) and 挡 (dǎng) mean to hinder or to block.

As this story illustrates, when you pit the best 矛 (máo spears) aginst the best 盾 (dùn shields), you would get a contradiction. 矛盾 (máodùn) is the word for contradiction, self-confliction, contradictory, or conflicting.

When you hear someone make a contradictory statement, you could say,

"这就矛盾了."
Zhè jiù máodùn le.
"This is self-conflicting."

Following are a couple more examples:

"他说的话前后矛盾."
"Tā shuō de huà qián hòu máodùn."
"His words contradict what he has said before."

"他又爱她, 又恨她. 真矛盾."
"Tā yòu ài tā, yòu hèn tā. Zhēn máodùn."
"He loves her and hates her at the same time. This is self-conflicting."

矛盾 (máodùn) is also used to indicate that one is in a dilemma, or torn between two conflicting choices. For instance:

"我想去看电影, 但明天要考试. 真矛盾."
"Wǒ xiǎng qù kàn diànyǐng, dàn míngtiān yào kǎoshì. Zhēn máodùn."
"I want to go to the movies, but there is an exam tomorrow. I'm torn."

Can you make a sentence containing the word 矛盾 (máodùn)?

How to Answer a Question

How you answer a question depends on how the question is posed. You might encounter the following types of questions.

1. Open questions

Open-ended questions really put your language ability to the test.

Question	Answer
他为什么没来? Tā wèishénme méi lái? Why did he not come?	他不舒服. Tā bù shūfu. He did not feel well.
她到花园去做什么? Tā dào huāyuán qù zuò shénme? What did she go to the garden for?	她去看花. Tā qù kàn huā. She went to enjoy the flowers.
这句话什么意思? Zhè jù huà shénme yìsī? What's the meaning of this sentence?	我不知道. Wǒ bù zhīdào. I don't know.

2. Questions that offer a choice

With such questions, simply pick the appropriate option.

Question	Answer		
你喜欢蓝的, 还是绿的? Nǐ xǐhuān lán de, háishi lǜ de? Do you like the blue or the green one?	蓝的. Lán de. The blue one.	*or*	绿的. Lǜ de. The green one.
你要不要吃西瓜? Nǐ yào bú yào chī xīguā? Do you care to eat some watermelon?	要. Yào. I would like to.	*or*	不要. 谢谢. Búyào. Xièxiè. No, thanks.

3. Questions that call for an affirmative or negative answer

When asked, "Will it rain to morrow?" in English, you would usually answer "Yes" or "No". With Chinese, the "Yes" and "No" are typically omitted. You would directly address the subject matter instead. If there is an auxiliary verb in the question, as in the first example below, then use that auxiliary verb to reply.

Question	Answer		
明天会下雨吗?	会.	*or*	不会.
Míngtiān huì xiàyǔ ma?	Huì.		Búhuì.
Will it rain tomorrow?	It will.		It won't.
你懂吗?	我懂.	*or*	我不懂.
Nǐ dǒng ma?	Wǒ dǒng.		Wǒ bù dǒng.
Do you understand?	I understand.		I don't.
他高兴吗?	高兴.	*or*	不高兴.
Tā gāoxìng ma?	Gāoxìng.		Bù gāoxìng.
Is he pleased?	He is pleased.		He's not pleased.
那是他的吗?	是.	*or*	不是.
Nà shì tā de ma?	Shì.		Búshì.
Is that his?	It is.		It's not.

In the last question above, the main verb is 是 (shì to be). Therefore, the answers correspond to "It is." and "It's not.", rather than "Yes." and "No.".

4. Questions that don't require an answer

Some "questions" are simply disapproving remarks in disguise.

Question	Answer
你怎么这样傻?	(Shrug.)
Nǐ zěnme zhèyàng shǎ?	
Why are you so gullible (foolish)?	

Exercise:

1. Please form question and answer pairs using the following pattern:

那只老虎很奇怪. 它没有眼睛.
Nà zhī lǎohǔ hěn qíguài. Tā méiyǒu yǎnjing.
That tiger is strange. It does not have eyes.

<u>为什么</u>那只老虎很奇怪?
Wèishénme nà zhī lǎohǔ hěn qíguài?
Why is that tiger strange?

<u>因为</u>它没有眼睛.
Yīnwèi tā méiyǒu yǎnjing.
Because it does not have eyes.

小猴子吱吱叫. 它肚子饿.
Xiǎo hóuzi zīzī jiào. Tā dùzi è.
The little monkey squeaks. It is hungry.

_____

_____ (pinyin)

_____

_____ (pinyin)

下雨了. 大家都在跑.
Xiàyǔ le. Dàjiā dōu zài pǎo.
It's raining. Everyone is running.

_____

_____ (pinyin)

_____

_____ (pinyin)

26. Punctuation   315

他怕冷. 他穿大衣. He tends to get cold. He wears an overcoat.
Tā pà lěng. Tā chuān dàyī.

_____

_____ (pinyin)

_____

_____ (pinyin)

Now, try to make a question-answer pair of your own.

_____

_____ (pinyin)

_____

_____ (pinyin)

2. Please add the proper punctuation marks to the following text.

啊为什么你掉眼泪
Ā Wèishénme nǐ diào yǎnlèi
Ah why are you weeping

要不是我们就要分开我眼泪不会掉下
Yàobúshì wǒ mén jiù yào fēnkāi wǒ yǎnlèi bú huì diào xià
Were it not that we are parting soon my tears would not be falling down

Answer:

1. Question and answer pairs

为什么小猴子吱吱叫?
Wèishénme xiǎo hóuzi zīzī jiào?
Why does the little monkey squeak?

因为它肚子饿.
Yīnwèi tā dùzi è.
Because it is hungry.

为什么大家都在跑?
Wèishénme dàjiā dōu zài pǎo?
Why is everyone running?

因为下雨了.
Yīnwèi xiàyǔ le.
Because it's raining.

为什么他穿大衣?
Wèishénme tā chuān dàyī?
Why does he wear an overcoat?

因为他怕冷.
Yīnwèi tā pà lěng.
Because he tends to get cold.

2. Punctuation marks

啊! 为什么你掉眼泪?
Ā! Wèishénme nǐ diào yǎnlèi?
Ah! Why are you weeping?

要不是我们就要分开, 我眼泪不会掉下.
Yàobúshì wǒmen jiùyào fēnkāi, wǒ yǎnlèi búhuì diào xià.
Were it not that we are parting soon, my tears would not be falling down.

26. Punctuation

27. Familiar Expressions

Every Chinese character (字 zì) is a word with a given meaning. For example, 大 (dà) means large or big, 中 (zhōng) means middle or medium, and 小 (xiǎo) means small.

Some Chinese characters have multiple meanings, each with its own intonation. Such words are called 破音字 (pò yīn zì split-sound words). For example:

好 hǎo (adj)　　　　　　**good, nice**

好吃 delicious　　　　好玩 fun　　　　好睡 comfortable
hǎochī　　　　　　　hǎowán　　　　hǎoshuì (for sleeping)

好　hào (v.)　　　　　　**to like to, to be fond of**

好吃 gluttonous　　　好玩 fun-loving　好睡 fond of
hàochī　　　　　　　hàowán　　　　hàoshuì sleeping

好吃懒做 (hàochī-lǎnzuò) is to be gluttonous and lazy.

种　zhǒng　(n.) seed, a kind of

种子 seed　　　　这种 this kind of 种种 all kinds of
zhǒngzi　　　　　zhèzhǒng　　　zhǒngzhǒng

种　zhòng　(v.)　to plant

种花 to plant flowers 种树 to plant trees 种田 to farm
zhòng huā　　　　zhòng shù　　　zhòngtián

量 **liáng (verb)**   **to measure**

测量 survey land   量体重 take body weight
cèliàng   liáng tǐzhòng

量 **liàng (noun)**   **quantity**

力量 strength   重量 weight   大量 copious
lìliàng   zhòngliàng   dàliàng

了 **le**   **(an auxiliary word)**

吃饭了! Time to eat!   不见了. It has disappeared.
Chīfan le!   Bújiàn le.

了 **liǎo**   **understand, being outstanding, finish**

了解 comprehend   了不起 extraordinary, amazing
liǎojiě   liǎobùqǐ

不得了 disastrous (adj.), exceedingly (adv.)
bùdéliǎo

更 **gèng**   **more, still more, even more**

更好 better   更多 more   更大 bigger
gènghǎo   gèng duō   gèng dà

更 **gēng**   **to change, to replace; one of the five 2-hour periods into which the night was divided in the past**

更换 replace   更改 alter   半夜三更 midnight
gēnghuàn   gēnggǎi   bànyèsāngēng
     (third period in the night)

Many Chinese terms (字詞 zìcí) are made up of two or more characters. They may be referred to as polysyllable words. A few examples are shown below. You can easily find additional examples from your own Chinese vocabulary notebook.

战争 zhànzhēng	war	战火 zhànhuǒ	war flame
燃起 ránqǐ	flare up	出征 chūzhēng	go to battle
上尉 shàngwèi	captain	求情 qiúqíng	beg for mercy
下跪 xiàguì	kneel down	嫌贵 xián guì	consider something to be too costly
星星 xīngxīng	star	亮晶晶 liàngjīngjīng	glistening
钻石 zuànshí	diamond	天顶 tiāndǐng	zenith
开玩笑 kāiwánxiào	to joke	笑眯眯 xiàomīmī	smiling
气呼呼 qìhūhū	sulking	兴冲冲 xìngchōngchōng	exulted, with joy
热呼呼 rèhūhū	warm	傻呼呼 sǎhūhū	simple-minded
脏兮兮 zāngxīxī	dirty, unclean	小气兮兮 xiǎoqìxīxī	stingy
醉醺醺 zuìxūnxūn	drunk	心脏病 xīnzàngbìng	heart disease

27. Familiar Expressions

321

With the following traditional song, pay special attention to the polysyllable words.

Cruel War
残酷的战争
Cánkù de Zhànzhēng

那战火又燃起,
Nà **zhànhuǒ** yòu **ránqǐ**,

The cruel war is raging,
(The **war flames** are **ignited** again,)

而强尼要出征.
Ér Qiángní yào **chūzhēng**.

And Johnny has to fight.
(And Johnny has to **go out to battle**.)

我要同他一起,
Wǒ yào tóng tā **yīqǐ**,

I want to be with him
(I want to be with him **together**)

从清早到三更.
Cóng **xīngzǎo** dào **sāngēng**.

From morning 'till night.
(From **early morning** to **mid-night**.)

我去见你上尉,
Wǒ qù jiàn nǐ **shàngwèi**,

I'll go to your captain,

向他求情, 下跪.
Xiàng tā **qiúqíng, xiàguì**.

Get down upon my knees.
(**Plead for mercy** and **kneel down**.)

要一万块金币,
Yào yī wàn kuài **jīnbì**,

Ten thousand gold guineas
(Even if it takes 10,000 **gold coins**,)

我都不会嫌贵.
Wǒ dōu **búhuì xián guì**.

I'd give for your release.
(I still **won't deem it too dear**.)

This popular children's song uses an old French melody and the lyric adapted from "The Star" (a poem written by Jane Taylor).

Twinkle, Twinkle, Little Star
星空 (Starry Sky)
Xīng Kōng

一闪, 一闪, 小星星.
Yī shǎn, **yī shǎn**, xiǎo **xīngxīng**.

Twinkle, twinkle, little star.
Twinkle, **twinkle**, little **star**.

谁能猜透你的心?
Shéi néng **cāi tòu** nǐ de xīn?

How I wonder what you are.
Who can claim to **know** your heart?

高高在上, 亮晶晶,
Gāogāo zài shàng, **liàngjīngjīng**,

Up above a way so high,
Way up high, and **glistening bright**,

好像钻石镶天顶.
Hǎoxiàng zuànshí xiāng **tiāndǐng**.

Like a diamond in the sky.
Like a **diamond** set in the **sky**.

一闪, 一闪, 小星星.
Yī shǎn, **yī shǎn**, xiǎo **xīngxīng**.

Twinkle, twinkle, little star.
Twinkle, twinkle, little **star**.

谁能猜透你的心?
Shéi néng **cāi tòu** nǐ de xīn?

How I wonder what you are.
Who can claim to **know** your heart?

猜 (cāi) means "to guess". 透 (tòu) means "seeping through" or "penetrating".

Here, 猜透 (cāi tòu) can be translated as "see through", "discern", or "know perfectly".

镶 (xiāng) is to inlay a precious metal or to mount a jewel onto some substrate.

Note the radial, 金 (jīn gold, metal), on the left side of this word.

A number of English words have been incorporated into modern Chinese. You have already encountered a few of the Chinese transliterations shown below:

巴士 bus
bāshì

坦克 tank
tǎnkè (vehicle)

摩托车 motorcycle
mótuōchē

的士 taxi
díshì

马达 motor
mǎdá

雷达 radar
léidá

雷射 LASER
léishè

派对 party
pàiduì

吉他 guitar
jítā

迷你 mini
mínǐ

咖啡 coffee
kāfēi

巧克力 chocolate
qiǎokèlì

雪茄 cigar
xuějiā

沙拉 salad
shālā

小苏打 baking soda
xiǎosūdǎ

盎士 ounce
àngshì

磅 pound
bàng

米 meter
mǐ

拜拜 bye-bye
báibái

维他命 vitamin
wéitāmìn

X 光 x-ray
àikēsīguāng

Most Chinese transliterations of English words are a collection of Chinese characters that sound similar to the English words. They do not have meaningful connotations in Chinese. However, there are some exceptions, where the ingenious choice of Chinese characters has created words that also make sense in Chinese. For example, "mini", as in "mini-skirts", is translated as 迷你 (mínǐ). 迷 (mí) means to enchant or to fascinate. Therefore, 迷你裙 (mínǐ qún mini-skirts) is a skirt that is supposed to fascinate you. Another good one is 维他命 (wéitāmìng), which is the word for vitamins. 维 (wéi) means to protect or maintain. 他 (tā) represents a person. 命 (mìng) means "life" or "fate". Therefore, 维他命 (wéitāmìng vitamin) aptly represents something that helps maintain one's life (or health).

Following are some common phrases 片语 (piànyǔ) and expressions that you might hear in everyday speech.

哎呀! Āiyā!	Oh! Wow!
真好! 太好了! Zhēn hǎo! Tài hǎo le!	Wonderful! Great!
好了! 好啦! Hǎo le! Hǎo lā!	Done! Finished!
这下可好了! Zhè xià kě hǎo le!.	Well, now what! What a fine mess (sarcastically).
天呀! 天啊! 我的天! Tiān yā! Tiān ā! Wǒ de tiān!	Heavens! Goodness, gracious!
我的老天爷! Wǒ de lǎotiānyé!	Good heavens!
要命! Yàomìng!	Awful! Terrible! Confounded! (It'll drive one to his death.)
救命呀! 救人呀! Jiùmìng yā! Jiù rén yā!	Help! (Save my life! Save a person!)
糟糕! 糟了! Zāogāo! Zāo le!	Oh-oh, too bad, darned! (all messed up)
我完了! Wǒ wán le!	I'm doomed. (I'm finished.)
怎么了? 怎么啦? Zěnme le? Zěnme lā?	What's the matter?

怎么办?	What shall I (we) do?
Zěnme bàn?	
怎么样?	How was it? How about it?
Zěnmeyàng?	What do you think?
不可思议.	Inconceivable; crazy.
Bùkěsīyì.	
有道理.	It makes sense.
Yǒu dàolǐ.	
岂有此理!	Preposterous!
Qǐyǒuzǐlǐ!	
毫不讲理.	Totally unreasonable; crazy.
Háo bù jiǎnglǐ.	(cannot be reasoned with)
算了; 算了吧.	Forget it; never mind; let it go.
Suàn le; suàn le ba.	
对不起. 抱歉.	Excuse me. I'm sorry.
Duìbùqǐ. Bàoqiàn.	
没关系.	It doesn't matter; never mind.
Méiguānxi.	
不要紧.	It doesn't matter; it's not serious.
Búyàojǐn.	
没问题.	No problem.
Méiwèntí.	
我不管!	I don't care!
Wǒ bù guǎn!	

讨厌!
Tǎoyàn!

Disgusting! Annoying!

火大
Huǒ dà

furious (like a blazing fire)

气死人!
Qì sǐ rén!

Infuriating! (familiar form)
(I'm so mad I could die.)

气坏人! 真气人!
Qì huài rén!   Zhēn qì rén!

Outrageous! (more polite form)

真是的!
Zhēnshì de!

Goodness! Really! I'd say!
(reproachful, or displeased)

你怎么搞的!
Nǐ zěnme gǎo de!

What's wrong with you!
(You've messed up.)

你看! 都是你! 都怪你!
Nǐ kàn! Dōu shì nǐ! Dōu guài nǐ!

Look! It's all because of you!
(You are to blame.)

赖皮
Làipí

not playing by the rule, not fair,
acting like a rascal (accusative)

废话.   胡說.
Fèihuà.   Húshuō.

Rubbish. Non-sense.

甭想!   梦想!
Béng xiǎng! Mèngxiǎng!

Don't even think about it.
You're dreaming!

作梦.   作白日梦.
Zuòmèng.   Zuò bái rì mèng.

Don't even think about it.
(Dream or day-dream all you want.)

做什么? 什么事?
Zuò shénme? Shénme shì?

What do you want? What's up?
(neutral, agreeable)

干什么! Gàn shénme!	What do you want (disgusted)! What are you doing (disgusted)!
吹牛 Chuīniú	to boast, to brag, or to talk big (to blow one's own horn)
等著瞧. Děng zhe qiáo.	Let's wait and see. Just wait and see.
不客气. Búkèqì.	You're welcome. Don't mention it. (Don't be courteous.)
不用了. 不必了. Búyòng le. Búbì le.	That's okay; never mind. Forget it. (It's not necessary.)
糊里糊涂 Húlǐhútú	confused; muddle-headed
吃了豹胆 Chī le bào dǎn	unjustifiably bold, foolhardy (as if one had eaten a panther's gall bladder)
鸡蛋里挑骨头. Jīdàn lǐ tiāo gǔtóu.	Extremely picky (looking for bones in an egg).
奉承 (拍马屁) Fèngchéng (pāimǎpì)	to flatter, toady to, or fawn upon (lick somebody's boots)
得寸進尺. Dé cùn jìn chǐ.	Give him an inch and he takes a foot.
小不补, 大尺五. Xiǎo bù bǔ, dà chǐ wǔ.	A stitch in time saves nine. (If not mended when small, it'll grow to a foot and a half.)
各式各样 Gè shì gè yàng	all styles and sorts (of something)

一模一样　　　　　　　　exactly alike
Yīmúyīyàng　　　　　　　(as if coming out of the same mold)

一时一刻　　　　　　　　for a single moment (usually in "not
Yīshí-yīkè　　　　　　　doing something for a single moment")

时时刻刻　　　　　　　　at every moment, constantly
Shíshí-kèkè

Exercise - Using Expressions

Draw a line to match each situation with the appropriate Chinese expression. Please refer to the previous pages to find the expression that you need.

Someone spilled coffee on your shirt.
To be nice, you would say:

讨厌!
Tǎoyàn!

Your mother wants you to fix a problem
before it gets worse. She says:

做什么?
Zuò shénme?

Your kid brother keeps bothering you.
You are frustrated, and say:

不要紧.
Búyàojǐn.

Your father announces that the family will go
to Mexico for the summer vacation. You exclaim:

我完了!
Wǒ wán le!

You hear your sister calling you from
upstairs. You ask:

小不补, 大尺五.
Xiǎo bù bǔ, dà chǐ wǔ.

You find out there is a test in the afternoon,
but you are not prepared. You mutter:

有道理.
Yǒu dàolǐ.

The building is on fire. You run outside
and scream:

救命呀! 失火了!
Jiùmìng yā! Shīhuǒ le!

Your elder brother tells you that you should
Measure the board before sawing. You say:

太好了!
Tài hǎo le!

Answer:

Someone spilled coffee on your shirt.
To be nice, you would say:

不要紧.
Búyàojǐn.

Your mother wants you to fix a problem
before it gets worse. She says:

小不补, 大尺五.
Xiǎo bù bǔ, dà chǐ wǔ.

Your kid brother keeps bothering you.
You are frustrated, and say:

讨厌!
Tǎoyàn!

Your father announces that the family will go
to Mexico for the summer vacation. You exclaim:

太好了!
Tài hǎo le!

You hear your sister calling you from
upstairs. You ask:

做什么?
Zuò shénme?

You find out there is a test in the afternoon,
but you are not prepared. You mutter:

我完了!
Wǒ wán le!

The building is on fire. You run outside
and scream:

救命呀! 失火了!
Jiùmìng yā! Shīhuǒ le!

Your elder brother tells you that you should
Measure the board before sawing it. You say:

有道理.
Yǒu dàolǐ.

28. Chinese Idioms

Idioms are pre-packaged thoughts, descriptions, observations or statements of fact. Each idiomatic phrase may take on a deeper meaning than that imparted by the individual words. For instance, suppose someone translates "hit the sack" literally into Chinese. Then when it is translated back to English, it may have turned into: "beat up the bag".

In ancient China, there was a Duke of Zhou who served as regent for the son of his deceased brother, King Wu of the Zhou Dynasty, until the young king was ready to rule. The Duke of Zhou defeated the young king's brothers who sought to usurp the throne. He also set up a system of government that helped restore order in the kingdom. In addition, he wrote many poems, which later greatly influenced the philosophy of Master Confucius. The Duke of Zhou is highly respected and idolized by the Chinese people, not only for his wisdom and military triumphs, but also for completing the classic canon, "I Ching" (The Book of Changes), for establishing the Rites of Zhou, and for his important contributions to Chinese classical music. The Duke of Zhou has also become a mythical figure among the Chinese folks who believe that he will visit them in a dream to give them a sign of any major event that is about to happen to them. In present days, 见周公 (jiàn Zhōu Gōng meeting with Master Zhou) is a humorous way of saying: "going to sleep" or "hitting the sack". For example:

我要去见周公了.   I'm ready to hit the sack.
Wǒ yào qù jiàn Zhōu Gōng le.

Idioms are used extensively in the written as well as the spoken Chinese language. Many of the Chinese idioms 成语 (chéngyǔ) are phrases borrowed from classical Chinese. These are terse expressions typically made up of four characters. Each packet of words may invoke an image, a feeling, a familiar situation or an entire story.

The following lists represent but a small sample of the commonly used Chinese idioms. Select a few Chinese idioms that you like and learn them by heart. Then launch them at the appropriate moments to impress your Chinese friends.

As you can see below, there are many Chinese idioms that contain numbers.

一针见血
yī zhēn jiàn xuě

Hit the nail on the head. (One poke with the needle draws blood - said of a poignant remark.)

一心一意
yī xīn yī yì

heart and soul; whole-heartedly

一刀两断
yī dāo liǎng duàn

make a clean break; break up with
(sever into two with one cut)

一鼻孔出气
yī bíkǒng chū qì

singing the same tune, siding with someone
(breathing through the same nostril)

一干二净
yī gān èr jìng

thoroughly, completely
(spic-'n-span, squeaky clean)

一不做, 二不休.
Yī bú zuò, èr bù xiū.

being determined to go all the way
(One either doesn't start, or one goes all the way.)

三番两次
sān fān liǎng cì

repeatedly (thrice and twice)

四分五裂
sì fēn wǔ liè

to be broken into pieces, or totally disintegrated
(divided into four and split into five)

七手八脚
qī shǒu bā jiǎo

everyone scrambling together to do something
(seven hands and eight feet pitching in)

半斤八两
bàn jīn bā liǎng

half a pound and eight ounces
(Two of a kind. Neither is better.)

八九不离十
bā jiǔ bù lí shí

pretty close, most likely, 80%-90% correct
(about 8 and 9, not far from 10)

十全十美
shí quán shí měi

perfect in every way

千真万确　　　　　　　absolutely true
qiàn zhēn wàn què　　　(1,000 times true and 10,000 times accurate)

The following idioms describe the manner of doing things.

开门见山　　　　　　　going straight to the point
kāimén jiàn shān　　　　(Open the door and see the mountain right away.)

手忙脚乱　　　　　　　running in circles, frantically
shǒu máng jiǎo luàn　　(busy hands and feet in a muddle)

有板有眼　　　　　　　in an orderly or methodical way
yǒu bǎn yǒu yǎn　　　　(like playing on the frets or open strings
　　　　　　　　　　　of a musical instrument)

有声有色　　　　　　　with a bang (full of sounds and colors)
yǒu shēng yǒu sè

分工合作　　　　　　　cooperate; collaborate by division of labor
fēngōng hézuò

同心协力　　　　　　　with one heart, joining efforts, working together
tóng xīn xié lì

同流合污　　　　　　　gang up with shady people and go with the flow
tóng liú hé wū

愚公移山　　　　　　　using a laborious, ineffective method,
yú gōng yí shān　　　　like a foolish old man trying to move a mountain,
　　　　　　　　　　　one shovel at a time

Here are a few idioms that relate to time or timing.

光阴似箭　　　　　　　Time flies (like an arrow).
guāngyīn sì jiàn

铁树开花   Once in a blue moon; not in a thousand years.
tiěshù kāihuā   (when the iron tree blooms)

生米煮成熟饭.   What's done cannot be undone. Too late.
Shēng mǐ zhǔ chéng shú fàn.   (The rice has been cooked. The milk has spilled.)

Many Chinese idioms refer to animals. For example, ask somebody,
"您近来好吗? (Nín jìnlái hǎo ma? How have you been recently?)", you may
get the perfunctory reply, "马马虎虎. (Mǎmǎ-hūhū. Horse, horse, tiger, tiger -
nothing special. So, so." 马马虎虎 (mǎmǎ-hūhū) also means passable, careless,
or doing things in a splash-dash manner. When used in this sense, it can be
expressed as: 马虎 (mǎhu). For example:

他做事很马虎.   He does things carelessly.
Tā zuò shì hěn mǎhu.

According to a folk legend, once upon a time, an artist was hired to paint a dragon
on a pillar at a newly erected temple. Many people stood around to watch this man
paint the colorful body of the dragon wrapped around the tall pillar. They oohed and
aahed as the artist detailed the dragon's flamboyant head. Finally, the artist stepped
back to examine his work. He then carefully aimed his brush and dotted the dragon's
eyes. All of a sudden, the dragon swooshed into the sky, leaving everyone behind in
total amazement. This is the story behind the following idiom, which sums up the
fact that adding the proper finishing touch can have a fantastic effect on a work or a
project.

画龙点睛   to add the crucial finishing touch (like dotting the
huà lóng diǎn jīng   eyes of a painted dragon to bring it to life)

Another story tells of a man participating in a brush-painting competition. He
painstakingly painted a true-to-life snake that seemed ready to slither away at any
moment. Quite pleased with his work, he looked around and saw that the other
artists were still busy working on their projects, none of which promised to be a
winner like the snake that he had painted. With extra time on hand, he smugly

proceeded to enhance his painting. When the judges announced the winner, it was not this man. The judges were impressed with this man's artistic skills, but, alas, they had never seen a snake with feet before. The moral of this story is to leave well enough alone. It is captured in the following idiom:

画蛇添足
huà shé tiān zú

to mess up by adding or doing something unnecessary (like adding feet to a painted snake)

Following are a few additional idioms that involve various kinds of animals.

一石二鸟
yī shí èr niǎo

killing two birds with one stone

一箭双雕
yī jiàn shuāng diāo

shooting two hawks with one arrow

一马当先
yī mǎ dāng xiān

take the lead; be in the forefront (like the leading horse)

马不停蹄
mǎ bù tíng tí

nonstop (like a galloping horse); very busy

骑虎难下
qí hǔ nán xià

hard to back down (or get off a tiger's back)

狼吞虎咽
láng tūn hǔ yàn

to wolf down (to swallow like a wolf and gobble like a tiger)

虎头蛇尾
hǔ tóu shé wěi

a job with a good start but poorly finished (with a tiger's head but a snake's tail)

打草惊蛇
dǎ cǎo jīng shé

act rashly, alerting one's adversary (beating the grass and disturbing the snake)

如鱼得水
rú yú dé shuǐ

to be in one's element, like a fish in water

亡羊补牢
wáng yáng bǔ láo

too late (like mending the pen after having lost the sheep).

狗眼看人低
gǒu yǎn kàn rén dī

damned snobbish (like a dog looking down upon the wretched)

猫哭老鼠
māo kū lǎoshǔ

the cat grieving for the rat (crocodile tears)

The following idioms all start with 不 (bù not) or 没 (méi without).

不打自招
bù dǎ zì zhāo

to confess without duress, or to admit inadvertently

不请自来
bù qǐng zì lái

self-invited (not necessarily welcome)

不大不小
bú dà bù xiǎo

just the right size (not too large, not too small)

没大没小
méi dà méi xiǎo

disrespectful (not minding one's elders)

不知不觉
bù zhī bù jué

unwittingly, unknowingly, unawares

不闻不问
bù wén bú wèn

to be unconcerned (not bothering to listen or to ask)

Here are a few more miscellaneous idioms. If you would like to learn additional ones, please pick up a book on Chinese idioms.

心想事成
xīn xiǎng shì chéng

All wishes come true. (All wishes are fulfilled.)

胡思乱想
hú sī luàn xiǎng

to let one's thoughts run wild (to imagine things)

28. Chinese Idioms

胆大包天
dǎndà bāo tiān

bold; audacious (with a gall bladder large enough to encompass the sky)

隔墙有耳
gé qiáng yǒu ěr

Walls have ears. (There are ears next-door, on the other side of the wall.)

以牙还牙
yǐ yá huán yá

A tooth for a tooth. Retaliation. (Use a tooth to repay a tooth.)

落井下石
luò jǐng xià shí

Add injury to insult. (to drop stone onto a perosn who has fallen into a well)

How would you go about using these idioms in a conversation? Generally, you can precede many of the idioms with an introduction, as shown in the following examples. You could also blurt out such self-contained idioms without any introduction.

这可以說是: "一石二鸟."
Zhè kěyǐ shuō shì: "Yī shí èr niǎo."
One could say this is like "killing two birds with one stone".

这叫作: "亡羊补牢."
Zhè jiào zuò: "Wáng yáng bǔ láo."
This is called "mending the fence after the sheep is gone".

俗话說: "一不做, 二不休."
Sú huà shuō: "Yī bú zuò, èr bù xiū."
As the saying goes, "Either you don't start it, or you go all the way."

Some idioms are more appropriately used as descriptive phrases, as in the following examples:

这件衣服不大不小, 正好.
Zhè jiàn yīfu bú dà bù xiǎo, zhènghǎo.
This garment is not too big and not too small, just right.

他们手忙脚乱地把她抬到医院.

Tāmen shǒu máng jiǎo luàn de bǎ tā tái dào yīyuàn.

They frantically carried her to the hospital.

他们做事马马虎虎.

Tāmen zuòshì mǎmǎ-hūhū.

They do things rather haphazardly.

Some idioms are action phrases, and you would simply use them like verbs.

不要胡思乱想.

Búyào hú sī luàn xiǎng.

Don't imagine things (and trouble yourself needlessly).

Following are the first two stanzas of a British ballad that's fun to sing.

Stewball

司都伯是匹好马,

Sīdūbó shì pǐ hǎo mǎ,

Stewball was a good horse.

他趾高气扬;

Tā zhǐ gāo qì yáng;

He held a high head;

(He strut about and **gave himself airs**.)

而他头上的鬃毛

Ér tā tóu shàng dē zōng máo,

And the mane on his foretop

(And the mane on his head)

就像银丝一样.

Jiòu xiàng yín sī yīyàng.

Was as fine as silk thread.

(Was **same as** silver thread.)

我带它去伦敦,

Wǒ dài tā qù Lúndūn,

I took him to London,

和其他赛马场.

Hé qītā sàimǎ chǎng.

Dublin and Budapest.

(And other **horse race tracks**.)

他每回得冠军,
Tā měi huí dé guànjūn,

Always winning the first place,
(**Each time** he was the **champion**.)

是天下第一棒.
Shì tiānxià dìyī bàng.

He was really the best.
(He's **the best under the sky**.)

趾高气扬 (zhǐ gāo qì yáng) is a way of saying "cocky". The literal translation is "with toes held high and spirits soaring". 神氣 (shénqì) has a similar meaning.

冠军, 亞军, 殿军 (guànjūn, yàjūn, diànjūn) correspond to the first place (champion), runner-up, and the last place, respectively.

第一棒 (dìyī bàng the first baton) refers to the first (and best) runner in a relay race, in which a baton is passed from one runner to the next. When people use this expression in praise of someone, they usually hold up their thumb to accentuate their point. The interjection "棒! (Bàng!)" means "Neat!" or "Great!"

Exercise in Making Rhymes

Try making a rhyme in Chinese that corresponds to the English verse. Feel free to change the English to anything that makes sense. It would be nice if you can make the Chinese verse rhyme.

司都伯是匹好马,
Sīdūbó shì pǐ hǎo mǎ,

Stewball was a good horse.

And I wish he were mine.

He never drank water.

He always drank wine.

Answer:

Following are a couple possibilities.

司都伯是匹好马.   Stewball was a good horse.
Sīdūbó shì pǐ hǎo mǎ.

每人都想拥有.   That everyone wanted to own.
Měirén dōu xiǎng yōngyǒu.

他从来不喝水；   He never drank water.
Tā cónglái bù hē shuǐ;

他只喝葡萄酒.   He always drank wine.
Tā zhǐ hē pútáojiǔ.   (He only drank wine.)

司都伯是匹好马.   Stewball was a good horse.
Sīdūbó shì pǐ hǎo mǎ.

他是我的朋友.   And a good friend of mine.
Tā shì wǒ de péngyǒu.

他从来不喝水；   He never drank water.
Tā cónglái bù hē shuǐ;

他只喝葡萄酒.   He only drank wine.
Tā zhǐ hē pútáojiǔ.

29. Names of Places

As with people's names, the English names of places can only be approximated in Chinese. As you can see in the following examples, some translations are based on the meaning of the English words.

海洋 hǎiyáng Oceans and Seas

太平洋	Tàipíngyáng	The Pacific Ocean
大西洋	Dàxīyáng	The Atlantic Ocean
印度洋	Yìndùyáng	The Indian Ocean
爱琴海	Àiqínhǎi	The Aegean Sea
地中海	Dìzhōnghǎi	The Mediterranean Sea

洲 zhōu Continents

北美洲	Běiměizhōu	North America
南美洲	Nánměizhōu	South America
亚洲	Yàzhōu	Asia
澳洲	Aùzhōu	Australia
欧洲	Ōuzhōu	Europe
非洲	Fēizhōu	Africa
南极洲	Nánjízhōu	Antarctica

河流 héliú **Rivers**

密西西比河	Mìxīxībǐhé	The Mississippi River
哥伦比亚河	Gēlúnbǐyàhé	The Columbia River
长江	Chángjiāng	The Long River

国家 guójiā **Countries**

巴西	Bāxī	Brazil
加拿大	Jiānádà	Canada
印度	Yìndù	India
埃及	Āijí	Egypt
荷兰	Hélán	The Netherlands (Holland)
墨西哥	Mòxīgē	Mexico
挪威	Nuówēi	Norway
西班牙	Xībānyá	Spain
联合国	Liánhéguó	The United Nations

Historically, China has considered itself the center of the world, hence the name: 中国 (Zhōngguó), where 中 (zhōng) means the center or the middle.

The full name for the United States of America is: 美利坚合众国 (Měilìjiān Hézhòngguó). Aren't you glad you can just say, 美国 (Měiguó) instead? As 美 (měi) means beautiful, 美国 (Měiguó) can be interpreted as "a beautiful country".

州 zhōu   **States in the USA**

加州	Jiāzhōu	California State
肯塔基州	Kěntǎjīzhōu	Kentucky State
美茵州	Měiyīnzhōu	Maine State
纽约州	Niǔyuē zhōu	New York State
俄勒冈州	Èlègāngzhōu	Oregon State
德州	Dézhōu	Texas State
犹他州	Yóutāzhōu	Utah State
华盛顿州	Huáshèngdùnzhōu	Washington State
华府 (华盛顿)	Huáfǔ (Huáshèngdùn)	Washington, D.C.

府 (fǔ) means seat of government or official residence.

How would you say "Kentucky Fried Chicken" in Chinese? The answer is:
肯塔基烤鸡 (Kěntǎjī kǎojī). You may find this mnemonic for "Kentucky"
helpful: 啃他鸡 (kěntǎjī), which means: "Munch on his chicken."

Cities are called 都市 (dūshì). Capitals are called 首都 (shǒudū) or 首府
(shǒufǔ). 首 (shǒu head) is the formal word for 头 (tóu head), and represents
"first", "top", "main" or "chief".

As an exercise, please draw a line to join each capital listed below with the corresponding country:

华盛顿 Huáshèngdùn
Washington, D.C.

台湾 Táiwān
Taiwan

台北 Táiběi
Taipei

日本 Rìběn
Japan

北京 Běijīng
Beijing

美国 Měiguó
USA

东京 Dōngjīng
Tokyo

中国 Zhōngguó
China

伦敦 Lúndūn
London

英国 Yīngguó
England (Great Brittain)

柏林 Bólín
Berlin

法国 Fǎguó
France

莫斯科 Mòsīkē
Moscow

加拿大 Jiānádà
Canada

巴黎 Bālí
Paris

德国 Déguó
Germany

渥太华 Wōtàihuá
Ottawa

俄国 Èguó
Russia

Answer:

华盛顿 Huáshèngdùn
Washington D.C.

台北 Táiběi
Taipei

北京 Běijīng
Beijing

东京 Dōngjīng
Tokyo

伦敦 Lúndūn
London

柏林 Bólín
Berlin

渥太华 Wōtàihuá
Ottawa

巴黎 Bālí
Paris

莫斯科 Mòsīkē
Moscow

美国 Měiguó
USA

台湾 Táiwān
Taiwan

中国 Zhōngguó
China

日本 Rìběn
Japan

英国 Yíngguó
England (Great Britain)

德国 Déguó
Germany

加拿大 Jiānádà
Canada

法国 Fǎguó
France

俄国 Èguó
Russia

This lively and silly song was composed by Stephen Collins Foster (1826-1864). Here is the first stanza of the original song.

Oh! Susanna
噢, 苏珊娜!
Ō, Sūshānnà!

我来自阿拉巴马,
Wǒ láizì Ālābāmǎ,

I come from Alabama

带著班究走四方.
Dài zhe bānjiù zǒu sìfāng.

With my banjo on my knee.
(With the banjo, roaming free.)

我要去到路易西安那,
Wǒ yào qù dào Lùyìxīānnà,

I'm going to Louisiana,

去看我的好姑娘.
Qù kàn wǒ di hǎo gūniáng.

My true love for to see.
(My lovely girl to see.)

大雨瓢泼, 不断下落;
Dà yǔ piáopō, búduàn xiàluò;

It rained all night the day I left,
The pouring rain kept hitting the earth.

草原依旧干枯.
Cǎoyuán yījiù gānkū.

The weather, it was dry.
The prairie, it stayed dry.

太阳似火, 却冻死我,
Tàiyáng sì huǒ, què dòng sǐ wǒ,

The sun so hot I froze to death.
The sun, like fire, froze me to death.

苏珊娜, 你不要哭.
Sūshānnà, nǐ búyào kū.

Susanna, don't you cry.

噢, 苏珊娜!
Ō, Sūshānnà!

Oh! Susanna!

你不要泪汪汪.
Nǐ bù yào lèiwāngwāng.

Now, don't you cry for me.
(Don't dry me an ocean.)

我来自阿拉巴马，
Wǒ láizì Ālābāmǎ,

I come from Alabama

带著班究走四方.
Dài zhe bānjiù zǒu sìfāng.

With my banjo on my knee.
(With the banjo, roaming free.)

自 (zì), 己 (jǐ) and 自己 (zìjǐ) all mean "oneself". So, "myself" is: 我自己 (wǒ zìjǐ), and "my own" is: 我自己的 (wǒ zìjǐ de).

The word 自 (zì) is also used as an adverb that means "certainly". In addition, it serves as the preposition "from" or "since". In "我来自阿拉巴马. (Wǒ láizì Ālābāmǎ)", 来自 (láizì) means "to come from". Alternatively, you could say, "我从阿拉巴马来. (Wǒ cóng Ālābāmǎ lái. I come from Alabama)".

班究 (bānjiù) is a transliteration of banjo.

四方 (sìfāng) refers to the four directions, all sides, or all quarters.

The four directions are listed below. (They are also shown on some mahjong tiles.)

东　(dōng)　　East
南　(nán)　　South
西　(xī)　　West
北　(běi)　　North

东方 (dōngfāng) is the east or the East. 东方人 (dōngfāngrén) are people from the East. 西方人 (xīfāngrén) are people from the West. The latter are often called: 西洋人 (xīyángrén). 洋人 (yángrén) is a general term for "foreigners", conveying the fact that they are from across the ocean. Another term that refers to people from other countries is: 外国人 (wàiguórén).

姑娘 (gūniáng) is a girl or a young lady. Modern young ladies are addressed as: 小姐 (xiǎojiě Miss).

瓢 (piáo) is a ladle made from dried gourd. 泼 (pō) means splashing or spilling. 瓢泼 (piáopō) is used here to exaggerate the way the night rain poured.

You know that 不断 (búduàn) is an adverb that means "constantly". Here, it is used to modify the verb 下落 (xiàluò drop, come down or fall down).

草原 (cǎoyuán) is a prairie.

依旧 (yījiù) and 依然 (yīrán) mean "as before", "still", or "even now".

干 (gān) means "dry" or "dried up". 枯 (kū) means dried up, withered or shriveled.

却 (què) is a conjunctive that means "nonetheless", "yet", or "however".

冻死 (dòng sǐ) means to freeze to death. 饿死 (è sǐ) means to die of hunger or to be starving. 气死 (qì sǐ) means to die of anger, or to be furious. 笑死 (xiào sǐ) means to die of laugher or to be splitting one's sides. In most cases, these are just exaggerations, and no one actually dies. A more courteous way to express such sentiments is to use 坏 (huài damaged) in place of 死 (sǐ dead), such as in 冻坏 (dòng huài), 饿坏 (è huài), 气坏 (qì huài) and 笑坏 (xiào huài).

汪 (wāng) is an accumulation of liquid. It is also a Chinese surname. 汪洋 (wāngyáng) refers to a vast body of water, like an ocean. Therefore, 泪汪汪 (lèiwāngwāng) means to be brimming with tears, or shedding an ocean of tears.

30. Transportation

Nowadays, cars have become an indispensable part of our daily life. The word for vehicles is 车 (chē). You have already learned the names of a few motorized vehicles, such as 公车 (gōngchē public car, bus), 巴士 (bāshì bus), 的士 (díshì taxi), 火车 (huǒchē train) and 摩托车 (mótuōchē motorcycle). Another word for "taxi" is: 计程车 (jìchéngchē). Trucks are called 货车 (huòchē) or 卡车 (kǎchē). 票 (piào) is a ticket. 车票 (chēpiào) is a bus or train ticket.

The passenger cars that we drive around are called 汽车 (qìchē). The gasoline they run on is 汽油 (qìyóu). Please note that the character, 汽 (qì), in these words means: "steam". It is different from the 气 (qì) that means air, breath, odor, spirit, and vital energy. The latter is the energy of life that the Kung Fu 功夫 (gōngfū) masters talk about. 加汽油 (jiā qìyóu), or 加油 (jiāyóu), means to add some gasoline, or to refuel. 加油 (jiāyóu) has also taken on the meaning of making an extra effort. When a crowd is cheering their favorite sports team, they would shout, "加油! 加油! (Jiāyóu! Jiāyóu! Go! Go!)"

Bicycles are probably the most popular man-powered vehicles. They are called 单车 (dānchē single-wheeled vehicle), or 脚踏车 (jiǎotàchē foot-pedaled vehicle). The pedicab, 三轮车 (sānlúnchē three-wheeled cart) takes passengers. With the rickshaw, 人力车 (rénlìchē man-powered vehicle), the driver actually runs on foot. 牛车 (niúchē) is an oxcart. In Taiwan, people sometimes jokingly refer to "Bus Route Number 11", or "十一路公车 (shíyī lù gōngchē)", which sounds like a bus route, but actually, the "11" refers to the human being's two legs. One could always walk.

Imagine that you are a traveling salesperson riding on a camel's back. You arrive at a desert store and are greeted with the hospitality described in the following folk song from Xinjiang, China. In the verses, 沙里洪巴嘿呀嘿! (Shā lǐ hóng bā hēi ya hēi!) is a collection of syllables sung as a lively but nonsensical refrain.

Traveler on Camel's Back
沙里洪巴
Shā Lǐ Hóng Bā

哪里来的骆驼客呀? 沙里洪巴嘿呀嘿!
Nǎlǐ lái de luòtuó kè ya? Shā lǐ hóng bā hēi ya hēi!
Whence comes the traveler riding the camel?

马萨来的骆驼客呀. 沙里洪巴嘿呀嘿!
Mǎsà lái de luòtuó kè ya. Shā lǐ hóng bā hēi ya hēi!
From Ma-Sa comes the traveler on camel.

骆驼驮来的啥东西呀? 沙里洪巴嘿呀嘿!
Luòtuó tuó lái de shà dōngxī ya? Shā lǐ hóng bā hēi ya hēi!
What does the camel carry on its back?

骆驼驮的姜皮子呀. 沙里洪巴嘿呀嘿!
Luòtuó tuó de jiāngpízi ya. Shā lǐ hóng bā hēi ya hēi!
The camel carries ginger on its back.

姜皮子花椒啥价钱呀? 沙里洪巴嘿呀嘿!
Jiāngpízi huājiāo shà jiàqián ya? Shā lǐ hóng bā hēi ya hēi!
What price for the ginger and peppercorn?

三两三钱, 三分三呀. 沙里洪巴嘿呀嘿!
Sān liǎng sān qián sān fēn sān ya. Shā lǐ hóng bā hēi ya hēi!
3.3 ounces, 3.3 cents.

门上挂的破皮靴呀. 沙里洪巴嘿呀嘿!

Mén shàng guà de pò píxuē ya. Shā lǐ hóng bā hēi ya hēi!

A pair of torn boots hang over the shop door.

有钱没钱请进来呀. 沙里洪巴嘿呀嘿!

Yǒuqián méi qián qǐng jìnlái ya. Shā lǐ hóng bā hēi ya hēi!

All are welcome, wealthy or poor.

有钱的老爷炕上坐呀. 沙里洪巴嘿呀嘿!

Yǒuqián de lǎoyé kàng shàng zuò ya. Shā lǐ hóng bā hēi ya hēi!

You wealthy masters, sit on the warm hearth.

没钱的老爷地上坐呀. 沙里洪巴嘿呀嘿!

Méi qián de lǎoyé dì shàng zuò ya. Shā lǐ hóng bā hēi ya hēi!

Those not so wealthy, please sit on the earth.

骆驼 (luòtuó) is the camel. 驼 (tuó) means "hunchbacked", while 驮 (tuó) means to carry on the back, as a beast of burden would do.

客 (kè) usually means a guest or a visitor. It also refers to a traveler or a traveling merchant.

姜 (jiāng) is ginger. 皮 (pí) is leather, hide, or the peel or skin of something.

姜皮子 (jiāngpízi) probably refers to dried ginger. Ginger can enhance one's blood circulation. When you feel a chill, microwave two slices of ginger root in a cup of water for three minutes then drink it warm. (Sweeten the drink with sugar or honey as you please.) If feasible, get under your blanket, and you should be able to have a good sweat.

花椒 (huājiāo) is a spice called Chinese prickly ash. It is often used to flavor meats.

啥 (shà) is from a provincial dialect. It means "what", which in standard Chinese is: "什么 (shénme)". 价钱 (jiàqián) means price. 啥价钱 (shà jiàqián) in regular parlance would be: "什么价钱? (Shénme jiàqián?)", or "多少钱? (Duōshǎo qián?)"

三两三钱 (sān liǎng sān qián) refers to the weight of the merchandize. The word, 两 (liǎng two) is also a Chinese unit of weight that corresponds roughly to the ounce. Here, 钱 (qián) is a unit of weight equal to one-tenth of a 两 (liǎng).

三分三 (sān fēn sān) refers to the monetary value of the merchandize. You know that 三分 (sān fēn) means "three cents". In the old days, even a fraction of a cent was worth something.

门上挂的 (mén shàng guà de that which hangs over the door) is an adjective phrase that modifies the noun, the boots, 皮靴 (píxuē). The worn boots serve as a sign for the store.

The storekeeper respectfully addresses the visitors as 老爷 (lǎoyé master).

炕 (kàng) is a heated brick bed used in Northern China.

The Chinese word for ship is 船 (chuán). Add the word for sail, 帆 (fān), to get 帆船 (fānchuán sailboat). Similarly, add the word for steam, 汽 (qì), and you have 汽船 (qìchuán steam boat). In Taiwan, 帆 (fān) is pronounced as "fán".

Following are a few terms associated with ships and boats.

船长 chuánzhǎng	captain, skipper	水手 shuǐshǒu	sailor, seaman
轮船 lúnchuán	steamer	汽艇 qìtǐng	motorboat
军舰 jūnjiàn	military vessel	潜水艇 qiǎnshuǐtǐng	submarine
独木舟 dúmùzhōu	canoe	筏 fá	raft
船首 chuánshǒu	bow	船尾 chuánwěi	stern
龙骨 lónggǔ	keel	船桅 chuánwéi	mast
桨 jiǎng	oar	舵 duò	rudder, helm
锚 máo	anchor	汽笛 qìdí	steam whistle, siren

起锚 (qǐmáo) is to weigh the anchor or set sail, while 抛锚 (pāomáo) is to drop the anchor. When talking about a car, 抛锚 (pāomáo) refers to a breakdown of the vehicle. So, "他的车抛锚了. (Tā de chē pāomáo le.)" means "His car has stalled."

By the way, 出发 (chūfā) means to take off, start out, or set off, as on a trip or a journey, and luggage is called 行李 (xínglǐ).

Air travel, of course, is a lot speedier than sailing. The Chinese word for "aircraft" is 飞机 (fēijī flying machine). Following are a few different types of aircraft:

直升机 zhíshēngjī	helicopter	战斗机 zhàndòujī	fighter plane
喷射机 pēnshèjī	jet plane	滑翔机 huáxiángjī	glider
飞船 fēichuán	dirigible	火箭 huǒjiàn	rocket

The plane we take for a business trip, or to go on vacation, is usually the jetliner, 喷射客机 (pēnshè kèjī). At the airport, 机场 (jīchǎng), you will need to have your boarding pass, 登机卡 (dēng jī kǎ), ready. If you are going abroad, you will also need to bring your passport, 护照 (hùzhào), with a valid visa, 签证 (qiānzhèng), for the country you are visiting.

Do you like your seating, 座位 (zuòwèi), to be by the window, 靠窗 (kào chuān), or by the isle, 靠走道 (kào zǒudào)?

The flight crew usually includes the following people:

驾驶员 jiàshǐyuán	pilot	副驾驶员 fù jiàshǐyuán	co-pilot
空中小姐 kōngzhōng xiǎojiě	stewardess	空中少爷 kōngzhōng shàoyé	steward

The jetliners are equipped with seat belts, 安全带 (ānquándài safety belt). They don't normally provide parachutes , 降落伞 (jiàngluòsǎn), for each passenger.

At the Airport
在机场
Zài Jīchǎng

Susan is traveling to Taiwan with Wendy to visit the latter's family. They stop over in Hong Kong, 香港 (Xiānggǎng), to wait for the flight to Taiwan. Charlie and Nick also happen to be at the Hong Kong International Airport, 香港国际机场 (Xiānggǎng Guójì Jīchǎng), enroute to Beijing.

文蒂: 你看! 尼克在向我们招手.
Wéndì: Nǐ kàn! Níkè zài xiàng wǒmen zhāoshǒu.
Wendy: Look! Nick is waving at us.

尼克 嗨! 苏珊!文蒂! 真巧!
Níkè: Hāi! Sūshān! Wéndì! Zhēn qiǎo!
Nick: Hi! Susan! Wendy! What a coincidence!

查理: 没想到我们会在香港碰面.
Chálǐ: Méi xiǎngdào wǒmen huì zài Xiānggǎng pèngmiàn.
Charlie: I did not expect to run into you here in Hong Kong.

苏珊: 我们要去台湾玩. 你们呢?
Sūshān: Wǒmen yào qù Táiwān wán. Nǐmen ne?
Susan: We are visiting Taiwan. How about you?

查理: 我们要往北京去.
Chálǐ: Wǒmen yào wǎng Běijīng qù.
Charlie: We are heading toward Beijing.

尼克 我有一位朋友在北京.
Níkè: Wǒ yǒu yī wèi péngyǒu zài Běijīng.
Nick: I have a friend in Beijing.

他会带我们参观北京.
Tā huì dài wǒmen cānguān Běijīng.
He will show us around in Beijing.

文蒂: 我们就要上飞机了.
Wéndì: Wǒmen jiùyào shàng fēijī le.
Wendy: We'll be boarding the plane soon.

         苏珊, 把你的护照和登机卡拿出来吧.
         Sūshān, bǎ nǐ de hùzhào hé dēngjīkǎ ná chūlái ba.

苏珊: 好. 你们的班机几点起飞?
Sūshān: Hǎo. Nǐmen de bānjī jǐ diǎn qǐfēi?
Susan: Okay. What time does your scheduled plane take off?

查理: 我们还要等一个多小时.
Chálǐ: Wǒmen hái yào děng yī ge duō xiǎoshí.
Charlie: We still need to wait a little over an hour.

尼克   希望你们在台湾玩得开心.
Níkè: Xīwàng nǐmen zài Táiwān wán de kāixīn.
Nick: I hope you have fun visiting Taiwan.

文蒂: 一路平安.
Wéndì: Yīlù píng'ān.
         Bon voyage. (Have a safe trip.)

苏珊: 再见.
Sūshān: Zàijiàn.
Susan: Good-bye.

机场 (jīchǎng), or 飞机场 (fēijīchǎng), is an airport.

招手 (zhāoshǒu) is to beckon or to wave. 在招手 (zài zhāoshǒu) is the verb in progressive tense, that is, to be beckoning or to be waving. 向我们 (xiàng wǒmen) is the adverbial phrase, "at us", that modifies the action of beckoning.

巧 (qiǎo) means skillful, artful, or intricate. It also means coincidental, as in "真巧! (Zhēn qiǎo! What a coincidence!)" and "碰巧 (pèngqiǎo by coincidence)". 碰 (pèng) means to touch, meet or run into some thing or someone. 碰面 (pèng miàn) means to meet someone unexpectedly. 钉子 (dīngzi) are nails or snags. 碰钉子 (pèngdīngzi) refers to getting a mild rebuff.

玩 (wán) means to play, have fun, or to trifle with an object or someone's feelings. You can use this word to refer to visiting a place for pleasure, playing a sport, or playing any game.

参观 (cānguān) is to visit or to look around, as inside a museum or a factory.

就要 (jiùyào) means to be on the verge of doing something. To emphasize the immediacy of the occurrence, you could say: 马上就要 (mǎshàng jiù yào to be just about to).

In 上飞机 (shàng fēijī), 上 (shàng) is used as an action word that means to embark. 班机 (bānjī) specifically refers to a scheduled flight.

一个多小时 (yī ge duō xiǎoshí) means "a little over one hour".

As you know, 一路 (yīlù) means "all the way" or "throughout the journey". "一路平安 (Yīlù píng'ān. Be safe all the way.)" is what you could say when seeing someone off. Remember that your Chinese will sound more authentic when you say "一 (yī)" in the second tone when it is followed by a character with the fourth tone, as in 一位 (yī wèi), 一个 (yī ge), and 一路 (yīlù).

Do you know the song, *Aloha Oe (Farewell To Thee)*, that was composed by Queen L. K. Liliuokalani, the last Queen of the Hawaiian Islands? This is how you would say "Farewell to thee!" in Chinese:

珍重再见!   Take good care of yourself, and good-bye.
Zhēnzhòng zàijiàn!

Exercise:

The week before leaving for Taiwan, Wendy wrote an email to her second-eldest brother who lives in Taipei. Please fill in the blanks to complete the email.

____ ____ ____二哥:

_____ ____ Èrgē:

Dear Second Elder Brother,

我 ____苏珊将于六月五日____ ____.

Wǒ _____ Sūshān jiāng yú liùyuè wǔ rì _____.

Susan and I will set out on June 5th.

我们的____ ____ 上午____ ____ 起飞,

Wǒmen de _____ shàngwǔ _____ _____ qǐfēi,

Our plane will take off in the morning at eight o'clock, and,

____ ____ ____ ____ 下午四点半到达 ____ ____.

_____ _____ _____ xiàwǔ sì diǎn bàn dàodá _____.

on June 6th at four thirty in the afternoon, arrive in Taipei.

_____ 别忘了到 _____ ____来接我们. ____ ____.

_____ bié wàng le dào _____ lái jiē wǒmen. _____.

Please don't forget to come to the airport to pick us up. Thanks.

祝好.

Zhù hǎo.

Wishing you well,

妹

Mèi

Your younger sister,

文蒂 敬上

Wéndì jìng shàng

Wendy, respectfully submitting the above.

Answer:

亲爱的二哥:

Qīnài de Èrgē:

Dear Second Elder Brother,

我和苏珊将于六月五日出发.

Wǒ hé Sūshān jiāng yú liùyuè wǔ rì chūfā.

Susan and I will set out on June 5th.

我们的班机上午八点起飞,

Wǒmen de bānjī shàng wǔ bā diǎn qǐfēi,

Our plane will take off at eight o'clock in the morning, and

六月六日下午四点半到达台北.

liùyuè liù rì xiàwǔ sì diǎn bàn dàodá Táiběi.

arrive on June 6th at four thirty in the afternoon.

请别忘了到机场来接我们. 谢谢.

Qǐng bié wàng le dào jīchǎng lái jiē wǒmen. Xièxiè.

Please don't forget to come to the airport to pick us up. Thanks.

祝好.

Zhù hǎo.

Wishing you well,

妹

Mèi

Your younger sister,

文蒂 敬上

Wéndì jìng shàng

Wendy, respectfully submitting the above.

For the "plane", you may either use 飞机 (fēijī) or 班机 (bānjī).

30. Transportation

31. Visiting Taipei

Wendy's mother, has received Wendy and Susan at the Liu residence in Taipei, 台北 (Táiběi). Wendy's little brother, Willie, returns from a neighbor's house.

文龙:	姊姊从美国回来啦!
Wénlóng:	Jiějie cóng měiguó huílái lā!
Willie:	Sis has come back from the States!

文蒂:	弟弟, 快来向苏珊姊姊打招呼.
Wéndì:	Dìdi, kuài lái xiàng Sūshān jiějie dǎzhāohū.
Wendy:	Younger brother, come and say hi to Elder Sister Susan.

文龙:	苏珊姊姊好!
Wénlóng:	Sūshān jiějie hǎo!
Willie:	How are you, Elder Sister Susan?

苏珊:	好乖! 这盒巧克力糖送给你.
Sūshān:	Hǎo guāi! Zhè hé qiǎokèlì táng sòng gěi nǐ.
Susan:	Good boy! This box of chocolate candies is for you.

文龙:	谢谢. 我好喜欢!
Wénlóng:	Xièxiè. Wǒ hǎo xǐhuān!
	Thanks. I love it!

刘太太:	今天你们好好休息.
Liú tàitài:	Jīntiān nǐmen hǎohǎo xiūxī.
Mrs. Liu:	You two get a good rest today.

	明天可以去故宫博物馆参观.
	Míngtiān kěyǐ qù Gùgōng Bówùguǎn cānguān.
	You could visit the Palace Museum tomorrow.

文蒂:	后天我带你去逛百货店,
Wéndì:	Hòutiān wǒ dài nǐ qù guàng bǎihuòdiàn,
Wendy:	The day after tomorrow I'll take you to the shopping malls,

也让你尝尝路摊可口的小吃.

yě ràng nǐ cháng cháng lùtān kěkǒu de xiǎochī.

and also let you try the delicious snacks at the roadside stands.

苏珊: 太好了! 谢谢.

Sūshān: Tài hǎo le! Xièxiè.

Susan: Wonderful! Thank you.

二哥: 周末大家一同去野柳海边玩.

Èrgē: Zhōumò dàjiā yītóng qù Yěliǔ hǎibiān wán.

Second Brother: This weekend we all go together to the Yeliu beach.

文龙: 我们可以游泳和吃野餐!

Wénlóng: Wǒmen kěyǐ yóuyǒng hé chī yěcān!

Willie: We will go swimming and have a picnic!

刘太太: 姑姑下周要接你们去南部玩.

Liú tàitài: Gūgu xià zhōu yào jiē nǐmén qù nánbù wán.

Mrs. Liu   Auntie is coming next week to take you to the south for a visit.

文蒂: 真好! 我姑姑很和气. 你会喜欢她.

Wéndì: Zhēn hǎo! Wǒ gūgu hěn héqì. Nǐ huì xǐhuān tā.

Wendy: Great! My aunt is very amiable. You will like her.

苏珊: 那当然罗!

Sūshān: Nà dāngrán luō!

Susan: Of course!

二哥: 你们慢慢谈. 我有事, 先走了.

Èrgē: Nǐmen mànmàn tán. Wǒ yǒushì, xiān zǒu le.

Second Brother: You guys carry on. I have something to take care of; gotta go.

大家: 好, 再见!

Dàjiā   Hǎo, zàijiàn!

Everyone: All right. See you!

Taiwan, 台湾 (Táiwān), is a small island located near the southeastern coasts of China. Taipei, the largest city of Taiwan, is situated in the northern part, 北部 (běibù), of the island. It is appropriately named 台北 (Táiběi). Similarly, the main city in the central part, 中部 (zhōngbù), is named 台中 (Táizhōng). And, a major city in the southern part, 南部 (nánbù), is named 台南 (Táinán Tainan). 基隆 (Jīlóng Keelung) is a major seaport in northern Taiwan, and 高雄 (Gāoxióng Kaohsiung) is a major seaport in southern Taiwan.

The National Palace Museum, 故宫博物馆 (Gùgōng Bówùguǎn), is a world-famous tourist attraction in Taipei City that features a fine collection of Chinese artwork and artifacts, most of which were from the original collections of China's ancient emperors.

逛 (guàng) means to stroll or to ramble. 百货店 (bǎihuòdiàn) means department stores. 逛百货店 (guàng bǎihuòdiàn shopping) is what many people love to do on the busy modern streets of Taipei, often late into the night.

If you are adventurous, you could try the delicious, but sometimes sanitarily dubious foods and snacks offered at the roadside stands, 路摊 (lùtān).

野柳 (Yěliǔ Yeliu Park) is a scenic geological site located about 10 Km northwest of Keelung. This cape offers a view of the Pacific Ocean as well as relatively easy access to wind-eroded sandstones in various interesting formations.

野餐 (yěcān picnic) literally means "a meal in the wilds".

When you need to extract yourself from a multi-party conversation, simply say:

你们慢慢谈. 我有事, 先走了.
Nǐmen mànmàn tán. Wǒ yǒushì, xiān zǒu le.
You people carry on. I have some business to take care of. I've got to go.

The Chinese word for neighbor is: 邻居 (línjū).

The streets in Taipei are so busy they may seem mind-boggling to you. Taxis, buses, large and small cars, motorcycles and bicycles fill the multiple lanes flanked by skyscrapers on both sides. A large bus may suddenly screech to a halt just inches from the taxi in front. It can be a challenge for a newcomer to cross a major street on foot.

To fetch a taxi that is driving by, wave your hand and yell:

喂! 计程车!
Wèi! Jìchéngchē!
Hey! Taxi!

If you wish to go to the Palace Museum, say:

到故宫博物馆.
Dào Gùgōng Bówùguǎn.
To the Palace Museum.

Suppose the taxi driver did not understand you fully, and dropped you off too soon. You paid him and let him go. But now you realize that there is still a short distance to walk to the museum. You will need some directions. You stop a passerby:

请问, 到故宫博物馆怎么走?
Qǐngwèn, dào Gùgōng Bówùguǎn zěnme zǒu?
Please tell me how to get to the Palace Museum.

Can you follow these directions?

往前走到十字路口; 向右转.
Wǎng qián zǒu dào shízì lùkǒu; xiàng yòu zhuǎn.
Go forward until you get to the intersection; turn right.

再走大约五分钟, 到红绿灯左转.
Zài zǒu dàyuē wǔ fēnzhōng, dào hónglǜdēng zuǒ zhuǎn.
Walk about another five minutes, and at the traffic lights turn left.

不一会儿就可以看到了.
Bù yīhuǐer jiù kěyǐ kàndào le.
Before long, you will see it.

31. Visiting Taipei

Two Famous Mountains in Taiwan

台湾最高的山是玉山,

Táiwān zuì gāo de shān shì Yùshān.

The tallest mountain in Taiwan is **Yushan** (Jade Mountain),

海拔 3854 公尺.

Hǎibá sān qiān bā bǎi wǔshísì gōngchǐ.

with an elevation of 3854 meters.

玉山上积著白雪.

Yùshān shàng jī zhe bái xuě.

White snow accumulates on Yushan (Jade Mountain).

阿里山脉也在台湾中部.

Ālǐ shānmài yě zài Táiwān zhōngbù.

The **Ali Mountain Range** is also in central Taiwan.

阿里山上有神木;

Ālǐshān shàng yǒu shén mù;

There is a sacred tree (a Chinese juniper) on the **Ali Mountain Range**.

要十个人牵手才能把树围起来.

yào shí ge rén qiān shǒu cái néng bǎ shù wéi qǐ lǎi.

It takes ten adults to **encircle** the tree by joining their hands.

阿里山上也有原住民.

Ālǐshān shàng yě yǒu yuánzhùmín.

There are also **indigenous people** on the Ali Mountain Range.

他们很会唱歌跳舞.

Tāmen hěn huì chànggē tiàowǔ.

They are very good at singing and dancing.

涧水围著青山转; 非常美丽.

Jiàn shuǐ wéi zhe qīng shān zhuǎn; fēicháng měilì.

The ravine water flows around the **green mountains**; it's very beautiful.

31. Visiting Taipei

32. *Visiting Beijing*

Nick's friend, Dalton Lee, treats Nick and Charlie to a scrumptious dinner at a restaurant in Beijing, 北京 (Běijīng).

大同: 尝尝这皮酥, 肉嫩, 味美的北京鸭!
Dàtóng: Cháng cháng zhè pí sū, ròu nèn, wèi měi de běijīngyā.
Dalton: Try this Peking Duck with crisp skin, tender meat and savory flavor!

把烤鸭放在薄饼上,
Bǎ kǎoyā fàng zài báobǐng shàng,
Place a piece of the roast duck on the thin pancake,

加点儿甜面酱, 包起来吃.
jiā diǎnr tiánmiànjiàng, bāo qǐlái chī.
add a dollop of sweet soy paste then wrap it up to eat.

尼克: 也可以加一段大葱.
Níkè: Yě kěyǐ jiā yī duàn dàcōng.
Nick: You may also add a section of fresh leek.

查理: 谢谢! 味道好极了!
Chálǐ: Xièxiè! Wèidào hǎo jí le!
Charlie: Thanks. It's extremely tasty!

大同: 明天我们去动物园看熊猫.
Dàtóng: Míngtiān wǒmen qù dòngwùyuán kàn xióngmāo.
Dalton: Tomorrow, we will go to the zoo to see the pandas.

查理: 太好了! 我要同熊猫握手.
Chálǐ: Tài hǎo le! Wǒ yào tóng xióngmāo wòshǒu.
Charlie: Wonderful! I'd like to shake hands with a panda.

大同: 然后, 我带你们到紫禁城去参观.
Dàtóng: Rán hòu, wǒ dài nǐmen dào zǐjìnchéng qù cānguān.
Dalton: Then I'll take you to the Forbidden City for a visit.

尼克: 以前那是皇宫; 平民不能进去.
Níkè: Yǐqián nà shì huánggōng; píngmín bùnéng jìnqù.
Nick: It used to be an imperial palace, inaccessible to the common people.

查理: 长城距离这儿多远?
Chálǐ: Chángchéng jùlí zhèr duō yuǎn?
Charlie: How far is the Great Wall from here?

大同: 一个多钟头的车程.
Dàtóng: Yī ge duō zhōngtóu de chēchéng.
Dalton: A little over an hour's drive.

长城有些地方很陡,
Chánchéng yǒuxiē dìfāng hěn dǒu,
Some parts of the Great Wall are quite steep,

走起来很费力.
zǒu qǐlái hěn fèilì.
and the walk can be very strenuous.

查理: 我体力好, 不怕累.
Chálǐ: Wǒ tǐlì hǎo, búpà lèi.
Charlie: I'm physically fit. I don't worry about being fatigued.

尼克: 先别吹牛; 到时再看.
Níkè: Xiān bié chuīniú; dào shí zài kàn.
Nick: Hold the big talk for now. We'll see when the time comes.

尝 (cháng) means to taste. In urging someone to do something, the verb is often

repeated, as in "尝尝看. (Cháng cháng kàn. Taste it.)", "吃吃看. (Chī chī kàn.

Try a bite.)", "试试看. (Shì shì kàn. Try it out.)", "說說看. (Shuō shuō kàn. Tell me about it.)", and so on.

皮酥 (pí sū with skin so crispy), 肉嫩 (ròu nèn with meat so tender), and 味美的 (wèi měi de with taste so wonderful) are adjective phrases that describe the Peking Duck. Notice that when there are two or more adjectives describing the same noun, the particle 的 (de) is only attached to the last one.

北京鸭 (běijīngyā Peking Duck) is a roasted duck known for its crunchy skin, tender meat, rich aroma and lip-smacking flavor.

薄 (bó) means thin, slight or ungenerous. It is pronounced differently when used in the word for thin pancakes, 薄饼 (baúbǐng).

动物 (dòngwù) is a general term for animals. 动物园 (dòngwùyuán) is a zoo. On the other hand, 植物 (zhíwù) are plants, and 植物园 (zhíwùyuán) is a botanical garden. 熊猫 (xióngmāo panda) literally translates to "a cat that looks like a bear". In fact, pandas belong to the same family as raccoons.

距离 (jùlí distance), 距 (jù distance) and 离 (lí to part or depart) can all be used as a verb that means "to be at a distance from". To inquire about how far a place is from where you are, you could also ask, "距这儿多远? (Jù zhèr duō yuǎn?)" or "离这儿多远? (Lí zhèr duō yuǎn?)"

程 (chéng) could be a procedure, a distance or an itinerary. 车程 (chēchéng) refers to the distance traveled by car.

As a noun, 费 (fèi) means fees, expenses or costs. As a verb it means to spend or to waste. 费力 (fèilì) means strenuous, or requiring great effort or strength.

吹牛 (chuīniú) is to brag or to blow one's own horn.

Before leaving for Beijing, Nick and Charlie put together a cheat sheet. They wish to share it with you. You may wish to add to this language survival kit to cover other situations that you might encounter as you may not be as lucky as they are - to have a friend in Beijing who can show you around and help you with various needs. Bring this list along on your trip and show the relevant sentences to the local people if they fail to understand you, or you them. Please remember that not all people in China speak Mandarin Chinese, and quite a few of those who do may sport a local accent.

早! *or* 您早! *or* 早安! Zǎo!　　Nín zǎo!　　Zǎoān!	Good morning!
您好! *or* 您好吗? Nín hǎo!　　Nín hǎo ma?	Hi! Hello! How are you?
贵姓? *or* 您贵姓? Guìxìng?　　Nín guìxìng?	What's your name? (What's your respected name?)
很高兴见到您. Hěn gāoxìng jiàn dào nín.	Pleased to see you.
对不起. *or* 抱歉. Duìbùqǐ.　　Bàoqiàn.	Excuse me. Sorry.
再见. *or* 明天见. Zàijiàn.　　Míngtiān jiàn.	See you. See you tomorrow.
您说什么?　我听不懂. Nín shuō shénme? Wǒ tīng bù dǒng.	What did you say? I don't understand. (Pardon me?)
请讲慢一点. Qǐng jiǎng màn yīdiǎn.	Please speak a bit slower.
请再说一遍. Qǐng zài shuō yī biàn.	Please say it again.
啊! 我懂了. Ā! Wǒ dǒng le.	Ah! I get it now.

可以借用电话吗?
Kěyǐ jièyòng diànhuà ma?

May I borrow the phone?

电话簿借一下, 好吗?
Diànhuàbù jiè yīxià, hǎo ma?

Let me borrow the phone book for a bit, OK?

我想订个房间.
Wǒ xiǎng dìng ge fángjiān.

I would like to reserve a room.

我们要一间套房.
Wǒmen yào yī jiān tàofáng.

We'd like to have a suite.

单人房收费多少?
Dānrénfáng shōufèi duōshǎo?

What's the fee for a single room?

包括小费吗?
Bāokuò xiǎofèi ma?

Does it include the tips?

包括早点吗?
Bāokuò zǎodiǎn ma?

Does it include breakfast?

可以用信用卡吗?
Kěyǐ yòng xìnyòngkǎ ma?

May I use my credit card?

收旅行支票吗?
Shōu lǚxíng zhīpiào ma?

Do you accept traveler's checks?

请问, 汇率是多少?
Qǐngwèn, huìlǜ shì duoshǎo?

What's the exchange rate, please?

房间号码是多少?
Fángjiān hàomǎ shì duōshǎo?

What's the room number?

在第几楼?
Zài dì jǐ lóu?

On which floor?

抱歉. 我的房门钥匙掉了.　　　　　　Sorry, the key to my room is lost.
Bàoqiàn, wǒ de fáng mén yàoshǐ diào le.

我的房间太热.　　　　　　　　　　My room is too hot.
Wǒ de fángjiān tài rè.

有没有电风扇?　　　　　　　　　　Do you have an electric fan?
Yǒu méiyǒu diànfēngshàn?

请问, 洗手间在哪儿?　　　　　　　Where is the restroom, please?
Qǐngwèn, xǐshǒujiān zài nǎr?

我想喝一些水.　　　　　　　　　　I would like to drink some water.
Wǒ xiǎng hē yīxiē shuǐ.

哪儿有好的餐厅?　　　　　　　　　Where is a nice restaurant?
Nǎr yǒu hǎo de cāntīng?

哪儿有自动出纳机?　　　　　　　　Where can I find an ATM?
Nǎr yǒu zìdòng chūnàjī?

请你明早七点叫醒我.　　　　　　　Please wake me up at seven
Qǐng nǐ míng zǎo qī diǎn jiàoxǐng wǒ.　tomorrow morning.

请帮我叫一部计程车.　　　　　　　Please call a taxi cab for me.
Qǐng bāng wǒ jiào yī bù jìchéngchē.

谢谢你的帮忙.　　　　　　　　　　Thanks for your help.
Xièxiè nǐ de bāngmáng.

不客气.　　　　　　　　　　　　　You're welcome.
Búkèqì.　　　　　　　　　　　　　(No need to be courteous.)

In the Beijing dialect, 咱们 (zánmen) means "you and I", as in:

咱们一同去. (Zánmen yītóng qù.)　　Let's go together.

The local people in Beijing make distinct retroflex sounds 卷舌音 (juǎn shé yīn tongue-curling sound) when saying words beginning with zh, ch, sh or r. In addition, when a word is followed by 儿 (er), its last syllable is merged with the "curled" 儿 (er). Like the German suffix, "chen" or "lein", 儿 (er) is used to indicate smallness, cuteness, a minute amount, or an endearment. I will conclude our lessons with the following popular Chinese children's song, which I have modified somewhat to show how the Beijing locals love to add 儿 (er) to just about any other word.

Little Donkey
小毛驴儿
Xiǎo Máolǘr

我有一匹小毛驴儿，
Wǒ yǒu yī pī xiǎo máolǘr,

I had a little donkey once,
(I had a little donkey)

我从来也不骑儿.
Wǒ cónglái yě bù qír.

And ride it I never dared.
(I had never ridden before.)

有一天我高了兴儿.
Yǒu yītiān wǒ gāo liǎo xìngr,

That one day, on a whim,

我骑它去赶集儿.
Wǒ chí tā qù gǎnjír.

I rode it to the fair.

我手里拿著个小皮鞭儿；
Wǒ shǒu lǐ ná zhe ge xiǎo píbiānr;

I held a small whip in my hand;

我心里真得意儿.
Wǒ xīn lǐ zhēn déyìr.

I was feeling mighty swell.

不知怎么, 哗啦啦啦啦,
Bùzhī zěnme, huá lā lā lā lā,

Don't know how, but
splatter, splash,

我摔了一身泥儿.
Wǒ shuāi le yīshēn nír.

Into the slosh I fell.

毛驴 (máolǘ) is a donkey.

高了兴儿 (gāo liǎo xìngr) means to have gotten into a happy mood. The particle 了 (liǎo) helps to form the perfect tense. You could pronounce it as "le". 兴儿 (xìngr) is pronounced like "shirr". The Chinese idiom for "on a whim" is 心血来潮 (xīnxuèláicháo), which is used in the original song.

As a verb, 集 (jí) means to gather or integrate. For example, 集合 (jíhé) is to call together or to assemble people, and 集邮 (jíyóu) means to collect stamps. As a noun, it means a gathering, an assembly or a collection. In 赶集 (gǎnjí), the gathering is a farmer's market, and 赶 (gǎn) means to hurry to a place.

皮鞭 (píbiān) is a leather whip.

心里 (xīnlǐ) means in the heart or one's inner feelings. Please do not confuse this with the term 心理 (xīnlǐ), which refers to psychology or mentality. 里 (lǐ inside) indicates a location, while 理 (lǐ) means logic, truth, a natural science or a methodology. 得意 (déyì) means to be complacent, self-satisfied, cocky, or swelling with pride. Literally, this term translates to "having gotten one's wish". 真 (zhēn true, really) serves as an adverb that modifies the adjective, 得意 (déyì self-satisfied).

哗啦啦啦啦 (huá lā lā lā lā) mimics the sound of splashing.

摔 (shuāi) is to fall or to take a tumble. 一身 (yīshēn) means "all over the body", or "the whole body" rather than "one body". 一 (yī) is often used indicate all or the whole of something. In this sense, it is the same as 全 (quán all, whole, entire). 泥 (ní) is mud. Mashed fruits or vegetables are also referred to as 泥 (ní).

What Next?

You have amassed a basic set of Chinese words in your vocabulary chest (only about one thousand ☺). You have also acquired the essential tools for building sentences that make sense. I encourage you to review the lessons and sing the songs often. Practice what you have learned by engaging in a simple conversation with a Chinese-speaking person whenever you can. You could also rent Chinese movies with English subtitles and see if you can catch a few lines here and there. Ask your Chinese friends if they can recommend movies that feature clear and slow Mandarin dialogues. It would be nice if you could attend a Chinese instruction class. There you will learn additional words and expressions, and also have the opportunity to interact with other Chinese-speaking people. Your local library may have a few simple Chinese readers or storybooks that you could check out. There are also many resources available on the Internet for learning the Chinese language. Of course, to become fully conversant with a language, you must be thrown into an environment that forces you to use that language on a daily basis. Plan your next long vacation or career move accordingly.

The fact remains that Chinese is not an easy language to learn. Don't despair if you have not learned to write all the Chinese characters. As long as you can recognize a character when you see it, you could type it into a document by using a Chinese input software program, such as the NJStar Chinese Word Processor, which I'm using to enter the Chinese characters for this book. This involves entering the pinyin for the Chinese character then selecting the appropriate word from a list of characters sharing the same pinyin. (A short definition will pop up when you point to each word in the list.) This will be a slow process but you will gain speed with practice.

Before I let you go, here is another exercise I'd like you to do. Turn to any page in the Index at the of this book. Close your eyes, and let your index finger land on a random word or expression on the page. Open your eyes and see if you can say the Chinese equivalent of your find. Can you also make a sentence using that Chinese word? If not, then please turn to the page indicated in the Index, and review the usage of that word or expression. Repeat this exercise whenever you have nothing more important to do.

Last but not least, thank you for learning Chinese with me.

The supplemental audio files for this book are stored in the Microsoft®
Windows Live™ SkyDrive at the following location:

http://tinyurl.com/37m8dxm

You could save this address under "Favorites" in your web browser.
You could also download and save the audio files to your hard drive,
or burn them onto a CD for your personal, non-commercial use only.

List of Songs and Rhymes

Index

381

385

393

395

397

Made in the USA
Charleston, SC
27 April 2012